The
RISE
and
FALL
of the
ISRAELITE
KINGDOMS

The RISE and FALL of the ISRAELITE KINGDOMS

TWO CONTRASTING BIBLICAL STORIES

Leslie J. Hoppe, OFM

Paulist Press
New York / Mahwah, NJ

Cover / title-page image: Shutterstock.com
Cover and book design by Lynn Else

Library of Congress Cataloging-in-Publication Data
Names: Hoppe, Leslie J., author.
Title: The rise and fall of the Israelite kingdoms : two contrasting biblical stories / Leslie J. Hoppe, OFM.
Description: New York / Mahwah, NJ : Paulist Press, [2021] | Includes bibliographical references. | Summary: "This book shows how the story of the Israelite Kingdoms is told in strikingly different ways in Samuel-Kings and Chronicles, each version demonstrating theological aims that addressed the situation in which it was written. The book highlights how those contrasting purposes resonate with divisions present in the faith community today"—Provided by publisher.
Identifiers: LCCN 2020040436 (print) | LCCN 2020040437 (ebook) | ISBN 9780809154883 (paperback) | ISBN 9781587688843 (ebook)
Subjects: LCSH: Bible. Samuel—History of Biblical events. | Bible. Kings—History of Biblical events. | Bible. Chronicles—History of Biblical events. | Jews—History—To 70 A.D.
Classification: LCC BS1325.52 .H67 2021 (print) | LCC BS1325.52 (ebook) | DDC 222/.095—dc23
LC record available at https://lccn.loc.gov/2020040436
LC ebook record available at https://lccn.loc.gov/2020040437

ISBN 978-0-8091-5488-3 (paperback)
ISBN 978-1-58768-884-3 (e-book)

Published by Paulist Press
997 Macarthur Boulevard
Mahwah, New Jersey 07430
www.paulistpress.com

Printed and bound in the
United States of America

Contents

Abbreviations vii

Introduction 1

    Why Two Stories 1

    The Relationship between Samuel/Kings
       and Chronicles 7

    Story and History 9

    The Endings 10

Chapter 1: The Preludes.. 23

    Joshua 1—1 Samuel 7 23

    1 Chronicles 1—9 34

    Conclusion 37

Chapter 2: The Early Israelite Monarchy................................... 38

    Saul 39

    David 42

    Solomon 73

    Conclusion 84

Chapter 3: The Two Israelite Kingdoms 85

    The Beginnings... 85

Contents

Excursus: The *gəbîrâ* 95

The Rise of the Kingdom of Israel 98

The Rise of the Kingdom of Judah 111

Conclusion 122

Chapter 4: The Decline and Collapse of the Two Kingdoms 124

The Role of the Prophets 124

The Fall of the Kingdom of Israel 133

The Fall of the Kingdom of Judah 141

Conclusion 165

Epilogue 167

Appendix: Table of Israelite Kings 171

Notes 175

Bibliography 197

Abbreviations

AB	Anchor Bible
ABD	*Anchor Bible Dictionary*. Edited by David Noel Freedman. New York: Doubleday, 1992.
ANET	*Ancient Near Eastern Test Relating to the Old Testament*. Edited by James B. Pritchard. 3rd ed. Princeton: Princeton University Press, 1969.
AOAT	Alter Orient und Altes Testament
BAR	*Biblical Archaeology Review*
Bib	*Biblica*
BWANT	Beiträge zur Wissenschaft vom Alten und Neuen Testament
CBA	Catholic Biblical Association
CBQ	*The Catholic Biblical Quarterly*
CBQMS	Catholic Biblical Quarterly Monograph Series
FRLANT	Forschungen zur Religion und Literatur des Alten und Neuen Testaments
HSM	Harvard Semitic Monographs
IEJ	*Israel Exploration Journal*
JBL	*Journal of Biblical Literature*
JSOT	*Journal for the Study of the Old Testament*
JSOTSup	Journal for the Study of the Old Testament Supplement Series
MT	The Masoretic Text
NABRE	The New American Bible, revised edition

NEAEHL	*The New Encyclopedia of Archaeological Excavations in the Holy Land*. Edited by Ephraim Stern. New York: Simon & Schuster, 1993.
NCBC	New Century Bible Commentary
NRSV	The New Revised Standard Version
OTL	Old Testament Library
RB	*Revue biblique*
SBL	Society of Biblical Literature
SBT	Studies in Biblical Theology
TA	*Tel Aviv*
VT	*Vetus Testamentum*
VTSup	Supplements to Vetus Testamentum
WBC	Word Biblical Commentary
ZAW	*Zeitschrift für Alttestamentliche Wissenschaft*

Introduction

WHY TWO STORIES

The Bible tells the story of the rise and fall of the two Israelite kingdoms in two versions. One appears in the Books of Samuel/ Kings and the other in the Books of Chronicles. Both versions focus on the monarchs that ruled in two kingdoms. In the culture of the time and period, kings were the embodiment of the states that they ruled. They, of course, bore personal responsibility for decisions they made and actions they took, but these decisions and actions shaped the destiny of the people they ruled. The fate of king and people were bound together. To tell the story of the monarchs of Israel and Judah is to tell the story of the people they ruled. This book is about the differences between the two versions of the story, differences that reveal something about what the writers of each sought to accomplish.

Some clarification of terminology is necessary before proceeding. The expression *Israel and Judah* refers to the two Israelite kingdoms. The *Kingdom of Israel* or *Northern Kingdom* refers to the Israelite kingdom that was formed by the ten northern tribes. The *Kingdom of Judah* or *Southern Kingdom* refers to the Israelite kingdom that encompassed the territory of the tribe of Judah. The term *Israel* refers to all the people who considered themselves descendants of Jacob, who was renamed Israel (Gen 32:28). Jacob had twelve sons who were considered to be the ancestors of the tribes. The tribe of Levi did not receive an allotment of land since the members of that tribe were to receive their support from their service of the cult. To maintain the number twelve, the tribe of

Joseph was split into two half-tribes: Ephraim and Manasseh, which become the dominant tribes in the north. The territory of Simeon was surrounded by that of Judah, and the towns of Simeon were absorbed by the larger tribe of Judah by the time of David (see 1 Chr 4:31).

The older account of the Israelite kingdoms is found in the Books of Samuel and Kings. This version, which dates to the middle of the sixth century BCE, describes the beginnings of the Israelite monarchy with Saul, followed by the flowering of the Israelite kingdom under David and Solomon and the dissolution of that kingdom following Solomon's death. Kings then traces the rise and fall of the two Israelite kingdoms, Israel and Judah, that were the heirs of the Davidic-Solomonic kingdom. That story ends by noting the fate of the last king to rule over Judah. Samuel and Kings present ancient Israel's monarchy as a failed institution. Kings depicts the monarchs of the Northern Kingdom (the Kingdom of Israel), without exception, as ignoring the status of the Jerusalem temple and promoting idolatry. Kings' portrait of the Judahite monarchy asserts that almost all of Judah's kings failed in their responsibilities to keep the people of Judah loyal to YHWH alone. With just two exceptions, the kings of Judah allowed worship at "the high places," that is, rural shrines that Kings considers at the least an illegitimate form of Yahwistic worship and at most tantamount to idolatry. The effect of the monarchy's failure was the collapse of both kingdoms and the forced migration of their people to Mesopotamia. Kings' story of the two Israelite kingdoms is a sad and even a tragic story. What began with such promise and hope for the future ends with the fall of Jerusalem, the end of the Davidic dynasty, the destruction of the temple, and the exile of a portion of the kingdom's population to agriculturally marginal regions in Mesopotamia.

The emphasis in the judgment on the kings of Israel and Judah appears to focus almost exclusively on matters of correct worship. The kings are condemned for promoting and even participating in patterns of worship that Samuel/Kings and Chronicles considers illegitimate and idolatrous. There was an important difference between the worship of Baal, Asherah, and other Canaanite deities and the worship of YHWH. The gods of Canaan provided a theological support for a stratified social and economic system.

In such a system land belonged to the king, who would distribute it to his supporters. What the ordinary farmer produced was subject to taxation to support the king, his court, and army, who are consumers but not producers of food. YHWH, however, was a God who took the side of slaves against their masters, who gave the freed slaves a land that provided them with the means of production, enabling them to live in peace and prosperity. Yahwism supported a social and economic system that was familial rather than stratified. When Deuteronomy speaks to its readers/hearers of their fellow Israelites, it calls them their "brothers."[1] The conflict between Baal and YHWH was played out not only in worship but in life. A good illustration of the social and economic effects of this conflict is the story of Naboth's vineyard (1 Kgs 21:1–29). In that story Jezebel, who promoted Baal worship in Israel, took action to deprive Naboth of his rights and his life because she believed that she was entitled to do so. Her husband Ahab at first recognized that Naboth was within his rights until she upbraided him by asking, "Do you now govern Israel?" (1 Kgs 21:7). Jezebel took charge and Naboth was murdered and his land confiscated.

The story of the Israelite monarchy told in Samuel and Kings is part of the larger work that recounts the story of the people of Israel in the land promised to their ancestors. That larger narrative begins with the Book of Joshua recounting the story of the Israelite tribes' acquisition of the land of Canaan, which was to be the setting for the rest of their story. The Book of Judges tells the tales of tribal heroes who acted in times when the tribes' control of Canaan became increasingly tenuous due to internal and external forces that threatened not only the tribes' acquisition of the land but also their very existence. The increasing level of these threats—especially incursions of the Philistines into Israelite territory—led the tribal elders to consider monarchy as the one institution that could provide the leadership necessary to respond to the Philistine menace. Saul died during a battle with the Philistines, but David was able to end their incursions into Israelite territory. David handed on to his son Solomon a kingdom that was at peace. This provided Solomon the opportunity to build a temple for YHWH, the ancestral Deity of the Israelite tribes. Solomon's political and economic policies bred discontent and led to the division of his kingdom following his death. The two kingdoms fought with each other and the other small states in the southern Levant for control of the region's resources. The rise of the Mesopotamian kingdoms led to the end of the two Israelite kingdoms, Israel falling to Assyria and Judah to Babylon.

Although this book will focus on the final form of Samuel/ Kings, a brief review of scholarship reveals attempts to understand how these books came together in response to significant historical events. Martin Noth suggested that the books from Joshua to 2 Kings were the work of an individual writer, who, of course, used sources to tell the story of the people of Israel in their land and to offer an explanation for the collapse of the Israelite kingdoms and the exile of their people.[2] Noth identified a common theological thread that wove together the narratives from Joshua to 2 Kings. This theological thread was derived from the Book of Deuteronomy. That book called upon Israel to be loyal to YHWH, its patron Deity. It identified love for YHWH as the mark of that loyalty (Deut 6:4). In addition, Deuteronomy asserted that Israel must avoid all forms of idolatry and worship YHWH in the one place that God has chosen (Deut 12:1–5). Fidelity would bring a blessing, but a curse would follow upon disobedience (Deut 30). Noth coined the term *Deuteronomistic History* to refer to the Books of Joshua to 2 Kings as a literary work that told the story of the Israelites in their land, deriving its identifying theological perspective from the Book of Deuteronomy.

Some scholars found it difficult to see the Books of Joshua to 2 Kings as the work of a single individual. They theorized that the Deuteronomistic History went through more than one edition. Frank Moore Cross suggested that there were at least two such editions.[3] The first was written in the seventh century to support the religious reform of Josiah. The fall of Jerusalem necessitated a second edition to account for that disaster. Rudolf Smend and other scholars from the so-called Göttingen Group asserted that the original document described by Noth underwent two postexilic redactions—one that highlighted the prophets and another that emphasized obedience to the Torah.[4] This book, however, will focus on the final form of Samuel/Kings.

Another problem that scholars had with Noth's hypothesis is his claim that Joshua–2 Kings describes why the people of the two kingdoms lost the land that was promised to their ancestors without providing any hope for the future of Israel. Scholars wondered why someone would devote so much time, energy, and creativity only to end with no positive message. The final form of Joshua–Kings, with Deuteronomy as its theological introduction, was composed during the exile or shortly afterward. It sought to provide an explanation of the disaster that befell in two Israelite kingdoms. This work eschews a mythological explanation that would have seen the fall of the two kingdoms as the fallout from a conflict among the gods in which YHWH proved to be less powerful than Asshur and Marduk, the patron deities of the Mesopotamian kingdoms that subjugated the Israelite kingdoms. Joshua–2 Kings lays the blame on Israel itself—principally on Israel's leadership that promoted and participated in the service of gods other than YHWH. Deuteronomy 30:15–20 describes the choice set before Israel: "life and prosperity, death and adversity." Joshua–2 Kings makes it abundantly clear that by choosing to serve other gods, Israel chose "death and adversity."

The Deuteronomistic History makes brutally clear the consequences of the choice that Israel has made. Led by the kings of Israel and Judah, the people will enter a dark, unfamiliar world. It is a world without the institutions that gave them their identity. It is a world without king and kingdom, without temple and priesthood, without prophetic intervention. The only light in this darkness is the book of the Law given by God to Moses—the Law that calls Israel to serve YHWH alone (Deut 5:6; 6:4–5). That Law promises blessing to the obedient, but the reader/hearer of Joshua–2 Kings is left to wonder if YHWH has revoked that promise. Reading the account of the rise and fall of the Israelite kingdoms, with its recitation of the infidelities of king after king after king with few exceptions, does not encourage hope and confidence but, at the very most, the question, "Have you not rejected us, O God?" (Pss 60:10; 108:11). Chronicles offers a later version of the story of the two Israelite kingdoms—a version that respects the Deuteronomistic account but is convinced that there was a future for Israel beyond judgment.

Chronicles offers an alternate approach to the story of the two Israelite kingdoms. First Chronicles begins with detailed genealogies of the Israelites tribes—genealogies that go back to Adam. The narratives, which are dependent on those of Samuel and Kings, begin in 1 Chronicles 10 with the fall of the house of Saul and the rise of the house of David.[5] Chronicles tells the story of the Davidic dynasty and the Kingdom of Judah (the Southern Kingdom) while almost completely ignoring the Kingdom of Israel and its kings. The story in Chronicles also ends with the Judeans outside their homeland in exile, though they are encouraged by Cyrus, the Persian king, to return to Jerusalem. The narratives in the Samuel/Kings and Chronicles overlap to some extent since they both cover the period of the monarchy. Each, however, tells the story of the monarchic period in its own way.

The story of the Israelite kingdoms in Chronicles shows that Judaism of the early postexilic period is ready to adjust to changing situations in response to the experience and the needs of a new generation that has accommodated itself to Persian hegemony. Yehud was a theocratic society centered on the service of YHWH in the temple of Jerusalem. Chronicles highlights points of continuity with the time of David and Solomon to give legitimacy to the patterns of belief and practice characteristic of early postexilic Judaism.

Although Chronicles does borrow extensively from Samuel and Kings, the voice of Chronicles is distinctly different from that of Samuel and Kings. The rhetoric of the latter is clearly Deuteronomic with its emphasis, for example, on the failure of Judah's kings to limit sacrificial worship to the single sanctuary that God has chosen.[6] Chronicles does not reject the authority of Samuel/Kings but it does challenge that work as the *only* way to understand Judah's past. This is clear from its construction as a history of the Judean monarchy from David to the fall of the Judean state. The genealogies in 1 Chronicles 1—9 provide a universalist context for that history, and the conclusion in 2 Chronicles 36:20–23 offers hope for Judah's future. Chronicles presents itself as the proper way to understand the story of the Judean national state and its monarchy as found in Samuel and Kings. For Chronicles, Yehud's political standing in the wider context of the Persian Empire is not important. Chronicles sees the identity of the Jewish people as a "religio-cultic community seeking acknowledgement within the wider sociohistorical context."[7]

THE RELATIONSHIP BETWEEN SAMUEL/KINGS AND CHRONICLES

The story of the two Israelite kingdoms as told in Samuel and Kings was certainly known to the priestly circles responsible for Chronicles. Samuel and Kings were in existence for about 150 years before Chronicles made its appearance. The following three observations explain some of the ways that Chronicles makes use of the earlier account of the two Israelite kingdoms.

Chronicles sometimes simply adopts the account of a particular king's reign from Kings. The account of Jehoahaz's reign in 2 Chronicles 36:1–4 is substantially the same as that found in 2 Kings 23:30–34. More often, Chronicles adapts the account in Kings. For example, the account of the border war between Abijah (called Abijam in 1 Kings) and Jeroboam I is mentioned without any elaboration in a single verse in 1 Kings 15:7. Second Chronicles 13:2a–22 devotes twenty-two verses to that war, employing the motif that the advantage of numbers does not guarantee victory (Judg 7:2–8; 1 Sam 14:6; 17:45–47). Addressing the forces of Israel, Abijah asserts that his army will prevail because the worship that Judah offers to YHWH is led by "the descendants of Aaron, and the Levites," who perform the appropriate rituals at the prescribed times. Since Abijah expresses such pious sentiments, it is not surprising that 2 Chronicles portrays him as one of Judah's more successful kings though 1 Kings 15 passes over his reign without comment. Chronicles also expands on Kings' account of the reigns of Jehoshaphat (compare 2 Chr 17—20 with 1 Kgs 22:42–50) and of Amaziah (compare 2 Chr 25:1–28 with 2 Kgs 14:2–20).

The version of Nathan's oracle in 1 Chronicles 17 illustrates how Chronicles can nuance the theological views of Samuel/Kings to accord with the changing circumstances of the Jewish people in the Persian period. In 2 Samuel, Nathan's words to David end with promise of an eternal dynasty: "Your house and your kingdom shall be made sure forever before me; your throne shall be established forever" (2 Sam 7:16). First Chronicles has Nathan speaking in God's name to David about his son Solomon: "But I will confirm him in *my* house and in *my* kingdom forever, and his throne shall be established forever" (17:14, emphasis added). When this verse was written, the Davidic dynasty and the Judahite national state no longer existed, but God's sovereignty perdures in the thought of Chronicles. Under God's sovereignty, the Jewish people continue to exist though its monarchy and national state had fallen.

Chronicles sometimes opposes the presentation given in Kings. The clearest example of the contrasting portrait of Manasseh given in Kings and Chronicles. Kings clearly identifies Manasseh as the worst of all the kings of Israel and Judah. He engages in forbidden practices such as divination, and he builds altars for "the host of heaven" that are to be worshiped alongside Yhwh in the temple. He is responsible for shedding innocent blood. He leads Judah to the practice of idolatry. Manasseh's actions are responsible for the fall of the kingdom and the destruction of the temple, though these happened many years after his reign (2 Kgs 21:1–18). Chronicles too presents Manasseh as a wicked king but with one significant difference (2 Chr 33). During his exile in Babylon, which is not mentioned in Kings, Manasseh repents.[8] Upon his return to Judah, he institutes religious reforms. Another example is the sanitizing of the stories of David and Solomon as found in Kings. Chronicles focuses on the role that these kings had in the establishment of the cult of Yhwh in Jerusalem and chooses to ignore stories about their personal lives.

Chronicles, then, sees the story of the two Israelite kingdoms through the lens of Judah's situation in the Persian Period. The exile is part of Judah's past, but the Jewish people need to move forward. The temple has been rebuilt and the worship of Yhwh under the direction of priests and Levites has resumed. The descendants of those who returned from the exile and rebuilt the temple have found their identity in the proper worship of God in the place God has chosen. The worship taking place in the Second Temple finds its legitimacy in its continuity with the pattern of worship established centuries before by David.

Chronicles also offers Judah a new definition of divine justice. Kings presents the fall of the Kingdom of Judah as a manifestation of God's justice in the face of the idolatry and infidelity that was characteristic of the final years of the Kingdom of Judah. The promise of an eternal dynasty has been abrogated and the inheritance of the land promised to Israel's ancestors has been irretrievably lost. Chronicles presents Cyrus's decree allowing the

Jewish exiles to return to their homeland, and the support that the Persian kings give for the reconstruction of the temple, as a new manifestation of divine justice. Although Chronicles recognizes the value of the narratives in Samuel and Kings, it also recognizes that these do not speak to the life situation of Jews of the Persian Period. This new situation requires a retelling of the story of the rise and fall of the two Israelite kingdoms.

STORY AND HISTORY

The actual events of history do not fully correspond with the literary depiction of those events. This book does not seek to offer a historical reconstruction of the Israelite monarchies and national states. The primary goal of this work is to shed light on how two ancient literary works present the story of the rise and fall of the Kingdom of Israel and the Kingdom of Judah. Both these stories attempt to provide those who first heard/read them with a way to make sense of what happened when the religious and political institutions of these two kingdoms collapsed, when their towns and villages were ravaged, and when many of their people were forced to migrate to other parts of the ancient Near East. Although it is possible to use some of the biblical narratives in the effort to reconstruct the history of Israel, their original purpose was more religious in nature. This book will follow the lead of the biblical narratives, which tell their respective stories primarily by assessing the reigns of the kings over the two Israelite kingdoms. When appropriate, I will supplement the biblical accounts by references to data coming from archaeological work and from other ancient Near Eastern literary sources. The purpose of these references is to provide a context for the biblical narratives—not to support or reject the historical value of the biblical stories.

Some contemporary readers of the biblical narratives assume that their religious value is supported by demonstrating the historical value of those narratives, and conversely their religious value is undermined by suggesting that a particular narrative is simply the literary creation of the ancient authors. Of course, some of the events mentioned in the biblical stories, such as the siege of

Jerusalem by the Babylonians in 597 BCE as described in 2 Kings 24:8–17, did take place.[9] Other stories such as the account of how David was able to take Jerusalem (2 Sam 5:8; 1 Chr 11:5–6) are likely legendary.[10] At the same time, extreme skepticism regarding the historical value of biblical accounts is not warranted, such as doubting the historical value of accounts of any event before the exile, or suggesting that all biblical narratives are the product of writers in the Hellenistic period to justify Hasmonean claims on territory in the southern Levant.[11]

In the Bible, story functions as a mode of theological discourse. The narratives of the Hebrew Bible make up a sizeable portion of its text. Contemporary Christian believers are accustomed to a more philosophical mode of theological discourse, despite the importance of narrative in the New Testament. The biblical narratives are forms of theological discourse rather than historical accounts of events in the life of ancient Israel.

These biblical narratives were shaped by religious beliefs; individual and communal memories; the cultural, social, political, and economic contexts in which the writing took place; and rhetorical skills of the ancient writers. Thus, this book seeks not to assess the reliability of the biblical narratives about the rise and fall of the Israelite kingdoms but to explore the stories of the two kingdoms *as story*. In addition, this book allows readers to give Chronicles a fair hearing, recognizing that the story of ancient Israel's life in its land has been dominated by the study of the Books of Joshua, Judges, Samuel, and Kings. There has been a growth of interest in Chronicles in the last twenty years.[12] Students of the Bible ought to consider both stories of the Israelite kingdoms. This book provides an introduction to both these stories with the footnotes to direct readers to important studies of specific aspects of these stories.

THE ENDINGS

It may seem strange to begin a study of the two stories of the Israelite kingdoms by taking a close look at the way each story ends. But the respective endings of these two stories serve to highlight the different horizons of each story and provide a key to appreciating their individual goals. The first to be considered is the ending of Kings:

2 Kings 25:27–30

[27]In the thirty-seventh year of the exile of King Jehoiachin of Judah, in the twelfth month, on the twenty-seventh day of the month, King Evil-merodach of Babylon, in the year that he began to reign, released King Jehoiachin of Judah from prison; [28]he spoke kindly to him, and gave him a seat above the other seats of the kings who were with him in Babylon. [29]So Jehoiachin put aside his prison clothes. Every day of his life he dined regularly in the king's presence. [30]For his allowance, a regular allowance was given him by the king, a portion every day, as long as he lived.[13]

After thirty-seven years as a prisoner, King Jehoiachin of Judah is released on parole by Amel-Marduk (known in the Bible as Evil-merodach),[14] Nebuchadnezzar's son and successor. Not only does Amel-Marduk release Jehoiachin from prison but he accords the deposed king of Judah special status above that of the other kings held by the Babylonians. He also provides Jehoiachin with a regular allowance, and invites the former Judean king to dine with him. This was one of several actions taken by Amel-Marduk at the beginning of his reign in 561 BCE that reversed some of his father's harsh policies toward conquered nations like Judah. Babylon's ruling class may have interpreted such actions as a sign of weakness, which may have led to Amel-Marduk's assassination by his brother-in-law Neriglissar a year later. Verses 29–30 suggest that Jehoiachin had died by the time the note of his parole was appended to 2 Kings 25.[15] With Jehoiachin's death, the Davidic dynasty came to an end. Whatever Jehoiachin's life after his release from prison may have been, it is past and gone. Nothing is said about a son or successor for Jehoiachin. God's promise to David of an eternal dynasty (2 Sam 7:15) had been abrogated. The text of 2 Kings does not say this explicitly, but the attentive reader/hearer must wonder about the future of the Davidic dynasty and the Kingdom of Judah. Jehoiachin may have received preferential treatment from Amel-Marduk, but the biblical text does not suggest that the former king's improved status had any effect on the other Judeans in Babylon. They remained as they were—exiles in a land far from their homes with no prospects for any change in their status.[16]

The last four verses of 2 Kings have attracted considerable attention from students of the Bible over the years.[17] The readers/hearers of Joshua to 2 Kings naturally expect the conclusion of this story of Israel in its land to bring a satisfying conclusion. It is, after all, the final words of a major block of biblical material. But this bland notice of Jehoiachin's parole provides little satisfaction. For Martin Noth, whose seminal study of the Books of Joshua to 2 Kings first suggested that these books form a theologically coherent story of Israel and its land, the last four verses of 2 Kings do little more than tie up loose ends.[18] The note about Jehoiachin's parole was nothing more than the last bit of information available about the fate of the last surviving king of Judah, and 2 Kings simply hands on that information. By way of contrast, Gerhard von Rad finds the ending of 2 Kings affirming what he considers to be the linchpin of the story of Israel in its land: the promise made to David of an eternal dynasty (2 Sam 7:11–16).[19] He regards the preferential treatment given to Jehoiachin a subtle but clear signal that Judah will be rehabilitated as was Jehoiachin, and that the promise made to David was not abrogated but will be fulfilled in the future. Over the years, most students of the Old Testament have aligned themselves with one of these two positions, though others have suggested alternatives. For example, Christopher Begg has suggested that both Noth and von Rad failed to read these final four verses of 2 Kings against the backdrop of the treatment of Babylon in 2 Kings, which does not condemn Babylon for its actions against Judah. Second Kings, according to Begg, sees submission to the king of Babylon as offering the best possibility for a tolerable Jewish life following the fall of the Judean state.[20]

Taking a literary approach, David Janzen claims that the ending of 2 Kings is an example of deliberate ambiguity. He argues that ambiguity allows readers to understand the end of the Judean state in a variety of ways, given the story's depth and complexity. Without ambiguity, that last four verses of 2 Kings would be mere reporting that describes things that no longer are. It is important to recognize that ambiguity is not obscurity or lack of clarity. Ambiguity offers the reader the opportunity for reflection and interpretive creativity. It can be a catalyst for comprehension beyond what a surface reading can offer. It promotes discovery beyond the obvious.

Janzen maintains that while it appears that ambiguity is inherent in a text, it is actually an effect of the engagement between the text and its readers/hearers. In fact, textual ambiguity depends on the alertness of the readers/hearers. The quest for meaning of the ending of 2 Kings has been fueled by the pursuit of certainty about what that text was affirming or denying about Judah's future. The search for clarity on the part of interpreters has not been entirely successful because the text is not an object from which the reader extracts meaning; rather, the process of interpreting a text is something that happens when the reader looks for affirmations and negations, emphases and patterns in the text. In the case of 2 Kings 25:27–30, the text itself says nothing about the future of the Davidic dynasty or the people of Judah. Because reading often is in pursuit of knowledge, there is the inevitable push toward resolution. Does the way 2 Kings ends offer hope for the restoration of Judah or not? Of course, readers/hearers instinctively push for resolution, but they should be open to not finding any. Readers/hearers of texts that are considered "sacred" are not always open to perceiving ambiguity in those texts.

When engaged in the task of interpretation, it is essential to see that text in context—not simply the immediate context (2 Kgs 24—25) as Begg suggests, but against the larger context of Joshua to 2 Kings. Seen in that larger context, 2 Kings 25:27–30 is not ambiguous, as Janzen claims. The reader/hearer of Joshua to 2 Kings cannot help but consider its story of Israel in its land anything but a tragic epic. What began with such promise with the Israelite tribes crossing the Jordan River to take possession of the land promised to their ancestors—a land flowing with milk and honey—ends with the elite citizens of the Kingdom of Judah, the sole remnant of the twelve tribes, being forced to migrate to agriculturally marginal areas of Mesopotamia.

The ending of 2 Kings does reflect the tragic story of Israel in its land that is told in Joshua to 2 Kings, and the readers/hearers of that story were prepared for its ending. The story of the tribes united under Joshua going from victory to victory in the Book of Joshua devolves into an account of an internecine warfare as the tribes turn against each other in the Book of Judges. The imposing figure of Saul in 1 Samuel 9 becomes the tortured, paranoid monarch trying to hold on to his throne. The ruddy-cheeked, handsome youth of 1 Samuel 16 whom Samuel anoints as Saul's successor and who defeats the Philistine giant becomes a feeble old man manipulated by his wife and her allies in naming her son Solomon as his successor. The king who asked for wisdom to govern his subjects with justice becomes a much-married idolater to please his many foreign wives. The kingdom of David and Solomon, which extended from the Euphrates to the border with Egypt (1 Kgs 4:21, 24), devolves into two petty Levantine states, which exhaust themselves in fighting over their mutual border. In the Kingdom of Israel, kings and dynasties rise and fall until the territory of that kingdom is absorbed into the Assyrian provincial system with the elite of its population forced to migrate to Assyria.

Despite the Assyrian expansionism, the Kingdom of Judah ruled by a Davidic king was able to at least maintain nominal independence under Assyrian hegemony. With just a few exceptions the kings of Judah tolerated and, in some instances, promoted idolatry. Josiah initiated a reform (2 Kgs 22—23), but it died with him. With Josiah's death, the Kingdom of Judah became a vassal first of Egypt and then of Babylon. The kings who followed Josiah were religious and political disasters. In 597, King Jehoiachin was taken to Babylon after an ill-conceived and short-lived rebellion against Babylonian hegemony. After another futile attempt to reclaim its independence a few years later, Judah fell to the military might of Babylon. Jerusalem and its temple were destroyed, its priesthood scattered, the national state ceased to exist, the members of the royal house were executed, and Zedekiah, the last of Judah's kings, was taken to Babylon along with many of Judah's people. Second Kings does not speak of Zedekiah's fate. Presumably, he died in exile.

This story illustrates the fundamental theological affirmation of the Book of Deuteronomy, namely that commitment and loyalty to YHWH brings blessing while the abandonment of that commitment leads to disaster. The consequences of the failures of

Judah—of its kings and people—are the destruction of Jerusalem and its temple, the scattering of the priests, the forced migration of the king along with Judah's elite to Babylon, the end of the national state whose territory was absorbed into the Babylonian provincial system, and the end of the Davidic dynasty.

The final chapters of 2 Kings suggest that the institutions that gave Judah its religious and political identity were gone. Indeed, they had to go. The prophet Hananiah believed that the fall of Jerusalem and the exile of some of its citizens in 597 were nothing more than a temporary blip (Jer 28:2–4). Jeremiah, of course, recognized that Judah's internal problems were more serious than people realized. Second Kings 25 suggests that Judah's religious and political superstructure will have to come down before it is possible to think of any future. Second Kings 25:27–30 offers no suggestion about Judah's future but rehearses the sorry end of the Kingdom of Judah and the Davidic dynasty. The people of Judah have collectively "hit rock bottom." It was necessary for that reality to sink into Judah's consciousness. Second Kings offers no *deus ex machina* to make things better. It offers no "cheap grace." The story of Israel in its land (Joshua–Kings) ends not with an answer but with a question. Its readers/hearers are left to think about what their future may be. Has our infidelity led to God's revoking the promises made to our ancestors? Has God rejected us?

Christians, who accept the affirmations and negations of the Scriptures as normative for their faith and life, are led to ask, "Can this happen again?" Is the church—especially but not exclusively in Europe and North America—witnessing the dying of the institutions that once gave expression to its vitality? Lay folk, especially the young, are leaving the church in great numbers. Some who remain are trying to re-create the church's long-lost "golden age." The bishops are no longer seen as credible moral leaders. The priesthood is living under a cloud that is not dissipating. Religious communities no longer attract idealistic women and men in numbers that suggest sustainability of this way of life. The Catholic school system is only a skeleton of what it once was. The parochial system is without sufficient personnel and financial resources necessary to ensure its viability. Are Catholics today living in circumstances that are in some way similar to those of sixth-century

Judah? Are we witnessing the death of the institutions that once were a sign of life?

2 Chronicles 36:22-23

[22]In the first year of King Cyrus of Persia, in fulfillment of the word of the LORD spoken by Jeremiah, the LORD stirred up the spirit of King Cyrus of Persia so that he sent a herald throughout all his kingdom and also declared in a written edict: [23]"Thus says King Cyrus of Persia: The LORD, the God of heaven, has given me all the kingdoms of the earth, and he has charged me to build him a house at Jerusalem, which is in Judah. Whoever is among you of all [God's] people, may the LORD his God be with them! Let him go up."

The second story of Israel in its land is found in Chronicles. The ending of Chronicles may be surprising, but it is certainly not ambiguous. The Persian king who ended Babylonian hegemony in the ancient Near East asserts that his victories were engineered by YHWH, for whom he intends to build a temple in Jerusalem. To achieve this purpose Cyrus encourages the Judean exiles to return to Jerusalem.

The Greek name for the Books of Chronicles is *Paraleipomena*, "that which was left out of (the Books of Samuel and Kings)." That title suggests a relationship of sorts between the Books of Samuel and Kings and the Books of Chronicles. Although it is clear that the latter used the former as a source, the tone and purpose of Chronicles differs markedly from those of Samuel/ Kings. Chronicles comes from a time when Judah's fortunes had changed considerably. The national state and the Davidic dynasty had not been restored. Judah was known by its Aramaic name Yehud, and it constituted only a small part of the Persian satrapy (province) of "Beyond the River" (Euphrates). At the same time, new possibilities had emerged. The people of Yehud were able to live according to the traditions of their ancestral religion, and the Persian government recognized the Mosaic Torah as imperial law for Yehud. Just as the story of Israel in its land as told in Joshua to 2 Kings reflects the tragic loss of monarchy and land with which the story ends, that narrated in Chronicles reflects hope in the renewal of YHWH's people under Persian rule.

The change in Judah's fortunes came from an unlikely source. An event twenty-two years after Jehoiachin's parole, which Chronicles does not mention, changed the Judean exiles' prospects dramatically: the city of Babylon fell to Cyrus the Great, the king of Persia. Nabonidus, the last Babylonian king, was extremely unpopular. Among other things, he promoted the worship of the god Sin in place of Marduk, the patron deity of Babylon. He brought the images of the gods from temples of the principal cities of his kingdom to the city of Babylon in the hope that this would unite the people of his realm in the defense of his capital against the Persians. This strategy backfired. The people of Babylon opened the gates of their city and welcomed Cyrus as a liberator. The fall of Babylon, combined with Cyrus's earlier conquests over the Medes, effectively left him in control of the entire ancient Near East.

Cyrus did not adopt the policy followed by the Assyrians and Babylonians, who exchanged populations by forced migrations as a means of pacifying the nations that they conquered. Cyrus encouraged exiles to return to their respective homelands and gave them a measure of autonomy as long as they accepted Persian rule and paid their taxes. Finally, he encouraged the worship of local patron deities, whom he saw of local representations of the Persian god, Ahura Mazda. These policies worked to the benefit of the Judean exiles in Babylon. They opened for them the possibility of reconstituting Jewish life in their homeland.

Some Judeans saw the hand of God in Cyrus's victory over Babylon. The unnamed exilic prophet whose words are found in Isaiah 40—55 identified Cyrus as YHWH's shepherd who would rebuild Jerusalem and lay the foundation of a new temple (Isa 44:28). The same prophet, speaking in the name of God, called Cyrus "my Messiah" (Isa 45:1)—a title that was associated with the kings of Judah. Second Kings sees the political role of the Davidic dynasty as a thing of the past, with no relevance for the present situation of the Judean exiles. Isaiah goes one step further by asserting that Cyrus is Judah's legitimate ruler—by divine choice.

The belief that the rise of Cyrus portended a new moment in Judah's life with God led Judean priestly circles to take another look at the story of Israel in its land as told in Joshua to 2 Kings.

The ending of their retelling of that story is found in 2 Chronicles 36:22–23. The belief that the decree of Cyrus was the fulfillment of a prophecy by Jeremiah (2 Chr 36:21; see also Jer 25:11–12) prompted retelling of the story of the Israelite kingdoms. The prophet maintained that the exile was the judgment of God on an unfaithful people (Jer 29:19), but that the consequences of that judgment would be limited in time.

The Bible's portrayal of Cyrus as God's instrument to restore proper worship in a rebuilt temple was not unique. The Cyrus Cylinder preserves a Babylonian text that claims that Cyrus was fulfilling the will of Marduk and restoring the images from several temples to their original homes. Cyrus's victory over Babylon meant that the "exiled" images were to return to their "homes" (temples). According to the Cyrus Cylinder, Marduk chose Cyrus to restore the proper worship of the patron deities of various Babylonian cities.[21]

The ending of Chronicles, unlike that of Kings, offers its readers concrete hope for the future of Judah. It assumes that judgment was not God's last word to Judah. The exiles of Judah are to return to Jerusalem to rebuild the temple for the worship of their ancestral Deity. After initial hesitancy on the part of the returnees from the exile, the temple was rebuilt with the encouragement of the prophets Haggai and Zechariah and the support of Darius I.[22] Chronicles attempts to convince the people of Judah that the rebuilt temple was the tangible evidence of God's mercy and love for them. What remains for the people to do is support the temple, to worship in the temple, to pray in the temple. A central concern for Chronicles, then, is the temple and its personnel. This central concern serves to shape Chronicles' version of Israel's story. Chronicles begins its story of Israel with the death of Saul and the rise of David (1 Chr 10:1–14), focusing its attention on the preparations David made for the worship of Yʜᴡʜ in the temple that his son Solomon was to build, omitting those stories found within the Books of Samuel and Kings that present the dark side of the reigns of David and Solomon. Chronicles depicts these kings as totally consumed with temple-related matters. Though Chronicles is dependent on Samuel and Kings, it sanitizes the stories of David and Solomon, creating an early Jewish myth of a golden age. Chronicles implies that renewing the worship of

YHWH in the temple of Jerusalem will constitute the beginnings of a new golden age when the people of Judah find their identity and destiny.

Chronicles also ignores the Kingdom of Israel and its fate, except when Judah's kings are in some way involved in the story of the Northern Kingdom. After all, the Kingdom of Israel abandoned the temple of Jerusalem in favor of temples at Dan and Bethel. Second Chronicles 13 encapsulates Chronicles' attitude toward the Kingdom of Israel. The setting of the story is a border conflict between Judah and Israel. Chronicles depicts King Abijah of Judah addressing the army of Jeroboam I, the King of Israel, on the night before the battle was to begin. Abijah tells the forces arrayed against his army that they cannot succeed since their nation was founded on the rejection of the divinely established Davidic dynasty and the cult of YHWH in the Jerusalem temple. Addressing Jeroboam's army, Abijah exclaims, "Do you not know that the LORD God of Israel gave the kingship over Israel forever to David...?" (2 Chr 13:5). Abijah goes on to characterize the worship of the Kingdom of Israel as idolatrous and conducted by "priests of no-gods" (13:9; au. trans.). The Judean king concludes his diatribe against the Northern Kingdom's political and religious system by warning Jeroboam's army: "you cannot succeed" (v. 12). Second Chronicles 13 goes on to describe Judah's victory over Israel, the death of Jeroboam I, and Abijah's growing economic status evidenced by his fourteen wives, twenty-two sons, and sixteen daughters (vv. 13–21).

Chronicles did not intend to describe events, persons, or institutions as they really happened in the life of the two Israelite kingdoms. This work sought to offer a version of the story of Israel in its land that reflected the changed fortunes of the people of Yehud. Given those changed circumstances, those responsible for Chronicles believed that the story found in Joshua to 2 Kings no longer reflected the life of the Jewish community.[23] John Van Seters calls Chronicles "revisionist history."[24] Van Seters regarded the story of the two kingdoms found in Joshua to 2 Kings as an example of genuine historiography. He recognized that Chronicles makes use of that earlier story but refashions it to support its own view of the history of the two Israelite kingdoms, offering readers a view of David, Solomon, Manasseh, Josiah, and other characters from Samuel/Kings that is clearly at odds with the way those books portray them. With the rebuilding of the temple and resumption of sacrificial worship, a key institution of Jewish life in the land promised to Abraham and his descendants was restored. Chronicles calls people to rally around the temple and join in the worship of YHWH there. That Chronicles omits the account of Jehoiachin's parole suggests that it was not perceived as a harbinger of the restoration of Jewish life in the land. It was the decree of Cyrus that made that a possibility. That decree begins the process of reversing of fortunes of the exiles and Jerusalem. The exiles are free to return to Jerusalem and begin restoring Jewish life in the land. In addition, a foreign king (Nebuchadnezzar) brought about the temple's destruction, and a foreign king (Cyrus) called for its reconstruction, beginning a new era in the life of the Jewish people.

The final book in the rabbinic Bible is 2 Chronicles. This ensures that the Bible ends on an explicitly hopeful note: YHWH, "the God of heaven...has charged me to build him a house at Jerusalem....Whoever is among you of all [God's] people, may the LORD his God be with him! Let him go up" (2 Chr 36:23). For Jewish believers, Chronicles' vision continues to find fulfillment in the immigration of Jews from around the world to the modern state of Israel. In fact, the modern Hebrew word for immigration (ʾăliyâ) is derived from the Bible's final word: yāʿal (let him go up).

Does the ending of 2 Chronicles offer hope for Christian readers of this book? Can they find in these words a path to the future of the church's troubled institutions? Will any of these institutions reemerge in a reconstituted, reformed, renewed church? Who will be the instrument of the church's reconstitution? What will that reconstitution look like? What can the church leave behind? The problem with Chronicles is its reliance on a myth of a golden age. Chronicles ignores the realities of the Davidic/Solomonic kingdom in favor of creating a story of two pious kings totally committed to the proper worship of YHWH in the place that God chose, Jerusalem. The implication is that the Jewish people could enjoy another golden age if they follow the lead of David and Solomon.

The restoration of temple worship, however, did not end the internal problems of Yehud—in particular, the disparity between rich and poor (see Isa 58). The Jewish community found itself divided because of the false expectations created by those who saw the future of the Jewish people inexorably tied to temple worship (see Isa 66:1–5). Chronicles is not well represented among the Dead Sea Scrolls. Just one tiny fragment preserves a few words from Chronicles. Mika Pajunen suggests this may be due to the centrality of the temple in Chronicles and its significance for the Hasmonean dynasty.[25] It was resistance to the Hasmoneans that led "the sons of light" to seek refuge in a settlement along the northwestern shore of the Dead Sea.

The Jerusalem temple was not able to respond adequately to the people's religious needs. The pious began to gather in small groupings to read the Scriptures and to pray together. This was the beginning of the synagogue. This institution enabled Judaism to survive and reconstitute itself after the destruction of the Second Temple and the scattering of its priesthood in 70 CE by the Romans. The vision of Chronicles with its myth of a golden age, though important in the Persian Period, was not the key to Judaism's future. That key would be found in the Deuteronomic tradition with its emphasis on the commitment to YHWH and obedience to the Torah.

Some Catholics today attempt to find refuge in the myth of the golden age. They find the solution to the problems they perceive as threats to the church's existence in the restoration of old liturgical practices and forms of popular piety. They are uncomfortable with the church's involvement in social and economic issues. They want the church's rituals led by male clerics alone. They are uncomfortable with lay ministry. But the way to the church's future is to move forward and not backward.

Chapter One

The Preludes

Each of the two stories of the rise and fall of the Israelite kingdoms has its own prelude. In the case of Samuel/Kings, that prelude includes the Books of Joshua, Judges, and 1 Samuel 1—7. The genealogies of 1 Chronicles 1—9 make up the prelude to Chronicles' story of the two kingdoms. As one might expect, each of these preludes provides a glimpse into the direction that the stories themselves will take. Joshua and Judges serve to prepare readers/hearers for the disaster with which the story of the two kingdoms end in 2 Kings 25. First Chronicles 1—9 serves to direct the reader's attention to David, who serves as the model for the postexilic Jewish community, implying a continuity between David's preparation for construction of Solomon's temple and the worship that will take place there with the experience of the Jewish community in the Second Temple. Chronicles maintains that such continuity provides legitimacy for that Second Temple. The genealogies provide explicit evidence of continuity.

JOSHUA 1—1 SAMUEL 7

The Book of Joshua

The Book of Joshua opens with the Israelite tribes encamped in the plains of Moab on the eastern shore of the Jordan River shortly after the death of Moses. The book's opening chapter begins with four discourses. In the first discourse, God commissions Joshua as the successor of Moses, ordering Joshua to take up the task of leading the Israelites across the Jordan to take possession of the land promised to their ancestors and Moses. God gives the expansive dimensions of the territory that the Israelites were to inherit: from Lebanon in the north to the Euphrates in the east and the Mediterranean to the west.[1] God reminds Joshua that the key to fulfilling his charge successfully is obedience to what Moses wrote in the "book of the law" (Josh 1:1–9). In Samuel and Kings, the kings of Israel and Judah will be judged by their observance of two prescriptions of that law: first, loyalty to YHWH and the avoidance of idolatry (Deut 5:6–10), and second, worship at the place that God will choose for God's name (Deut 12). The readers/hearers know that the people of the two Israelite kingdoms were not in possession of the land, and God's speech at the beginning of Joshua makes clear why.

Following his commissioning, Joshua addresses tribal leaders in the second discourse. He orders them to prepare the people for the crossing of the Jordan (Josh 1:10–11). He then addresses the tribes of Reuben and Gad along with the half-tribe of Manasseh in the third discourse. Their tribal inheritance will be on the east side of the Jordan. Joshua orders the military muster of these tribes to join with those of the other tribes in the effort to take possession of the region west of the Jordan (1:11–15). The scene closes with a fourth discourse as fighters from the eastern tribes agree to follow Joshua's orders (1:16–18).

The scene is set for the tribes' crossing the Jordan into "the land of Canaan." Canaan is a geographical term rather than a political one. It encompasses the territories represented by the modern nonpolitical term *the Levant*. Upon crossing the Jordan in Canaan, the Israelites encounter the region's indigenous population, which resists the Israelites' incursion. In quick order the Israelite tribes take control of Canaan in three principal thrusts. The first to come under Israelite control is the central area with its cities of Jericho, Ai, and Shechem (Josh 2—28).[2] There was a temporary setback when Achan kept some of the booty from Jericho for himself. He was found out and dealt with (7:1—8:29), and the Israelite tribes were able to take control of the region.

Following the successful campaign in central Canaan, Joshua leads the tribes to take the south of Canaan (Josh 9:3—10:43).

Though a coalition of the city-states in the south opposed the Israelites, Joshua's forces prevailed. When the tribal militias turned to the north, they faced another coalition, which was led by Jabin, the king of Hazor. Again, the Israelites prevailed (11:1–15). A recurring motif in the stories of the land taking was that the victories of the Israelite tribes were won for them by YHWH. The Israelite tribes confess that they are victorious only because "the LORD has given all the land into our hands; moreover, all the inhabitants of the land melt in fear before us" (Josh 2:24). Evidence of the book's emphasis on the priority of God's actions in the land taking is the 227 times the name YHWH appears in Joshua.

Following the account of the land taking, the bulk of the Book of Joshua recounts the division of the land among the tribes (Josh 13:1—21:45). The assumption behind this portion of Joshua was that each tribe, clan, and family would have a specific allotment of land. Possession of that land made it possible for the Israelites to produce the food necessary to sustain themselves. The account of the distribution of the land among the tribes, however, begins with a listing of the regions of Canaan that were not under Israelite control (13:1–7). Among those regions is the land controlled by the five Philistine city-states. The Philistines will prove themselves to be Israel's most intractable opponents. The Israelite tribes could not be secure in Canaan until the Philistine threat was neutralized.

The book ends with three concluding sections. The first is a warning against disputes that can undermine the unity of the tribes (Josh 22:1–34). The dispute is over an altar built east of the Jordan River by the tribes that settled there. The tribes that settled west of the Jordan regarded the altar at Shiloh as the sole legitimate place of worship (Josh 22:19).[3] This is a harbinger of the dispute between the Kingdom of Israel and the Kingdom of Judah over the proper place to offer sacrificial worship. This dispute continued even after the fall of both kingdoms, well into the first century CE (see John 4:19–20). The worship of their ancestral Deity ought to unite the tribes, but from the very beginning of their life in the land promised to their ancestors, the tribes are at odds with one another over the proper place of worship. Of course, this dispute had political ramifications. The tribes from east of the Jordan feared that they would be dominated by the rest of the Israelite community, so they asserted their independence by having their own altar for sacrifice. The conflict ended when the Transjordanian tribes relented and assured the other tribes that no sacrifices would be offered on their altar. It will be simply a memorial of their belief in YHWH (Josh 22:29, 34). The story of this intertribal dispute lays the groundwork for a recurring motif in Kings: there is only one place for legitimate sacrificial worship—the place God will choose—a belief central to the Book of Deuteronomy (see Deut 12). For Kings this place is the temple of Jerusalem.

The Book of Joshua concludes with a pair of exhortations (23:1–16; 24:1–28) that turns Israel's past into a "sermon" that urges the people to recommit themselves to their ancestral Deity. These exhortations are similar to the testaments of revered figures of the past who give a final charge to their children before their deaths, namely, Jacob in Genesis 48—49 and Joseph in Genesis 50:22–26. In the case of Moses, the entire Book of Deuteronomy, especially 32—33, may be considered Moses's testament to all the people of Israel. The testament is a literary form that purports to contain the final words of a well-known figure of the past. Testaments usually contain moral exhortations and blessings. This form became popular in the Second Temple period as exemplified by such pseudepigraphical works as the *Testament of Moses* and the *Testaments of the Twelve Patriarchs*. An example from the New Testament is Jesus's Farewell Discourse in John 13:31—17:26.

Joshua 23:1–16 is Joshua's testament directed to the leaders of the Israelite tribes. Joshua reminds them of what YHWH has done for Israel and calls them to observe "all that is written in the book of the law of Moses" (v. 6) and to love YHWH (v. 11). Joshua also warns the tribal leaders of the consequences of disloyalty and disobedience: "You [will] perish quickly from the good land that YHWH has given you" (23:16). This warning is an example of *vaticinium ex eventu*, that is, prophecy after the fact. It reminds the readers/hearers of the Book of Joshua that the people of the Israelite kingdoms were well aware of the consequences of their infidelity. God's forbearance was exhausted by Israel's kings and people. The rise of the Mesopotamian kingdoms with military might and expansionist politics brought an end to the two Israelite kingdoms. The Book of Kings sees the fall of the kingdoms as a direct consequence of the infidelity of Israel and Judah.

Joshua's final words are addressed to the entire Israelite community assembled at Shechem.[4] After rehearsing the mighty deeds of God on Israel's behalf, he calls the people to recommit themselves to the service of YHWH alone (Josh 24:1–15). Without hesitation, the people promise to be loyal to YHWH (24:16–18). Joshua, then, reminds the people of implications of their choice: they are to foreswear the service of any other god. The people agree and Joshua leads them in renewing their covenant with YHWH (24:19–28).

The book ends with a notice of Joshua's death and burial in central highlands in the territory of Ephraim. It also notes that Israel remained loyal to YHWH during Joshua's lifetime and that of the tribal elders who survived him. The Book of Joshua sees the time of the settlement as an ideal period in Israel's life. The tribes were united under a single leader chosen by God. While that leader was alive, Israel remained loyal to the God who gave them the land promised to their ancestors. This underscores the significance of leaders who themselves are loyal to God in maintaining Israel's commitment to YHWH.

The Book of Judges

The story of Israel's settlement in Canaan takes a dark turn following the death of Joshua. The Book of Judges suggests that the settlement was not as successful as portrayed in the Book of Joshua. Judges begins by listing the regions of Canaan that were not under Israelite control (Judg 1:1–34). This meant that some Israelites had to live among the Canaanites. This had an unfortunate effect of weakening their commitment to serve YHWH alone. A "messenger from God"[5] points out the failure of people in that situation to remain loyal to YHWH. Without hesitation, the people express sorrow and regret over their infidelity (Judg 2:21–25).

The plot of the remaining stories in Judges is laid out in Judges 2:1—3:6. This section of the book describes the downward path taken by the people of Israel as they come under the influence of the indigenous peoples of Canaan. This led to a deadly spiral that threatened to bring an end to Israel's life in its land. After the death of Joshua, the Israelites are drawn to the worship of "the Baals" (Judg 2:11).[6] Baal is not a proper name but a title, meaning

"Lord," for the god Hadad, a storm god who brought rain and fertility to the land. Rain was critically important for agriculture in Canaan. The moisture essential for the growing of crops had to come in the form of rain. It is likely that the Israelites did not see that the cult of Baal was necessarily incompatible with their service of YHWH. This failure to remain loyal to YHWH alone had consequences for their continued presence in the land. The Israelite tribes began losing their grip on the land, as the indigenous peoples raided their villages (Judg 2:13). Before Israel's enemies could end Israel's presence in Canaan, "YHWH raised up judges" who responded to the threats to Israel's existence. These judges were military leaders who were able to rouse the tribal militia to stand up against those who attacked Israelite settlements. But upon the death of a judge, the tribes relapsed. When they repented, God would raise up another judge. The Book of Judges depicts a cycle of idolatry, followed by repentance only to be followed by idolatry. The question any reader/hearer would have is how long this cycle can go on.

Chapters 3—13 contain a collection of stories about tribal military leaders, whom the text never calls "judges." Though the Book of Judges names twelve such leaders, only six receive more than a passing mention: Othniel (3:9–11), Ehud (3:15–37), Deborah (4—5), Gideon (6—8), Jephthah (11—12), and Samson (13—16). Some are unlikely leaders because of their low social position: Deborah is a woman, Gideon a simple agricultural worker, Jephthah a son of a prostitute. Each of the judges comes from a different geographical locale, for example, Othniel was from Judah, Ehud and Jephthah were from the Transjordan, Deborah was from the central highlands, and Samson was from the region just north of the Philistine cities. The Book of Judges is an assemblage of stories about tribal heroes that are set out in an artificial chronological order. None of the judges was able to muster a fighting force from all the tribes. The militia from tribes immediately affected by a threat responded to the judge's call to arms. Deborah complains about the tribes that did not join in the battle against Jabin, the king of Hazor. Jabin wanted to keep control of the Jezreel Valley because of its agricultural, commercial, and strategic importance (Judg 5:15b–17). Unless Israel could wrest the Jezreel Valley from Jabin, the tribes north of the valley would be cut off from the rest of the tribes. Gideon took reprisals against the elders of Succoth, who did not support his army in the conflict with the Midianite raiders (Judg 8:13–17). Jephthah fought with the Ephraimites when they did not join in his conflict with Ammon. In Joshua, the tribes are united in their efforts to take control of Canaan. In Judges, the unity among the Israelite tribes has broken down.

The Book of Judges ends with an appalling story of the gang rape of a secondary wife of a Levite from Ephraim by men from the town of Gibeah in the tribal territory of Benjamin. The Levite's wife died after a night of horror. The Levite called upon the Israelite tribes to avenge this crime. All Israel "from Dan to Beersheba" responds to his call. Ironically, the Levite was more successful at mustering the Israelite tribes than any of the judges. Thus, began a cycle of internecine warfare that threatened to do what the indigenous population of Canaan was unable to do: end Israel's existence in the land promised to their ancestors. The tribe of Benjamin was hit the hardest and it appeared that it was threatened with extinction. The other tribes then allowed the men of Benjamin to kidnap women of Shiloh to repopulate their tribe. There were to be no reprisals against Benjamin for what was nothing less than kidnapping and rape. Thus, the Book of Judges ends with a civil war sandwiched between accounts of brutal rapes that show no regard for women as human beings. In shock and wonder, the reader/hearer asks if things could get any worse. Judges ends with a rather weak explanation for the morass that the tribes of Israel created for themselves: "In those days there was no king in Israel; all the people did what was right in their own eyes" (Judg 21:25).

The story of how the tribes of Israel came to possess the land began well and ended terribly. The period of Joshua's leadership was presented as the ideal. A united Israel serving YHWH alone and observing all that was written in the Torah succeeds in settling in the land promised to their ancestors. YHWH gives the tribes victory over the Canaanites. The Book of Judges, however, portrays the settlement period in ominous tones. Periods of idolatry followed by oppression alternate with periods of repentance followed by restoration. The tribes are no longer united but act out of self-interest alone. The settlement period ends with what Phyllis Trible characterized as "texts of terror."[7] The fallout from these outrages leads the reader/hearer to wonder about Israel's future.

The stories connected with the settlement of the Israelite tribes are stories of violence and war. Reconstructing this period is a problem for historians, archaeologists, and biblical theologians. What was going on in Canaan at the time the Israelite tribes sought to gain a foothold in the region? It has been long recognized that the period of the Israelite settlement was a time of disruption and collapse in the eastern Mediterranean world. There has been no agreement among scholars regarding the cause of this generalized disruption, the collapse of urban centers and political entities, and the mass migration of peoples that followed. Recent examination of the lake bed of the Sea of Galilee has produced evidence of a local climate change in the region that brought about a severe diminishment of food production. It was this climate change that led to conflicts among the people of Canaan over food.ᵉ The groups that eventually recast themselves as the *banê yiśrā'ēl* (the children of Israel) were among the people struggling for survival in most difficult of circumstances. This assumes that the bulk of the people making up the *banê yiśrā'ēl* were Canaanites who left the urban centers of Canaan and resettled in the lightly populated central highlands as part of the migrations and shifting populations during the 150 years of the climate change.

The story of the Israelite tribes in their land shifts from the period of settlement to a time of disintegration. The problems that the tribes faced are both internal and external. The issue of leadership is still an important one. Without strong and effective leadership Israel may not survive the most serious threat it has yet to face: the expansion of the Philistines from the strongholds in the southwest of Canaan to the area where the Israelite tribes have made their home. This part of Israel's story begins in the Book of 1 Samuel.

1 Samuel 1–7

The judges did lead the Israelite tribes in responding to military threats, but they were not able to maintain the unity of the tribes nor their commitment to YHWH. Samuel enters the story and becomes the person who served as the bridge between the period of the judges and the beginning of the monarchy. He was judge, priest, and prophet and led the Israelite tribes, when the

Israelites still had not established themselves firmly in the southern Levant. Samuel came on the scene following the disaster of the civil war that almost destroyed the tribes and as the Philistines, whose origin was likely in southern Europe, emerged as the most powerful and determined of Israel's rivals for dominance in Canaan.[9] When the Philistines inflicted a stinging defeat on the tribal militia, the Israelite elders came to the conclusion that a strong centralized leadership was needed, so they asked Samuel for a king. This request was the first step in the establishment of a national state whose population was made up of primarily people who thought of themselves as *banê yiśrā'ēl*.

Samuel's story begins at Shiloh. His parents went to the shrine there for the annual pilgrimage. His mother Hannah, who had been unable to conceive, prayed for a child, promising to dedicate a male child to God's service (1 Sam 1:9–11). Hannah did have a son and once he was weaned, she took him to the shrine at Shiloh, leaving him there in fulfillment of her promise (1 Sam 1:27—2:1a). Samuel served at the shrine under the direction of the priest Eli. The circumstances of Samuel's birth marked him for greatness in the service of God. Eli blessed Hannah and her husband Elkanah, and they had five more children (1 Sam 2:18–20).

The next scene in Samuel's story takes place when he is an adult and Eli is old. An unnamed "man of God" visits Eli and reminds him of the promise made to his ancestor that he and his descendants would always be priests, but he announces that God will revoke the promise because of the conduct of Eli's sons. Both have proved themselves unfit for the priesthood because of their greed (1 Sam 2:12–17). They will die before Eli himself does, and God will "raise up...a faithful priest" in their stead (1 Sam 2:35). The man of God does not name the ancestor who was chosen by God to serve as God's priest, though it is likely Levi (see Exod 32:29; Deut 33:8–11).

The revocation of the promise made to Eli's ancestor of an eternal priestly dynasty (1 Sam 2:30) alerts the reader/hearer of the possibility that God can and will revoke promises. In 2 Samuel 7:16, God promises David an eternal dynasty, but following the fall of Judah to Babylon, the Davidic dynasty is extinguished— another of God's promises that was revoked.[10] The void created by God's rejection of Eli's sons is filled when God calls Samuel in a dream (1 Sam 3:1–18). This divine designation is coupled with the popular acclamation of Samuel, whom the people of Israel acknowledge as a prophet through whom YHWH's word comes to Israel (1 Sam 3:19–20).

Samuel's story is put on hold as 1 Samuel 4:1b begins describing the odyssey of the ark of the covenant (1 Sam 4:1b—7:1). The ark of the covenant was a rectangular (45 in. x 27 in. x 27 in.) box made of acacia wood that was a symbol of the Deity's presence among the Israelite tribes. It was also known as "the ark of God," "the ark of testimony," and "the ark of YHWH." Its most elaborate designation is found in 2 Samuel 6:2: "the ark of the covenant, which is called by YHWH of hosts who is enthroned on the cherubim." This phrase reflects the notion that God sat invisibly above the ark on the outstretched wings of two cherubim that were depicted in gold on the top of the ark. The ark itself, then, served as a footstool for YHWH. Chronicles explicitly calls the ark "the footstool of our God" (1 Chr 28:2). Deuteronomy, however, considers the ark simply a box made by Moses to contain the two tablets of the law (Deut 10:1–6).

Originally the ark served as a palladium. As such it was taken into battle by the Israelites, who believed that its presence offered them protection and ensured their victory as it did at Jericho (Josh 6:12). This is precisely the conception of the ark that underlies 1 Samuel 4—6. The Israelite militia takes the ark from Shiloh, where it was housed in a tent, as they prepare to confront the Philistines, but the Philistines defeat Israel and capture the ark (1 Sam 4:10–11). The ark then begins its travels. First, it is taken to the temple of the Philistine god Dagon in Ashdod.[11] The failure of the ark to effect a military victory over the Philistine army was simply a prologue to the story of YHWH's cosmic victory over Dagon. The image of Dagon collapses in the presence of the ark (1 Sam 5:1–5). The Philistines then move the ark to other cities in their territory—first to Gath and then to Ekron. The ark brought devastation to wherever it went in Philistine territory. After seven months, the Philistines decide to return the ark to the Israelites, accompanied by an indemnity of several golden images (1 Sam 6:1–9). The ark arrives in the Israelite town of Beth-shemesh. The people of this town, in fear, pass the ark on to Kiriath-jearim, a village twelve miles northwest of Jerusalem. There it remained for twenty years in the house of Abinadab (1 Sam 7:1–2). Leonhard Rost suggested that the story of the ark's odyssey was originally an independent saga that he termed "the Ark Narrative."[12] For a long time, scholars agreed with Rost. More recently the tide has shifted so that fewer scholars now hold that position, preferring to read the story in its larger literary context as depicting David's attempt to consolidate his position as king.[13]

The Philistine victory resulted not only in the loss of the ark, but also in the loss of a substantial portion of the Israelite militia. Among the fallen were Hophni and Phineas, Eli's sons. When Eli received the news of the Israelite defeat, the death of his sons, and the loss of the ark, the shock was too much for the old man to bear. He died after having judged Israel for forty years (1 Sam 4:12–18). This sets the scene for the emergence of Samuel as the undisputed leader of the Israelite tribes.

The Philistines remained in a dominant position for twenty years. Samuel called Israel to repentance, which would induce YHWH to take Israel's side against the Philistines. Samuel assembled the people at Mizpah,[14] where the people fasted and prayed (1 Sam 7:5–6). The Philistines sought to take advantage of this gathering and attacked the Israelites while they were worshiping YHWH. A sudden bolt of thunder surprised the Philistines who fled. The Israelites pursued them and inflicted a serious defeat on the retreating Philistines. Israel was able to recover some lost territory because of their victory, which Samuel memorialized by setting up a commemorative stone. First Samuel 7 ends by summarizing Samuel's career as a judge. He made an annual circuit of towns in Benjamin to facilitate this administration of justice.

The Israelite tribes managed not only to gain a foothold into the land promised to their ancestors but also to survive the internal and external threats to their continued existence in that land. They were able to do this without the benefit of a centralized leadership provided by a monarchy. The period before the rise of the Israelite monarchy was marked by a decentralized political system in which each tribe guarded its independence. When specific threats developed, a judge arose who provided effective but temporary leadership, but elders of the Israelite tribes wanted a monarchy. Evidently, they thought that this institution would bring permanence and stability. Samuel sought to ensure continuity of leadership by appointing his sons as judges, but they proved themselves to be unfit since "they took bribes and perverted justice" (1 Sam 8:1–3). The elders of Israel then approached Samuel with a request that he appoint a king.

1 CHRONICLES 1–9

The genealogies found in 1 Chronicles take up about one-third of that book. Obviously, a lot of time and effort were expended in assembling this material. It is clear, then, that the genealogies play a significant role in the book despite the tedium that afflicts the contemporary readers of these chapters. Those readers also may wonder about the point of beginning the story of the Israelite monarchy with such detailed information about the ancestors of its first readers/hearers. At first glance, all this information appears to be intrusive in a story about the rise and fall of the Israelite kingdoms. Actually, this is not an unusual way to introduce an important story in the Bible at all. For example, the story of the flood (Gen 6—9) is preceded by the genealogy from Adam to the sons of Noah (Gen 5). A genealogy that traces the descendants of the sons of Noah as they repopulated the earth introduces the Tower of Babel story (Gen 10—11). The patriarchal narratives (Gen 12—50) are preceded by the genealogy representing descent of Abram and his family from Shem (Gen 11:10–32). In the New Testament, a genealogy of Jesus introduces the story of his birth and infancy (Matt 1—2). A second genealogy introduces the story of his ministry (Luke 4:23–38).

The genealogies are an indispensable component of Chronicles' story of the Israelite kingdoms. Chronicles sheds new light on the older account of the two kingdoms and their fate as found in Samuel and Kings. By beginning with Adam, Chronicles broadens the horizons of his readers by implying that God has concerns that go beyond the fate of Judah alone. In view of Israel's election, this suggests that Jewish people struggling to recover their identity are to see their responsibility to be a light to the nations as essential to that identity.

The arrangement of the genealogies of the Israelite tribes is significant. Several scholars have identified a chiastic structure

for chapters 1—9.[15] The one feature of the structure of the genealogies, however, that does stand out is the placement of Judah's
genealogy in the first position (2:1—4:23). Chronicles ignores the
birth order of the sons of Jacob. The genealogy of Reuben, Jacob's
firstborn, appears *after* those of Judah and Simeon.[16] Judah is given
pride of place because it is the tribe to which David belongs. The
rehabilitation of David's reputation is a major concern of Chronicles. David becomes the ideal king and the ideal Israelite because
he is so devoted to all aspects of the worship of Yhwh in the temple
to be built by his son Solomon. Simeon's genealogy comes immediately after that of Judah, probably because the tribe of Simeon
early on loses its identity and is absorbed by the tribe of Judah
(Josh 19:1–9; Judg 1:3; 1 Chr 4:27, 31). In addition to Judah's
placement at the head of the tribal genealogy, Chronicles devotes
as much space to Judah as to the rest of the tribes combined.

The genealogies are not mere lists. They are interspersed with
comments that reflect important motifs in the book. In explaining
the standing given to Judah, Chronicles recounts, "Judah became
prominent among his brothers and a ruler came from him" (1 Chr
5:2). This, of course, is an allusion to David, a central figure in
Chronicles' story of the Israelite monarchy. Chronicles lists David's
fifteen sons (1 Chr 3:9) and his descendants who succeeded him
on the throne up to the return from Babylon under Zerubbabel
(1 Chr 3:10–19). The list of David's descendants concludes with
several generations from the Second Temple period. These Davidides are otherwise unknown. Chronicles displays great interest in
the tribe of Judah and in David and his descendants. There is no
indication that Chronicles expected a restoration of the Judahite
state and the Davidic dynasty; rather, the focus on David serves to
legitimate the cult of Yhwh in the temple that will be constructed
by order of Cyrus (1 Chr 36:33). That cult will duplicate the pattern of temple worship set by David.

The genealogy of Levi is placed at the center of the tribal
genealogies (1 Chr 6:1–81) and at the end as well (9:10–34).
Chronicles devotes more space to Levi than it gives to the other
tribes (except for Judah) combined. This is not surprising given
the role the priests and Levites play in Yehud at the beginning of
the Second Temple period. It is important to remember that the
setting for the end of 2 Chronicles is the time of Cyrus the Great

of Persia.[17] Chronicles sees the identity of the people of Yehud refashioned according to the parameters set out by the Persians. There will be no restoration of the Judahite state or of its native dynasty. Yehud will be a theocratic entity whose principal concern is the service of YHWH in the temple of Jerusalem. Under these circumstances, priests were to have a prominent position in Yehud, and so it is understandable that Levites hold significant places in the genealogies of the tribes. The association of the Levites with Jerusalem (9:1–34) and its temple serves to enhance the status of the city. One consequence of Yehud's status as a theocratic entity whose principal function is the worship of YHWH in the temple is that, freed from its political connections, Jerusalem becomes a "holy city" (Neh 11:1, 18). The holiness of the temple is attached to the city as a whole. This is a significant moment in the evolution of Jerusalem's status in Jewish thought and piety. Levi and Judah combined have 50 percent of the listings in the genealogies of Chronicles. This is a clear indicator of the lens through which Chronicles views the story of Israel in its land. It also prepares the reader/hearer for the Chronicles' version of that story with its emphasis on David and his connection with the temple and related institutions. Samuel and Kings turn Israel's past into a sermon on fidelity and commitment. By contrast, Chronicles underscores the importance of continuity with David's plans for the worship of YHWH in Solomon's temple as providing legitimacy for the patterns of the worship of YHWH in the Second Temple.

Though Saul, Israel's first king, gets scant attention in the narratives of Chronicles (1 Chr 10), the genealogy of Benjamin, his tribe, is given twice (7:6–12; 8:1–40), and a specific genealogy for Saul appears as well (9:35–44). The reason for the specific attention to Saul in the latter genealogy is to give Israel's first king his due. The list of Saul's descendants extends to about the middle of the eighth century. The concern that Saul is getting lost in the mass of data given in the genealogies demonstrates one of the principal theological contributions that the genealogies of Chronicles makes. Though the story of the two Israelite kingdoms will focus on kings, royal advisors, prophets, and priests, the genealogies testify to the significance of the individual, ordinary Israelite. Their names are remembered and recorded. It would have been impossible to tell the stories of all these people; nevertheless, their inclusion in the genealogies is a mark that they as individuals are important.

Like Saul, the Kingdom of Israel is only on the periphery of Chronicles, whose principal focus is on the Kingdom of Judah. The presence of the genealogies of all the tribes, however, indicates that Chronicles still regards "all Israel" as the ideal. Second Kings 17 regards the population in the territory of the former Kingdom of Israel as not authentic Israelites but the result of intermarriage with non-Israelite immigrants into that territory. Chronicles does not contain a story about the fall of the Kingdom of Israel and its immediate impact. It has Hezekiah celebrate a "national Passover" to which the people of Ephraim and Manasseh, the most populous northern tribes, are invited (2 Chr 30:1). Similarly, at Josiah's Passover "all Judah and all Israel" were present (2 Chr 35:18). Although Chronicles is Jerusalem-centered, this does not mean that the people of the former Northern Kingdom are excluded. Chronicles' vision of the future includes all who trace their genealogy to Jacob.

CONCLUSION

The preludes to the two stories of the rise and fall of the Israelite kingdom have two different horizons. The prelude to the story in Samuel and Kings focuses its attention on specific individuals: Joshua, the judges, and Samuel. The emphasis here is on effective leadership, which is marked above all by the leader's commitment to YHWH and to "the book of the law." The prelude to the story in Chronicles too focuses on individuals but as members of the people of Israel. The latter emphasis is significant for both the ancient and modern reader/hearer. Chronicles' inclusive vision is an emphasis that serves to broaden the horizons of all readers, ancient and modern. It reminds them that barriers, borders, and walls that separate people from each other are not the future of the human family.

Chapter Two

The Early Israelite Monarchy

The Israelite tribes managed not only to gain a foothold into the land promised to their ancestors but also to survive the threats to their continued existence in that land. They were able to do this without the benefit of a centralized leadership provided by a monarchy. The period before the rise of the Israelite monarchy was marked by a decentralized political system in which each tribe guarded its independence. The leaders of the Israelite tribes believed that this could not continue—that strong, effective, centralized leadership was necessary if the Israelites were to overcome the threats to their continued hold on the land. First–Second Samuel and 1–2 Chronicles both describe the beginnings of the Israelite monarchy, but they have different takes on Israel's first three kings: Saul, David, and Solomon. The concern of these texts is not to reconstruct the history of the monarchy's early years but to turn Israel's past into a sermon, that is, as a guide to their hearers/readers for their lives—as a guide for their future.

This chapter will profile how Samuel/Kings and Chronicles portray Israel's first three kings. First Samuel describes the tall, handsome Saul—every inch a king—who eventually was destroyed by his paranoia and depression that led him to take his life after a crushing military defeat. Chronicles virtually ignores Saul in its rush to focus on David and Solomon. First Samuel tells the story of a ruddy-faced youth who stood up to Goliath but who eventually became an old man manipulated by his wife and his courtiers. First Chronicles ignores David's failures as it portrays him solely committed to preparing for the worship of YHWH that would take place in the temple his son was to build. First Kings depicts Solomon as the wise and wealthy king who built the temple of YHWH in Jerusalem but who, in the end, became entangled in idolatry. Second Chronicles omits any mention of the dark side of Solomon's reign and focuses on the building of the temple in Jerusalem.

There is some tension in the way Samuel/Kings portrays Saul, David, and Solomon with their respective portraits in Chronicles. These differences can be explained against the backdrop of the different audiences first addressed by these texts. Samuel/Kings tells of the death of the religious and political institutions that gave the people of Israel their identity. These books address a people who asked their patron God, "Why have you forgotten us completely? Why have you forsaken us these many days?" (Lam 5:20). Chronicles, on the other hand, addresses the descendants of the people who returned to Jerusalem, rebuilt the temple, and hoped to reconstitute Jewish life in their ancestral homeland. Samuel, Kings, and Chronicles aim to have their readers/hearers see themselves and their experiences reflected in the lives of their first three kings.

SAUL

First Samuel demythologizes the monarchy. In Egypt, the Pharaoh was a divine being—the god Horus incarnate and the son of the god Re. In Mesopotamia, monarchy was part of the divinely established order. The Sumerian King List (18th cen. BCE) begins, "After the kingship descended from heaven...." First Samuel presents the monarchy in Israel as a human institution whose origin is the response to a request made by the elders of Israel. For 1 Samuel the story of Saul is the story of the Israelite monarchy's origin. Although the tribes were able to maintain control of their respective regions, the threat that the Philistines posed could not be ignored. The last of the charismatic leaders of the Israelite tribes was Samuel, and the tribes turned to him, requesting his help in establishing more centralized leadership for Israel. In other words, the tribes wanted a king "like other nations" (1 Sam 8:5). The Philistine heartland was in the southwestern region of Canaan, which was controlled by five city-states: Ashdod, Ashkelon, Gaza, Ekron, and Gath. The Philistines sought to extend their control over more of the territory and resources of Canaan by expanding to the north and east—into territory controlled by several Israelite tribes. Conflict between the Philistines and the Israelite tribes was inevitable.

Samuel sought to continue the pattern of leadership reflected in the Book of Judges by naming his sons as his successors, but the tribal leaders had no confidence in Samuel's sons. The elders of the tribes were adamant—they wanted a king since they believed that this was the only way to respond to the Philistine threat. Samuel was opposed, and he delivered three speeches in opposition to the request of the elders. In 1 Samuel 8:1–9, Samuel asserts that asking for a king is tantamount to rejecting YHWH as king. In 1 Samuel 8:10–22, Samuel enumerates the inroads the king will make in the personal and economic lives of his subjects. In 1 Samuel 10:17–19, Samuel reiterates his assertion that by asking for a king, the people are rejecting the rule of YHWH as their king. Samuel believed that the preference for a human king in place of a divine ruler was an act both of ingratitude and of folly.

Despite Samuel's opposition to the establishment of the monarchy, he recognizes that God has chosen Saul as king (1 Sam 9:1—10:16). Not only does Saul cut an imposing figure, he also has been chosen by God to end the Philistine threat. Samuel recognizes this and anoints Saul as king (10:1–2). Saul's reign begins well enough. The Ammonites threatened the Israelites living in the town of Jabesh in Gilead, a hilly region in the north of the Transjordan. Saul was able to marshal a small army and relieve the people of Jabesh-Gilead. Israel acclaims Saul as king once again following his victory over the Ammonites.

With the leadership of the Israelite tribes in Saul's hand, Samuel makes his farewell. He begins by asserting that his service was just and honest. It did not enrich him, as God is his witness (1 Sam 11:1–5). He then goes on to recount what God has done on Israel's behalf from the days of Moses to the days of the judges

(11:6–11). Again, the prophet asserts that Israel's request for a king represents a remarkable lack of trust in God's readiness to continue delivering Israel from its enemies. The request was sinful and calls for divine judgment (11:17). Samuel makes good on this threat by asking for rain during the harvest time for wheat. Rain at harvest time would be a disaster. It would make it impossible for the reapers to do their task, and the crop would rot in the field. The thunder and rain that came lead the people to ask for Samuel's intercession. The prophet assures the people that God will not abandon them, but he also warns them that they must be faithful. If they are not, they and their king "shall be swept away" (12:25). The prophet's warning is reminiscent of the warning Moses spoke as the Israelites were about to enter the land promised to their ancestors (Deut 30:13–20).

Both Moses and Samuel speak about the choice that Israel is to make—a choice between fidelity and infidelity, a choice that will determine Israel's future. This warning addresses Israelites of every generation. Their future is the product of the choice they make. Will it be a future of exile and of political, economic, and military impotence? It is Israel's choice. The Deuteronomic tradition reflected in Samuel's speech believes that Israel has its future in its hands. That future is not determined by chance, fate, politics, or military might. Samuel's farewell address, like that of Moses, intimates that there can be a future for Israel beyond judgment and exile.

Though Saul enjoyed some initial success in blunting the Philistine threat, matters soon took an ominous turn. In 1 Samuel 13:7–14, Saul offers a sacrifice that he had no right to do. It was the prerogative of Samuel the priest to offer the sacrifice before the battle with the Philistines. Samuel was late in arriving and Saul wanted to begin his attack. Samuel rebukes Saul and says that no son of his will succeed him as king. Saul falters again after his victory over the Amalekites. He failed to dedicate all the booty acquired to God, keeping some for himself (1 Sam 15:1–35). This failure results in Samuel's declaration that Saul is no longer the legitimate king of Israel. The story of Saul's fall from grace illustrates an important emphasis in Samuel and Kings: Israel's political leaders and people need to obey prophets sent to them. The story of Saul offers an example of what happens when a king fails to do so. The rest of Saul's story in 1 Samuel is told in connection with the story of David's rise to kingship. Still, the attentive reader/hearer will recognize that the story of Saul will not have a happy ending.

First Chronicles has nothing to say about the origins of the Israelite monarchy, assuming that its readers/hearers are familiar with the account given in 1 Samuel. Chronicles notes that Saul is a descendant of Benjamin (1 Chr 8:33). Chronicles' focus, however, is on the tribe of Judah. The story of Saul, Israel's first king, is passed over almost completely. Chronicles limits that story to an account of Saul's disastrous defeat by the Philistines at Mount Giboa and his subsequent suicide. Saul's death paves the way for David, who is Chronicles' main interest. Saul functions merely to introduce the story of David.

DAVID

First Chronicles devotes twenty chapters to David. First–Second Samuel also devotes a significant amount of attention to him, but depicts him as a much more complex individual than the David of Chronicles. First–Second Samuel shows that David was capable of great good but also great evil. Chronicles presents David as entirely taken up with preparations for the worship of YHWH that will take place in the temple that his son Solomon will build. First–Second Samuel allows its readers/hearers to recognize themselves in the story of David, while Chronicles seeks to convince them that their identity is bound up with the authentic and legitimate worship of YHWH that takes place in the temple of Jerusalem.

Both 1–2 Samuel and 1 Chronicles examine the process by which David became king of Israel. First–Second Samuel takes great pains to guide the reader from the anointing of David by the prophet Samuel (1 Sam 16) to the oracle of the prophet Nathan, who conveys the promise of an eternal dynasty (2 Sam 7). First Samuel portrays David as setting out to succeed Saul with careful planning and measured steps, which included his service in Saul's court and army, his insertion into Saul's family, his marriage with women of wealth and influence, his neutralizing other potential successors, his elimination of the Philistine threat, and his appropriation of Israelite religious symbols such as the ark. First Samuel has David actively pursuing the throne of Israel and making the prudent decisions necessary to ensure his succession to Saul. First Samuel paints this complex picture whose subtext is a subtle but clear critique of monarchy. This critique does not have an ideological origin. It was the result of the monarchy's failure to maintain Israel's relationship with YHWH, its ancestral Deity. From the perspective of Samuel and Kings, the monarchy was a failed institution. The story of the monarchy ends in 2 Kings with the death of the last remaining king of the Davidic dynasty (1 Kgs 25:30) and with no prospects for a restoration of the Judahite state and the Davidic dynasty. First Samuel tells the story of David's rise to power in connection with his troubled relationship with Saul (1 Sam 16:14—30:31). This is followed by the account of the war over the succession that pitted the remnants of Saul's army under the leadership of Abner against David's army under the leadership of Joab (2 Sam 2:8; 3:1, 6; 4:12) and the assassination of Ishbaal (2 Sam 4:5–8), Saul's son and successor as king of the Israelite tribes except for Judah. According to 1–2 Samuel, the succession to Saul was anything but smooth.

Chronicles' David hardly resembles the David of 1–2 Samuel. According to Chronicles, David's rise to kingship went very smoothly. Immediately following Saul's death, the elders of Israel anointed David as king (1 Chr 11:1–5). It is as if David's accession was foreordained. What occupies David in Chronicles is the preparation for the worship of YHWH in a temple to be built by his son and successor. This portrait too is shaped by experience—the experience of the Jews during the early Second Temple period. With encouragement and support from the Persian kings, Cyrus and Darius I, Jews who returned from exile built the Second Temple. In it the Jewish people of Yehud were able to do what their ancestors did in the First Temple whose personnel, their accoutrements, and rituals were the objects of David's concern. Continuity with the service of YHWH in temple as determined by David gave legitimacy not only to the rites and personnel of the Second Temple but also to the entire Judean restoration.

David's Rise to Kingship

The story of David's accession to the throne of Israel begins with Saul's falling out with Samuel. Once Samuel asserts that Saul is no longer the legitimate king, the prophet goes to Bethlehem, a town five miles south of Jerusalem. There he anoints David, the youngest of the eight sons of Jesse (1 Sam 16:1–13). David meets Saul for the first time after some of Saul's courtiers speak of the soothing effects of David's harp playing to the troubled king. Saul then adds David to his entourage as his armor bearer (1 Sam 16:18–23). First Samuel presents David as an unlikely candidate for the succession to Saul. After all, he was the youngest of eight brothers. Still, David plots out a path to the throne with care. He is wise enough to marry into the royal family and make of Jonathan, Saul's son and heir, a devoted friend. He became a successful and popular military leader in Judah, gathering a band of loyal followers. He married two wealthy women and ingratiated himself with the elders of Judah. First Samuel portrays David as a man who had designs on Saul's throne and the determination to take it.

Saul was occupied with the Philistine threat to Israel's existence. After all, he owed his throne to the popular expectation that he could handle that threat. The Philistines established a foothold in the southwestern portion of Canaan toward the end of the Late Bronze Age (13th–12th cen. BCE). From that foothold, they began expanding to the north and east. Soon they encountered the Israelite tribes who were trying to maintain their holdings in the region. First Samuel 17 describes one confrontation with the Philistines, in the story of a battle that took place in the Valley of Elah, which was located fifteen miles southwest of Bethlehem, David's hometown. Three of David's brothers were among the Israelite fighters facing the Philistines. David went to the Israelite encampment to bring provisions for his brothers. Circumstances led David not only to join the fight but to emerge as the hero, killing Goliath, the Philistine champion (1 Sam 17). Following David's victory, he became a personal friend of Jonathan, Saul's son and heir (18:1–4; 20:1–42). Saul appointed David to a command position in the Israelite army—a move that met with universal approval (18:13, 16). David inserted himself into the king's family by marrying Michal, Saul's daughter (18:20–29).

David's popularity engendered jealousy on Saul's part, which eventually led to attempts on David's life. Saul recognized that David was after his throne (1 Sam 18:6–16; 19:1–24). David had two opportunities to kill Saul, but each time he spared the king's life (1 Sam 24 and 26). Sandwiched between those two accounts of David's passing up the opportunity to assassinate Saul is the story of David's encounter with Nabal and Abigail. Nabal was a wealthy sheep farmer from whom David asked for help in feeding himself and his followers. David backs up his request with an implied threat to Nabal's flocks. Nabal misses the implication, but his wife Abigail does not. She gathers the provisions that David requested for his men and takes them to him before David can act on his threat. In speaking to David, Abigail addresses him as "my lord" fourteen times and she refers to herself as "your servant" five times. She acknowledges that David has been chosen by God to rule Israel and reminds him to show mercy and not shed innocent blood (25:17). Her words and actions lead David to call off the punitive measures that his men were ready to inflict on Nabal's household. David acknowledges that his encounter with Abigail was providential (25:32). She, in turn, asks David to keep her in mind. Abigail's husband, whose name means "fool," is given this name in the story to underscore the contrast between him and his wife, who proves to be wise and resourceful, preventing disaster on her household because of her husband's imprudent response to David.

Indeed, David did remember Abigail. He also knew that Nabal's death left Abigail a wealthy widow. David sent for her and married her. In marrying Abigail, David aligned himself with Nabal's clan. This helped prepare the way for David's claim to the throne of Judah.[1] Abigail herself was from Carmel in the Galilee and the marriage helped solidify support from the northern tribes. David also married Ahinoam from Jezreel, a town in southern Judah known for its vineyards (1 Sam 25:43). This marriage, too, strengthened his position in the tribe of Judah.

The conflict with Saul was becoming more serious, and David took a dangerous but bold step by becoming a Philistine vassal (1 Sam 27:1–7). This put him in a position to protect Judah from raids by the Amalekites, but it also allied him to the enemies of Saul and Israel. David was able to recover the plunder taken by the Amalekites during their raids into the territory of Judah and distribute that plunder to his followers and to the elders of Judah (30:1–31). This was another step in strengthening his position in Judah. As the Philistines were gathering for major confrontation with Saul and his army, the overall Philistine commander did not trust David and kept him from the battle on Mount Gilboa in the Galilee, which ended with the defeat of the Israelite forces and the death of Saul and his son and heir Jonathan (29:1–11; 31:1–13).

David's path to the throne becomes clearer due to the death of Saul and Jonathan following the defeat of Israel's forces by the Philistines (1 Sam 31). When the Philistines discover Saul's body, they hang it from the wall of Beth-shan (v. 10; 2 Sam 21:12). The people of Jabesh-gilead recover Saul's body and bury it in their city as a last act of gratitude for his actions on their behalf (1 Sam 31:12). When Chronicles tells the story of Saul's death and its aftermath (1 Chr 10), it omits the detail about the hanging of Saul's body from the Beth-shan wall. However, it does mention the kind deed of the people of Jabesh-gilead in burying Saul.

The beginning of 2 Samuel serves to soften the portrait of David as carefully calculating his path to Saul's throne as found in 1 Samuel. In 2 Samuel 1, David appears to be distraught at the news of the deaths of Saul and Jonathan. David hears of the circumstance of Saul's death from the Amalekite youth who had administered the coup de grace at Saul's request. David, however, cannot abide the Amalekite's action and orders his execution (2 Sam 1:6–16). Then David raises a moving elegy over Saul and Jonathan as he mourns the fallen father and son (1:17–27). Second Samuel acknowledges that the elegy first appeared in the no-longer-extant Book of Jashar (v. 17). The skeptical reader wonders if David's lament is sincere in light of his troubled relationship with Saul. The biblical text gives no hint of David's motives, allowing hearer and reader to draw their own conclusions.

Second Samuel tells of a civil war over the succession following Saul's death. Although David had his supporters, there were those who maintained that Saul's successor should be Ishbaal, the dead king's sole surviving son (2 Sam 2:8—3:1). Abner, Saul's uncle and the commander of his army, led those who supported Ishbaal (1 Sam 14:50). During the war of succession, Abner killed Asahel, the brother of Joab, who commanded the forces loyal to

David (2 Sam 2:8, 12). The civil war took an unexpected turn when Ishbaal and Abner had a falling out. Apparently, Abner made a move to claim the throne for himself by taking a woman from Ishbaal's harem. After being confronted by Ishbaal for this blatant act of disloyalty, Abner changed sides. Abner pledged to persuade the Israelite tribes to abandon Ishbaal. David demanded that Abner facilitate the return of Michal, Saul's daughter and David's wife. Michal represented a measure of legitimacy to his claim on Saul's throne. Abner then spoke with the elders of Israel in support of David. In particular, he managed to persuade the tribe of Benjamin, Saul's own tribe, to come over to David's side (2:12–32).

The war over the succession to Saul continued after Abner sided with David. Joab, however, killed Abner as an act of revenge for the death of his brother Asahel. Two of Ishbaal's supporters assassinated Ishbaal with the hope of gaining David's favor. David, however, had them executed to distance himself from the assassination of his principal rival for Saul's throne. With Ishbaal's assassination, the war over the succession ended, and the elders of Israel came to David at Hebron to offer him the throne. Second Samuel 5:1–3 gives a brief account of that encounter during which the elders rehearse David's achievements as a military leader and acknowledge his designation by God to rule over Israel. The elders made a covenant with David. The elders had a significant role in the choice of the monarch, and they and the king acknowledge their mutual rights and obligations, suggesting that the Israelite monarch was not to be an absolute ruler. David owed his throne, in part, to the support of the tribal elders.

Without making explicit comments, 2 Samuel shows its disapproval of the monarchy. A lot of blood was spilled before David managed to succeed Saul. In the ancient Near East, royal succession often did not proceed in an orderly fashion. Still, this internecine strife over the succession tarnished David's accession to the throne. He was forced to neutralize others who had a claim on the succession. There were those—especially from the tribe of Benjamin—who did not recognize the legitimacy of David's accession to the throne. Unrest and discontent lie just below the surface. That is the downside of the monarchic system. The centralization of political power often engendered competition and strife. The elders of Israel made a covenant with David because they had no realistic alternative. David was victorious in the war over the succession.

Chronicles makes no mention of any civil strife connected with David's succession to the throne, paying little attention to the time before David became king over Israel. It does, however, provide a list of David's warriors along with a brief account of their activities before David became king over all Israel in 1 Chronicles 11:10—12:41. The principal concern of Chronicles is what David did once he became king—not his path to kingship. Chronicles reprises 2 Samuel's account of David's covenant with the elders of Israel at Hebron (1 Chr 11:1–3; 12:24–30), providing an expanded account of the assembly and highlighting the role of the tribal militias—including that of the Levites—in acclaiming David as king. This underscores that David had popular support for his succession to Saul. Chronicles makes a special note of support from Benjamin, Saul's tribe. The Benjaminites previously maintained the allegiance to the house of Saul but now came over to David (12:30).

Chronicles sanitizes the story of how David consolidated his position as king, not even mentioning Ishbaal in its account of the succession. "All Israel" offers the throne to David immediately following Saul's death. This phrase appears forty-two times in Chronicles. This is surprising since the narratives in Chronicles focus on Judah almost exclusively. Evidently "all Israel" remained the ideal. Chronicles makes special mention of the Benjaminites, who join with the Judahites in support of David's accession (1 Chr 16:16–18). Chronicles also mentions by name the military leadership of the other tribes, all of whom "were of a single mind to make David king" (12:38).

The City of David

Jerusalem and its temple came to have central importance in postexilic Judaism. They became the linchpins of the Judahite restoration, though neither had any connection with the oldest Israelite religious traditions. Jerusalem first comes into the biblical tradition in the stories about the reign of David and how its temple was built by David's son and successor Solomon.[2] The Israelite tribes were in existence long before there was a temple and

48

before Jerusalem rose into prominence as a temple city and the seat of the Davidic kings. Both Samuel/Kings and Chronicles play significant roles in this development since these theological motifs have no foundation in the exodus/Sinai traditions. Deuteronomy limits sacrificial worship to the place where the Lord will choose to make his name dwell (Deut 12). Samuel/Kings makes it clear that this place is the Jerusalem temple. The territory of Yehud was considerably smaller than that of the Kingdom of Judah. Mizpah was Yehud's political center and Bethel was its most important religious center. In the middle of the fifth century BCE, Jerusalem recovers the prominence it enjoyed during the monarchic period when it served as the capital for the Davidic kings. The Book of Kings presents the fall of the Kingdom of Judah as the byproduct of the failure of king and people to adhere to the requirement that God be worshiped only in the place that God had designated, the temple of Jerusalem. Chronicles' focus on the tribe of Judah and the house of David led to the special attention given to Jerusalem and its temple. Chronicles also depicts Jerusalem as the seat of Judah's kings. By identifying the location of Solomon's temple as Mount Moriah (2 Chr 3:1), Chronicles attempts to connect that site with the story of the binding of Isaac, whose setting was "the land of Moriah" (Gen 22:2). All this served to enhance the status of Jerusalem, as in both the political and religious spheres for Jews of Yehud.

In 2 Samuel 5, the first act of David as the newly acclaimed king of Israel is to lead his men in the capture of the city of Jerusalem, which was still in the hands of the Jebusites (vv. 6–12). The historical kernel of this story is difficult to determine. It is true, as 2 Samuel 5:6 implies, that Jerusalem was easily defended, since the city was surrounded on three sides by steep slopes that gave the city's defenders a significant advantage. Second Samuel 5:8 implies that David's men made their way into the city by climbing up the shaft that enabled people inside the city to get water from the Gihon Spring, which was in the Kidron Valley below. When that shaft was discovered in the course of excavations on the Ophel, Alpine mountaineers were unable to make their way up the shaft; it was simply too wide.[3] Chronicles does not mention the use of the water shaft to gain entrance into the city. Rather, it credits the leadership of Joab with the successful capture of Jerusalem. The city did become identified with David and his dynasty, becoming known as "the city of David" (2 Sam 5:7).

Both 2 Samuel and 1 Chronicles mention the repair and expansion of the city following its capture, centering their attention on the Millo. The biblical text is unclear about the nature and function of the Millo. Apparently, it was some sort of a construction—a fortification perhaps—that was built at an unspecified location following the capture of Jerusalem from the Jebusites. The word *Millo* is likely derived from the Hebrew verb *ml'* ("to fill"). This has fueled the speculation regarding what this structure may be—a repair of the city wall that had been breached, or a partial filling of the Tyropoeon Valley to connect the eastern and western ridges of the city. Excavation of the Ophel Hill has led to other suggestions. Kathleen Kenyon uncovered what she called a "stepped stone structure" on the Ophel Hill south of the Temple Mount but identified it as a fourteenth- to thirteenth-century Jebusite terracing. Yigal Shiloh suggested that the Millo added 240 square yards to the top of the Ophel and supported a Jebusite citadel. More recently Eilat Mazar suggested that the Millo supported an Israelite palace, which she identified as David's palace. Israel Finkelstein maintains that the "stepped stone structure" represents at least two phases of construction: the downslope dates to the ninth century BCE, while the upslope to the Hellenistic period.[4] Solving the mystery of the Millo will require additional excavation.

The Ark of the Covenant

With the assassination of Ishbaal a significant political obstacle to the throne of Israel was removed. The elders of Israel offered David the kingship. He accepted and then took Jerusalem, a Jebusite enclave abutting the tribal territories of Benjamin to the north and Judah to the south. David received important international recognition from Hiram, the king of Tyre (2 Sam 5:11–12) and then defeated the Philistines who were threatening Jerusalem (2 Sam 5:17–25). Politically and militarily, David's rule was secure, allowing him to find religious support for his rule, so he turned to the ark of the covenant, which was all but forgotten. Once David took Jerusalem and made it his city, he took steps to relocate the ark of the covenant there, appropriating an ancient tribal symbol of God's presence and power in his efforts to strengthen his position as king. Second Samuel and 1 Chronicles agree on the significance of the transfer of the ark to Jerusalem, though they tell the story somewhat differently. Contrary to Leonard Rost's proposal that there was an originally independent "Ark Narrative"[5] (see chapter 1: "Joshua 1—1 Samuel 7" above), recent scholarship tends to prefer to read the story of the ark's transfer to Jerusalem in its larger literary context.[6] In that context, the Ark Narrative tells of another action taken by David to consolidate his rule over the Israelite tribes.

David's plan to bring the ark to Jerusalem was put on hold when Uzzah, one of the men responsible for transporting the ark to Jerusalem, died suddenly while engaged in the transfer. David did not want to take any chances with his own life, so he had the ark delivered to the house of a Philistine from Gath. It remained there for three months until David determined that the danger had passed. David brought the ark to Jerusalem, appropriating the important and ancient symbol of the divine presence in Israel's midst. Second Samuel implies that David brought the ark to his capital to shore up support for his accession to the throne of Israel.

Chronicles recounts the unfortunate death of Uzzah while the ark was being transported from Kiriath-jearim, but suggests that Uzzah died because he was not a Levite and so should not have been among those transporting the ark (1 Chr 15:13), a detail not mentioned in Samuel. David rectifies this by insisting that only Levites carry the ark when he finally brings it to Jerusalem (1 Chr 15:2). The Levites set the ark into the tent that David prepared for it. David then instructed the Levite Asaph and his family to sing the praises of YHWH. The song that they sang (1 Chr 15:8–36) is an amalgam of extracts from Psalms 96, 105, and 106. In addition to bringing the ark to Jerusalem, Chronicles has David make provisions for the shrine at Gibeon, a town that is five and a half miles northwest of Jerusalem. The shrine has both the tent of meeting and the altar that Moses built (1 Chr 21:29). Sacrifices were offered twice daily at Gibeon. Second Samuel does not mention David's support for the shrine at Gibeon, since this would give some legitimacy to a high place—something that was contrary to views of Samuel/Kings. A recurring criticism of Judah's kings in 1–2 Kings is their failure to end worship at "high places."

That not everyone was persuaded by this appropriation of the ark is made clear from the reaction of Michal, Saul's daughter and one of David's wives. Michal upbraids David for his display of religious enthusiasm as the ark was being transported to Jerusalem (2 Sam 6:23–30). Although 2 Samuel tells the story of Michal reproaching David for his behavior before the ark in some detail, Chronicles only mentions it in passing by commenting that Michal kept her critique of David's behavior "in her heart" (1 Chr 15:29).

David's transfer of the ark to Jerusalem and its placement in a tent that David had erected for it completed the steps that David took to consolidate his position as king. Second Samuel portrays David as engaging in acts that were clearly designed to place him in a position to succeed Saul. He fought against the Philistines with great success, he married into Saul's family and married several other women of wealth and social position, and he gathered around himself a formidable group of armed supporters. Upon Saul's death, he had himself proclaimed king over Judah, his own tribe. He took advantage of the assassination of Ishbaal, Saul's son and heir, and accepted the request of "all the tribes" to be king over them. David's defeat of the Philistines, the recognition of his accession by Hiram of Tyre, his capture of Jerusalem, and his installation of the ark there served to shore up his rule militarily, politically, and religiously. Second Samuel implies that David's rise to kingship was the consequence of farsighted planning followed by careful implementation. Again, this is the way 1–2 Samuel demythologizes the monarchy.

Nathan's Oracle

Framing 1–2 Samuel's account of David's rise to kingship and in some tension with it are two stories of encounters that David had with prophets: his anointing by Samuel (1 Sam 16) and Nathan's oracle (2 Sam 7:1–17). Both stories present David as chosen by God as king over Israel. The anointing by Samuel was treated above. The story of David's encounter with the prophet Nathan begins with the king noting the anomaly that while he lives in a "house of cedar," the ark "stays in a tent" (2 Sam 7:1–6). Nathan understands that David plans to build a monumental structure, that is, a temple to house the ark. Although the text reads as if David is motivated by piety, his plan to build a temple for YHWH is nothing less than the exercise of a royal prerogative. In ancient Near Eastern religious practice, only kings have the authority to build temples. By building a temple for YHWH, David is reinforcing his claim on the throne of Israel. The prophet, a long-time supporter of David, gave his support to David's plans.

During the night, the prophet hears the word of YHWH, raising an objection to David's plans. That word suggests that the king's desire to build a monumental structure speaks to his need to exercise his kingship in a dramatic fashion. God is satisfied with the portable sanctuaries that were in use from the time of the exodus from Egypt. There is no need for David to make a dramatic and outwardly pious gesture to legitimate his rule since he rules by God's choice. Indeed, God has made David's rule secure by giving him "rest from all [his] enemies" (2 Sam 7:11). With a play on words in Hebrew, the prophet asserts that David will not build a house (*bayit*) but that God will establish a royal dynasty (*bayit*) for David. The oracle continues as the prophet speaks about David's successor, who will build the temple. The prophet promises that God will establish "the throne of [David's] kingdom forever" (v. 13), promising David an eternal dynasty: "Your house and your kingdom shall be made sure forever before me; your throne shall be established forever" (2 Sam 7:16).

How was this text received by people who witnessed or knew of the fall of the Judahite state, the exile of Zedekiah, and the execution of the royal family by the Babylonians in the sixth century BCE? Dennis J. McCarthy sees Nathan's oracle "as a new beginning related to the past but essentially a program for the future."[7] The story of the Davidic dynasty in 2 Samuel to 2 Kings, however, is a story of self-destruction—beginning with David's immediate family (2 Sam 9—20; 1 Kgs 1—2) and ending with Zedekiah's ill-conceived revolt against Babylon (2 Kgs 4:20b). There is little in Samuel/Kings' story of the Judahite monarchy that gives reason for hope for the future of either the Davidic dynasty or the Judahite state. Still, there were those in Yehud who were convinced that Judah's future was tied up with that of the Davidic dynasty, so the story of a message that God gave the prophet Nathan concerning the dynasty was kept alive.

Psalm 89 is a poetic rendering of the ideology behind the belief in the eternity of the Davidic dynasty. Ironically, it was likely occasioned by the failure of an unnamed king of Judah in battle or international politics. This failure questions the validity of the promise that God would never reject David's successors. The belief in the eternity of the dynasty is undermined by the harsh experience of the Judahite state, its rulers, and its people. The psalm is a lament in which the people of Judah remind God that those who have humiliated the king and oppressed the people are God's enemies. Those who offer this lament pray that God take action against those enemies for the sake of David and the promise made to him. There have been several attempts to link the origins of this psalm to a specific historical event, but none of the suggestions is persuasive. The psalm does imply, however, that there are circumstances that could lead to the abnegation of the promise of an eternal dynasty. Those Judahites living in the shadow of the fall of Jerusalem and the annihilation of Judah's royal family would be led to conclude that such an eventuality did happen.

Chronicles' account of Nathan's oracle (1 Chr 17:1–15) is dependent on the account in 2 Samuel 7; it largely follows that version but with several important differences. First, Chronicles omits the note about God giving David "rest" from his enemies (see 2 Sam 7:1, 11).[8] Chronicles replaces this typical Deuteronomic phraseology with the assurance that God will give David victory over his enemies: "I...have cut off all your enemies before you; and I will make for you a name, like the name of the great ones of the earth" (1 Chr 17:8). Second, Chronicles alludes to David's military victories and suggests that the blood shed during David's wars makes him unfit for the task for building the temple. Such a task belongs to "a man of peace" (1 Chr 22:9). The building of the temple is a focus of both 2 Samuel 7 and 1 Chronicles 17. Since the temple is a principal concern in Chronicles, it is not surprising either that Chronicles' version of Nathan's oracle focuses more on David's "offspring" (1 Chr 17:11–14) than on David himself, or that Chronicles omits the allusion to any sin that Solomon will commit (see 2 Sam 7:14b). In portraying Solomon as without any fault, Chronicles is unlike Kings, which castigates him for his foreign wives who led him into idolatry (see 1 Kgs 11). Third, Chronicles does not assure David that his house and his kingdom will last forever; rather, it is God's house and God's kingdom that will endure: "but I will confirm him in *my* house and in *my* kingdom forever" (1 Chr 17:14). Chronicles' version of the promise appears to take into account the fall of the Davidic dynasty and the end of the kingdom over which that dynasty ruled. For Chronicles, the Davidic dynasty may have come to an end, but God's sovereignty remains. The temple was rebuilt and its cult was resumed under the direction of the priests and Levites. It is God's kingdom, not David's, that lasts forever. First Chronicles 17 appears to focus the promise on David's son who will succeed him and build "a house" for God. The oracle, then, serves to legitimate Solomon rather than the dynasty as a whole.[9]

Nathan's oracle as found in 2 Samuel 7, Psalm 89, and 1 Chronicles 17 has proven to be a magnet for scholarly investigation.[10] The secondary literature on these texts is sizeable. One reason for this interest in Nathan's oracle is that it appears to affirm the possibility of a future for Israel. The fall of the two Israelite kingdoms and the forced migration of some of their people to various sites in Mesopotamia appear to undermine the promise of a dynasty that will rule Israel forever. The restoration of Judah following the return from exile did not include the restoration of the dynasty. Some interpreters have suggested that Nathan's oracle was appropriated by some in the community in Yehud as a promise that sometime in the future a Davidic king will emerge and complete the restoration of the kingdom. One impetus for this line of interpretation is opposition to Noth's hypothesis that 2 Kings offered no hope for the future but served only to explain the reason for the fate of the two Israelite kingdoms. Although there may be some justification for Noth's position on 2 Kings, Chronicles does appear to direct its readers to hope for a change for the better in the future—a hope that had, as one of its foundations, belief in the promises made to David. Chronicles is in a position to offer hope because it reflects the experience of the Jewish community in Yehud that has rebuilt the temple and resumed the authentic worship of YHWH under the leadership of the priests and Levites, though that community was not ruled by a member of the Davidic dynasty.

The Gospels offer justification of an eschatological thrust to appropriation of Nathan's oracle by some Jews in the first century. "Son of David" is a title for Jesus that appears sixteen times in the Synoptics. Certainly the Gospels wish to portray Jesus as the fulfillment of all Israel's eschatological hopes. Of course, the Gospels describe Jesus's fulfillment of those hopes in ways that went far beyond the expectations of the Jewish community.

The Succession

The question of the succession to David is a major difference between 2 Samuel/1 Kings and Chronicles. Of course, both agree that David was succeeded by his son Solomon, whose mother was Bathsheba. Chronicles, however, deals with the succession in a single verse: "When David was old and full of days, he made his son Solomon king over Israel" (1 Chr 23:1). David asserts that his choice of Solomon as his successor was in obedience to "the word of the LORD" that he received (1 Chr 22:8). Neither a prophet nor the elders of Israel have a role to play in the succession. David simply informs Israel's military, tribal, and political leadership that God has chosen Solomon (1 Chr 28:1–8). Neither Samuel nor Kings asserts that Solomon was God's choice to succeed David until Solomon himself makes it in his prayer at Gibeon after he has become king (1 Kgs 3:7). The assembly of Israel's leadership then recognizes Solomon as David's heir and chosen successor (1 Chr 29:22b). Upon David's death, the succession and transition in power is smooth and without incident (1 Chr 29:28). Except for listing David's other sons in the genealogies, Chronicles gives no attention to any of David's sons and potential successors except for Solomon. David's other sons are simply listed without any elaboration (1 Chr 3:1–2; 14:3–7).

By way of contrast, the story of the succession to David's throne is a major component of the Samuel/Kings story of the early monarchy. The story of David's family and the succession is told in 2 Samuel 9—20, concluding in 1 Kings 1—2. It is a complicated and dark story with several twists and turns. At the same time, it is told in such an engaging way that it is among the most readable narratives in the Bible. In 1926, Leonhard Rost wrote the seminal monograph on what has become known as the "Succession

Narrative," which has engendered a small library of monographs and articles on this subject.[11]

The story of the succession to David in 2 Samuel and 1 Kings begins with what appears to be an act of kindness. The attentive reader/hearer, however, will recognize that the opening scene in the Succession Narrative describes another attempt by David to secure his own succession to Saul's throne. David asks if there are any survivors from the house of Saul. He learns that Mephibosheth, Jonathan's son, is still alive. David brings him to Jerusalem. Although Mephibosheth was disabled and probably posed no threat, David took no chances. David kept a potential rival where he could be watched. He wanted to be sure that Saul's supporters could not use Mephibosheth as a tool to undermine the legitimacy of his own succession to the throne of Israel. The story intimates that Mephibosheth is aware of David's real purpose, so he promises obedience to David and suggests that he poses no real danger to the king (2 Sam 9:6, 8). This episode underscores the great care David took to avoid questions of his right to succeed Saul. Second Samuel hints that support for David was not universal. There was an undercurrent of opposition—especially from the tribe of Benjamin—to the Judahite David's accession to the throne of the Benjaminite Saul.

Second Samuel 10 serves to provide the background for the Bathsheba incident that is the subject of the following chapter. After dealing with domestic politics in chapter 9, David moves into the international sphere when Nahash, king of the Ammonites, who was an enemy of Saul (1 Sam 11:1–11) but a friend of David (2 Sam 10:2), died. Nahash was succeeded by his son Hanun. In the ancient Near East, the death of a king was a time fraught with uncertainty. In this confused atmosphere, Hanun mistook David's ambassadors for spies, humiliated them, and sent them back to David (2 Sam 10:3–6). This led to a war between Ammon and Israel with Aram allied with the Ammonites. Joab, the commander of David's army, managed to defeat the coalition (2 Sam 10:9–19) while David remained in Jerusalem.

While Joab was besieging Rabbah, the Ammonite capital, an event took place that had profound and far-reaching effects on David's family and on the matter of the succession. David decides to add another woman to his harem. As he did in the past, the woman he chooses comes from a politically influential family. The woman who catches his eye is Bathsheba, the daughter of Eliam, who was a member of David's honor guard, which 2 Samuel calls "the Thirty" (2 Sam 23:24). Eliam's father was Ahitophel, David's principal advisor (2 Sam 15:12). Though God had given him Saul's kingdom, David continued his attempts at securing support for his succession to Saul by marrying women from prominent families. The reader/hearer recognizes the pattern of David aligning himself with wealthy and influential families through marriage. David uses these women for the purpose of facilitating his accession and propping up his throne. But in the case of Bathsheba, there was a serious obstacle in David's plan to add her to his harem. Bathsheba was married to Uriah, a mercenary in David's army. Traditional Israelite morality and personal loyalty to his soldiers held that David should have respected the marital bond between Uriah and Bathsheba. But David ignored his moral obligations in his quest to add Bathsheba to his harem. She became pregnant with his child. To deal with this complication David tried to induce Uriah, Bathsheba's husband, to spend the night with her. Despite Uriah's protestations of loyalty, the story intimates that Uriah knew of the circumstances of his wife's pregnancy and refused to participate in the charade that David concocted. David then arranges with Joab to make it likely that Uriah would fall in battle with the Ammonites. David's plan works and he is free to marry Bathsheba. In due course, Bathsheba has a son. Thus, 2 Samuel adds its most unflattering portrait of David, who disregards one of the most basic tenets of traditional Israelite morality.

The text includes an editorial comment following the story of the Bathsheba incident: "the thing that David had done displeased the LORD" (2 Sam 11:27b). The prophet Nathan had the task of informing the king that his behavior calls out for divine judgment. The prophet did so carefully—by setting out a fictitious case for the king's judgment that led David to pronounce judgment on himself (2 Sam 12:1–7). Once David gives his judgment on the case that Nathan put before him, the prophet then is free to confront the king with the crimes of adultery and murder that he committed. The words of Nathan's indictment of David are this: "You are the man!" (2 Sam 12:7). Nathan continues by announcing judgment in the name of God: "the sword shall never depart from your house" (2 Sam 12:10). Indeed, it never does. The rest of the story of succession relates one tragedy after another that fulfills the prophetic word.

To his credit David does not offer excuses or explanations but acknowledges his guilt: "I have sinned against the LORD" (2 Sam 12:13a). The prophet then assures that David would not die because of his sin but that the child Bathsheba bore will die. David fasted, prayed, and humiliated himself in his efforts to avert the judgment of death against his infant son—to no avail. After his son's death, David tried to console Bathsheba. She had another son whom David named Solomon (2 Sam 12:24). Nathan gave the child another name, Jedidiah ("the beloved of YHWH"; 2 Sam 12:24–25). Chronicles explains the name Solomon (*šəlōmōh*) as a pointing to Solomon's rule as king: YHWH "will give peace [*šālôm*] and quiet to Israel in his days" (1 Chr 22:9). A more likely possibility is that the name Solomon is derived from the Hebrew *šlm* (piel: "to replace") since Solomon compensates for loss of the first child of David and Bathsheba. The latter explanation fits the context of the story of Solomon's birth.

This story suggests to readers/hearers that acknowledging one's guilt can avert punishment. At the same time, doing what displeases God unleashes the power of evil, which cannot always be controlled. In this case, David and Bathsheba had to face the loss of their child, who is totally innocent in this situation. Those hearing this story at the beginning of the postexilic era have experienced the power of evil in their lives because of the failure of their forebears, whose infidelity led to the loss of Judah's independence and the end of the dynasty, the destruction of Jerusalem and the temple and the scattering of its priesthood, followed by the forced migration of many Judahites to Babylon. Though the exile might be over and the temple rebuilt, Judah is now firmly within the Persian Empire and is not in control of its own destiny. The people of Yehud were experiencing the effects of judgment that their forebears brought about.

Chronicles does not reprise the story of David and Bathsheba. Indeed, it never even mentions her name, but does include a "Bath-shua, daughter of Ammiel" in the list of David's wives and sons, identifying her as the mother of Solomon (1 Chr 3:5). The name Bath-shua means "daughter of nobility" and Ammiel is the name

Eliam (2 Sam 11:3) with the syllables reversed. Chronicles does not want to call attention to this matter because it mars the portrait of David that the book attempts to paint. Of course, Chronicles cannot ignore Bathsheba entirely since she is the mother of David's son and successor. Still, the text tries to mask Bath-shua's true identity. Chronicles is certainly aware of the sordid story of Bathsheba, Uriah, and David and manages to keep it under wraps.

The omission of this story is the most glaring difference between the portrait of David that appears in 2 Samuel and that which appears in 1 Chronicles. An obvious explanation for this omission is the idealization of David in Chronicles. This is achieved by omitting stories concerning David's personal life. What Chronicles includes are stories about David that relate to the Israelite community such as the story of David and the census (1 Chr 21:1—22:1). The idealization of David in Chronicles leads the book to lay the blame on Satan for leading David "to count the people." In the case of the incident with Bathsheba, there is no one to blame but David himself. This tragic story, of course, was well known, Chronicles thought it best not to repeat it since it would detract from Chronicles' aim to offer hope beyond tragedy.

With the death of the child conceived because of David's sin, his marriage to Bathsheba, and her giving birth to Solomon, one would think that this sordid episode was now closed. But that was not to be—the tragic pattern is repeated. There will be another instance of an illicit sexual encounter followed by a murder, resulting in the death of David's eldest son and heir presumptive, Amnon (2 Sam 13). Amnon was infatuated with his half-sister Tamar. Like his father, Amnon chose not to control his impulses. He raped Tamar but then wanted to have nothing to do with her. Tamar was left to deal with the loss of her virginity at the hands of her half-brother. When David heard of this outrage, he was angry but did nothing to discipline Amnon, his firstborn. This angered Absalom, Tamar's full brother. He nursed his anger for two years but never forgot what happened to his sister and David's failure to discipline Amnon. When it had appeared that David's family had put the outrage against Tamar behind them, Absalom arranged a banquet for all David's sons. During that banquet, Absalom had Amnon killed. In the disorder following Amnon's murder, the rumor spread that Absalom had all his brothers killed. David's surviving sons joined their father in lamenting Amnon's death, but Absalom fled (2 Sam 13:34–36).

Absalom sought refuge in the court of Talmai, the king of Geshur,[12] his maternal grandfather (see 2 Sam 3:3). Three years had passed since Absalom's self-imposed exile, and it appeared to Joab that David's anger toward Absalom abated. Joab induced an unnamed "wise woman from Tekoa," to tell a tale of a son lost in the course of a conflict with his brother, who then fled from the family's vengeance. David promises to protect the woman's supposed son from danger. She informs David that Joab had her tell her story to make it easier for David to restore Absalom to his favor. Much has been made of the "wise woman" regarding the role and status of women in ancient Israel's political sphere and the wisdom of rural folk. Still, in this episode the woman does not act on her own but is simply Joab's mouthpiece. It is Joab who concocts the tale she tells to manipulate David in allowing Absalom to return to Jerusalem.[13] David then allows Absalom to return to Jerusalem but not to the royal court. After an additional two years, Joab, at Absalom's suggestion, induces David to be fully reconciled with his son (2 Sam 14:28–33).

Again, it appeared as if the crisis in David's family had come to an end, but the reconciliation between David and Absalom was a sham. Five years after the rape of his sister and his own exile from the royal court, Absalom still nursed his grudges. After four years of carefully courting a following among people displeased with David's rule, Absalom led a revolt against his father and had himself acclaimed as king in Hebron, David's first capital (2 Sam 15). The rebellion against David's rule was gaining momentum. A crucial event was the defection of Ahitophel, David's principal advisor, who joined Absalom's entourage. David decided to leave Jerusalem. He crossed the Mount of Olives and headed east toward the Jordan Valley. Philistine mercenaries remained loyal to David and accompanied the king. The two priests, Zadok and Abiathar, remained loyal as well, but David urged them to return to Jerusalem and provide him with intelligence regarding the progress of the coup. Hushai, another of David's advisors who also remained loyal, would serve as the conduit for any information they might provide. Mephibosheth thought that Absalom's coup could be turned to his advantage. He believed that he had an opportunity to assert his claim on his grandfather's throne. When David heard this, he ordered all Mephibosheth's property to be confiscated and given to Ziba, Mephibosheth's servant, who remained loyal to David. During his retreat, David was confronted by Shimei, a supporter of Saul's family. Shimei cursed David, whom he called "a man of blood" (2 Sam 16:5–8). When Abishai, one of David's followers, sought to silence Shimei, David stopped him, so Shimei shadowed David and his entourage, pelting them with stones and shouting curses at them.

Encouraged by Ahitophel, Absalom went to the palace and assembled his father's harem on the roof, had intercourse with them in the sight of witnesses, thus claiming David's prerogatives and status as king. The text comments that this action fulfills the words of Nathan, condemning David for his taking of Uriah's wife into his harem (see 2 Sam 16:23; also see 12:11–12). This action was the high watermark of Absalom's rebellion. The tide soon turned against Absalom, and it was his own doing. Ahitophel advised Absalom to keep the momentum of the rebellion going by striking at David and his remaining loyal followers while they were tired after their hasty retreat that took them from Jerusalem to the River Jordan—a distance of twenty-one miles. Hushai, David's spy, managed to convince Absalom to wait and gather more warriors before confronting David. Hushai hoped that this pause would give David some breathing room. Absalom followed Hushai's advice, affording David time to cross the Jordan to safety. Ahitophel committed suicide (2 Sam 17:23), in all likelihood because he knew the grave mistake that Absalom made in providing David and his small force with time to recover after an exhausting retreat. He knew the price that David would exact from him for his defection to Absalom.

David was able to muster forces from the Israelites who lived east of the Jordan. These forces were provisioned and made ready for battle by Joab. David ordered Joab to "deal gently" with Absalom. The civil war between David's loyalists and Absalom's rebels took place in the forests of Ephraim, which is northwest of Jerusalem. David's forces carried the day and it was Absalom's turn to retreat. As he did so, his lush hair was entangled in a tree. When Joab saw Absalom hanging from a tree, he thrust three spears into him, ignoring David's orders to spare his son (2 Sam 18:9–15).

With Absalom dead, the rebels melted away, returning to their homes. David then received the best news he could hope for and then, a little later, the bad news he dreaded. Runners from the scene of the battle came announcing the victory of David's forces followed by a lone mercenary who brought news of Absalom's death. This news evoked an anguished lamentation from David: "O my son Absalom, my son, my son Absalom! Would I had died instead of you, O Absalom, my son, my son!" (2 Sam 18:33b).

After the revolt's collapse, David sought to allay the fears of the rebels, who invited David back to Jerusalem following the collapse of their rebellion. Moved by the people's invitation to rule over them again, David said, "Shall anyone be put to death in Israel this day? For do I not know that I am this day king over Israel?" (2 Sam 19:22). David recognizes that he is king not because of the careful plans he made to position himself as Saul's successor nor because his rival from Saul's family was eliminated. He is king because the people invited him back to the throne.

David forgave Shimei, who tormented him during his retreat from Jerusalem. The king's problems were not over, because there were other Benjaminites who were still smarting over David's accession to the throne of Israel, which they believed rightly belonged to their tribe. David had to face a second revolt. This one was led by Sheba ben Bichri, who opposed David and called Israel to join him in deposing David from a throne that rightly belonged to the tribe of Benjamin:

> We have no portion in David,
> no share in the son of Jesse!
> Everyone to your tents, O Israel! (2 Sam 20:1)

David thought that Sheba presented a greater threat than Absalom. Indeed, 2 Samuel asserts that "all the people of Israel" withdrew their support for David and joined Sheba's revolt. Amasa, the leader of the Judahite tribal militia, and Joab, the commander of David's mercenaries, pursued Sheba. In a fit of jealousy, Joab killed Amasa, whom he considered a rival. Joab managed to locate Sheba in the far northern town of Abel Beth-maacah. Joab began a siege, but an unnamed woman from the town began negotiating with Joab because she feared that the siege would be the end of her town. Joab promised to lift the siege if Sheba was handed over to him. The woman consulted with the townspeople, who killed Sheba, thus ending the siege and Sheba's revolution (2 Sam 20:16–22). This unnamed woman saved her town from suffering the fate that came to all those associated with the rebellion against David: the fate that came to all of Saul's heirs with the exception of Mephiboseth. David hoped that their execution would forestall any more trouble from the tribe of Benjamin (2 Sam 21:1–14).

Chronicles omits the story of the revolutions that David faced. In Chronicles David ruled over a united Israel. He did not have to deal with internal unrest and opposition. This freed him to attend to his principal task, as Chronicles saw it: preparations for the service of YHWH that would take place in the temple to be built by Solomon his successor. For Chronicles, this is the reason David became king. Second Samuel pays more attention to the problems of David's family and to the tensions in Israel between those who supported David's rule and those who did not consider that David's kingship had any legitimacy. Opposition to this rule was widespread, and it took a strong leader to bring this opposition to the surface. For Samuel/Kings the forces that threatened the existence of the Israelite national state were present from the very beginning. They were harbingers of the dissolution of a political system that Samuel/Kings saw as ultimately failing the people of Israel.

The story of the succession to David concludes in 1 Kings 1—2, as it fast forwards to David in his old age. There were two factions, each with its preferred candidate for the throne of Israel: the Hebron faction and the Jerusalem faction. Hebron was the principal town of the tribe of Judah and David's first capital. The leaders of the Hebron faction were Joab, David's nephew and his military commander, and Abiathar, David's priest. Both had a long association with David. Their candidate was Adonijah, who was born in Hebron and was David's eldest surviving son. The Jerusalem faction was made up of courtiers who first became associated with David after he made Jerusalem his capital. This faction included Bathsheba, David's wife and Solomon's mother; Zadok, the priest of Jerusalem; Nathan the prophet; and Benaiah, the commander of David's mercenary forces. The Jerusalem faction favored the candidacy of Solomon.

When Adonijah took actions that could be interpreted as making a claim on the throne (1 Kgs 1:5–6, 9–10), David made no objection. Nathan and Bathsheba, however, hatched a plot to have David explicitly designate Solomon as his successor. First, Bathsheba reminds David of a promise he supposedly made to her that her son Solomon would be his successor. Nathan follows by telling of Adonijah's acting as if he were already king with the support of Joab and Abiathar. Nathan then reminds David that he has not actually named his successor. David then tells Bathsheba that he will keep his "promise" to her and name Solomon as the heir to his throne. David orders Zadok and Nathan to anoint Solomon as king at the Gihon Spring. When the news of Solomon's anointing reached Adonijah's supporters, they scattered, leaving Adonijah to his fate. Adonijah was taken into custody, but when he acknowledged that Solomon was king, Solomon took no action against his brother.

The transition from one king to his successor was a dangerous period in the ancient Near East. Plots, assassinations, and revolts were always a possibility, as David's succession to Saul shows. The story of the succession to David ends by describing the actions taken by Solomon to make his hold on the throne secure. David gives Solomon advice on consolidating his rule. In 1 Kings 2:1–4, David asserts that obedience to the Torah of Moses is the way to ensure that God's promises to maintain the dynasty will be fulfilled. This is followed by instructions to purge Joab, who supported Adonijah, and Shimei, who favored the claims of Saul's family to the throne (1 Kgs 2:5–9). David's instructions regarding obedience to the Torah stand in tension with his advice on how best to neutralize opposition. It reflects the tension between traditional Israelite morality and the realities of the monarchic political system. The stories of the Israelite kingdoms demonstrate that in the end, kings chose to act in accord with what they perceived as political reality rather than in accord with the ethical ideals of their ancestral religious tradition.

After David concludes his instructions to Solomon about consolidating his position, he dies with Solomon's throne "firmly established" (1 Kgs 2:10–12). Still, the situation was very fluid. Apparently, Adonijah did not entirely give up his claims on the throne. He asks Bathsheba—of all persons—to persuade Solomon to allow him to marry Abishag, the most recent addition to David's harem. Solomon saw that such a marriage amounted to a renewed claim on the throne, and so he had Adonijah executed. Sparing Abiathar because he was a priest, Solomon sentenced him to internal exile in Anatoth, a Levitical city in the territory of Benjamin. Solomon did not spare Joab but had him executed. Zadok took Abiathar's place and Benaiah took Joab's. Solomon was willing to spare Shimei as long as he stayed in Jerusalem where his actions could be monitored. Shimei went to Gath, ostensibly to capture two runaway slaves. It was a fatal miscalculation. Solomon ordered Benaiah to find and execute Shimei (1 Kgs 2:46).

The Samuel/Kings story of the succession ends with a simple statement: "So the kingdom was established in the hand of Solomon" (1 Kgs 2:46b). The text then leaves it to readers to draw their own conclusion about the succession and about David, Solomon, and the institution of the monarchy. Scholars have made the subject of Samuel/Kings' attitude toward the Israelite monarchy a matter of considerable debate. Rost claimed that the story of the succession to David was written *ad maiorem Solomonis gloria* ("to the greater glory of Solomon").[14] Reading that story makes it difficult to regard it as anything but a biting critique of monarchy as an institution. Similarly, it contributes nothing to a positive view of Solomon. Indeed, it is a story without a genuine protagonist. What the story of the succession appears to say to its readers/hearers is, "If you want a monarchy, this is what you can expect." It is a saga that began with adultery and murder. Along the way there were several other murders that included two fratricides and an attempted parricide, rape, and two revolts against David's rule, with one led by his son Absalom. There were palace intrigues with two factions seeking the advantage over an elderly and ill monarch. Solomon consolidated his position by having his rival and brother Adonijah and his principal supporters executed. This story does not enhance the reputation of either Solomon or the institution of the monarchy.

In the end, Solomon owed his throne to the prophet Nathan and his mother, Bathsheba. Bathsheba does not appear in 2 Samuel after Solomon is born. Her reappearance in 1 Kings shows a remarkable transition from a victim of David's abuse of power to become a power broker herself. She was able to convince David that he had designated Solomon as his successor though the biblical text recounts no such promise. Bathsheba's role in having her son succeed David displays a high level of intelligence, authority, and influence. She is no puppet or mouthpiece for the men in the pro-Solomon faction. Bathsheba's authority grows after Solomon becomes king. Solomon bowed down to his mother and had a throne for her placed next to his own (1 Kgs 2:19). Bathsheba likely recognized the potential danger Adonijah's seemingly innocent request posed, so she conveyed Adonijah's petition to her son, providing him with the excuse to eliminate the one man who had a legitimate claim on the throne.

The crucial role of Bathsheba in the succession story leads to a consideration of the role of the other women in this story. They appear at significant moments in that story and what they do affects its progress and the final resolution of the succession question. David's daughter Tamar is a tragic figure—a victim of her half-brother's unchecked passion. When Amnon attempts to seduce her, she reminds him that what he proposes is contrary to traditional Israelite morality: "No, my brother, do not force me; for such a thing is not done in Israel; do not do anything so vile!" (2 Sam 13:12). Amnon rapes Tamar, his half-sister, and then has nothing more to do with her (2 Sam 13:14b–15). The action that Absalom takes to avenge his sister continues the downward spiral of David's family. David destroyed Uriah's family and now he experiences the destruction of his own family.

Two unnamed women have crucial roles in the story of the succession. The first is the "wise woman of Tekoa," who succeeded in moving David to end the exile of his son Absalom when David's male advisors failed to do so. The second is the woman of Abel Beth-maacah, who negotiated the end of Sheba's rebellion, saving David's throne and her town. These two women make their appearance at critical points in the story and their actions help shape the contours of that story. The efforts of the "wise woman of Tekoa" initiate a process of reconciliation between David and Absalom. The reconciliation failed because Absalom was not really committed to it. The town of Abel Beth-maacah was in danger of becoming collateral damage in Joab's attempt to put down Sheba's rebellion. A woman of the town confronts Joab and persuades the people of her town to end the threat to their town by killing Sheba.

Abishag, an attractive young woman from Shunem in the north of Israel, joins the king's service in his old age (1 Kgs 1:4, 15). She becomes an unwitting pawn in the final tragedy to befall David's family as Solomon, the successor to David, consolidates his position. Solomon's crime of fratricide is the final act in the story of the succession to David—which is also the story of the dissolution of David's family. Women play a crucial role in that story.

Compared to the political chaos, moral turpitude, and family strife of the story of the succession in Samuel/Kings, Chronicles' account of Solomon's succession to David's throne describes careful planning and methodical execution that led to smooth transition of power from David to Solomon. According to Chronicles, the final years of David's life were not filled with family strife, with revolts against his rule, or palace intrigues over the succession. The old king prepares for an orderly transition to Solomon's rule by summoning "all the leaders of Israel and the priests and the Levites" and organizing the civic, judicial, military, financial, priestly, and Levitical components of the Israelite community. Chronicles provides its readers/hearers with a window into the complexity of the Davidic national state (1 Chr 23:2—27:33). Though ancient Israelite society was not as complex as those in Egypt and Mesopotamia, it was no simple matter to have all the components of Israelite society working together for the common good. Chronicles portrays David as a "hands on" ruler who carefully and prudently prepared for the transition to the reign of Solomon, whom God has chosen to build "a house for the LORD" (1 Chr 22:6).

The focus on the monarchy in Chronicles is restricted primarily to that institution's relationship with Israel's worship of YHWH in the temple. The story of the succession to David does not directly relate to that focus. It obscures the image of the Davidic dynasty that Chronicles was trying to create. The sordid and tragic story of the succession found in 2 Samuel and 1 Kings is simply ignored by the Chronicles in favor of describing the roles of David and Solomon in preparing for the construction of the temple and the arrangement of its personnel so that Israel could worship its patron Deity properly.

Chronicles' account of the succession begins in 1 Chronicles 23:2: "David assembled all the leaders of Israel and the priests and the Levites." The rest of chapters 23—27 contain the specific instructions given to each group in preparation for the succession. Solomon needed not concern himself with the religious leadership of Israel—David made certain that all was in order. David established the divisions of the priests and Levites, appointed the singers and gatekeepers, and outlined their duties (1 Chr 24—25). David endowed the temple and appointed treasurers to oversee its finances (1 Chr 26:1–28), and he appointed regional officials and judges (1 Chr 26:29–32). Israel's military and political leaders also received their instructions: the leadership of the militia (1 Chr 27:1–15), tribal leadership (1 Chr 27:16–24), the stewards of the king's property (1 Chr 27:25–31), and David's counselors (1 Chr 27:32–34). It was important to ensure that the kingdom's political leadership support David's plans for the succession. Also, Solomon must rely on their loyalty if he is to consolidate his rule. Without the support of Israel's leadership, Solomon cannot hope to reign successfully.

David rehearses the promises that God made to him, assuring Solomon that God will treat him as a son and that his kingdom will endure forever "if he continues resolute in keeping my commandments" (1 Chr 28:7). Turning to the people assembled, David calls them to obedience, reminding them that the possession of the land is contingent on their obedience to YHWH's commandments (1 Chr 28:8). Chronicles and 2 Samuel are in agreement regarding the conditional nature of the relationship between Israel and YHWH. The principal difference between them in this matter is that Samuel/Kings attempts to motivate Israel's obedience by describing in detail the failure of Israel's leaders and people to be obedient to the YHWH's commandments. Chronicles, by way of contrast, attempts to show that there is, despite Israel's failure, a future with God for the people.

The succession story in Chronicles portrays David as a good king who arranges matters methodically in view of his own death and Solomon's accession. David leaves nothing to chance but ensures that the leadership of the nation supports Solomon. A central component of this preparation is appointment of proper temple personnel. In contrast to 2 Samuel's portrait of David, Chronicles' story of the succession reflects the idealization of David that became the norm in postbiblical Jewish literature.

The Census

Chronicles' portrait of David is so different from that found in Samuel/Kings that one wonders if the two stories are about the same person. Although 1 Chronicles 1—31 uses 1 Samuel 31 — 2 Samuel 24, Chronicles omits the episodes from 2 Samuel that can appear to detract from David's reputation as an ideal king. Chronicles portrays David as acclaimed by all Israelites as their king. He devotes himself to the cult of YHWH. He is victorious over the enemies of Israel and successful in politics. The one episode that appears to mar Chronicles' portrait of David is the story of the census ordered by David and the plague that subsequently comes upon Israel in 1 Chronicles 21:1—22:1. Scholars have noted this anomaly and have offered several explanations.[15] The inclusion of the census episode, however, should not be considered anomalous. Chronicles' portrait of David is not as one-dimensional as it may appear at first. The David of Chronicles is also a complex figure. He is more than the exemplary king; he is a repentant sinner.[16]

The story of the census and its aftermath is also found in 2 Samuel 24. The taking of a census is a necessary part of good administration. It is important to know the size of the tax base and number of men available for military service. Joab, however, suggests that a census is unnecessary (2 Sam 24:3; 1 Chr 21:3). Neither 2 Samuel nor 1 Chronicles explains the reason that the taking of a census displeased God, although 2 Samuel notes that God was angry with Israel before the taking of the census, and so God incited David to "count the people of Israel and Judah" (2 Sam 24:1). Chronicles, however, has the actions of an unnamed adversary leading David to order a census (1 Chr 21:1), although the responsibility is clearly on David. In both Samuel and Chronicles, David confesses he is solely responsible for the deed that led to the punishment that came to all Israel (2 Sam 24:16; 1 Chr 21:17).

Though David did accept responsibility and asked that God redirect God's anger from the people toward him and his family, both Samuel and Chronicles make it clear that God relented from executing judgment on Jerusalem (2 Sam 24:16; 1 Chr 21:15). Both accounts present David as a paradigm of a repentant sinner.

He accepts full responsibility for his sin. He is also aware that his sin has the potential of drawing innocent people into the vortex of divine judgment, and so he prays that God limit those effects to himself and his family. The people of the postexilic Jewish community recognized the power of evil to envelope both the innocent and the guilty. Indeed, they had to live with the consequences of their forebears' sins of infidelity. No doubt they understood the importance of repentance. They had to wonder if repentance was enough. They asked along with Jeremiah, "Have you completely rejected Judah? Does your heart loathe Zion?" (Jer 14:19). Both Samuel and Chronicles portray God relenting and preventing Jerusalem from experiencing the judgment that David brought upon the city by his sin. In the larger context of Samuel/Kings the question remains whether God will once again relent and restore Jerusalem. For Chronicles, the restoration of Judah began with the decree of Cyrus. The story of David's census and repentance portrays God as merciful and forgiving. That forgiveness anticipates David's repentance and ensures that his repentance will have its desired effect in saving Jerusalem from having to endure the consequences of David's sin. For Chronicles, David is a repentant sinner whom the people of Judah ought to emulate.

The story of the census in both Samuel and Chronicles ends with David's purchase of a threshing floor upon which he builds an altar. He offers sacrifices upon that altar to bring an end to the plague in Israel. According to 2 Samuel 24:18, he does so in obedience to the instructions of the prophet Gad; in 1 Chronicles 21:18, David was commanded to build the altar by "the angel of YHWH," a formula that implies that it was God who called for an altar to be built in Jerusalem. Chronicles notes that there was an altar at the high place in Gibeon where the tabernacle was located and sacrifices were offered (1 Chr 21:29). It is clear that this is only temporary, since the rest of Chronicles' story of David depicts him as preparing for the construction of the temple and developing an administrative structure that will facilitate the work of his successor, who will be responsible for executing David's plans. Second Samuel 24 does not mention the altar in Gibeon because it considers sacrificial worship at high places illegitimate.

Chronicles does not offer a monochromatic portrait of David as if his concern for the worship of YHWH was all that Chronicles wished to portray. The episode of the census testifies to the Chronicles' wish to depict David as a repentant sinner. As such, David offers to those who hear or read the account of David's reign an example of repentance—an example that believers of every age need. Chronicles is convinced that the people of Judah ought to follow David's example.

David's Farewell

A recurring motif in biblical narratives is the farewell address made by Israel's great leaders: Jacob (49:1–28), Moses (Deut 32:1–47; 33:1–29), Joshua (23:1–16; 24:1–28), and Samuel (1 Sam 12:1–25). Samuel/Kings recounts three farewells given by David. In the first (2 Sam 23:1–7), David speaks as a prophet uttering an oracle about the promise that bound God to support his dynasty by an "everlasting covenant." In the second (1 Kgs 2:1–4), David exhorts Solomon to observe the written authoritative Torah to ensure that Solomon would have a successor. This stands in tension with the farewell in 2 Samuel. In the third farewell, also addressed to Solomon (1 Kgs 2:5–9), David instructs Solomon to move against those men whom David was unable to eliminate during his reign: Joab, who murdered two of David's supporters, and Shimei, who led a rebellion against David, while rewarding Barzillai, who supported David during Absalom's revolt. David suggests that such actions were prudent since they would eliminate potential threats to Solomon's rule.

In 1 Chronicles 29:10–19, David's farewell is a prayer, acknowledging God's sovereignty over all that is and expressing sentiments found in two of David's prayers as found in 1 Chronicles 16:24–26 and 17:16–27. As David asserts that the sacrificial offerings made by him and his people are actually gifts from God, he prays for the people of Israel that they be devoted to God. He also prays that Solomon keep God's commandments and build the temple. There is no reference to the dynastic oracle or any enemies of the dynasty. David took steps to make the transition to Solomon smooth and his prayer reflects David's success in assuring that there would be no problems for Solomon or Israel as Solomon takes David's throne.

SOLOMON

The story of Solomon in Kings differs markedly from that in Chronicles. In 1 Kings 2—11, the story of David's immediate successor follows a familiar pattern: what begins with great promise is ultimately disappointing and even tragic in the end. Both Saul and David were anointed by Samuel at God's command. They both enjoyed success in neutralizing the threats to Israel's existence in the land promised to Israel's ancestors. But both Saul and David committed deeds that were seriously at odds with traditional Israelite morality, creating a downward spiral for both. Saul and his son Jonathan died during a battle with the Philistines. David witnessed the disintegration of his family and ended his reign as an old man subject to manipulation by his wife and courtiers. This pattern repeats itself in 1 Kings's story of Solomon. That story begins with narratives illustrating his unparalleled wisdom as a ruler. Also, it tells of his ambitious building projects and prodigious wealth that were the fruit of his successful commercial enterprises. All this led to his successes in international politics. Still, Solomon's singular achievement in 1 Kings is his building of the temple in Jerusalem. Then, in a dramatic and sudden shift, Solomon's story becomes another example of a shocking failure as he falls into idolatry. In Chronicles, however, Solomon is the very opposite of a failure.

Chronicles portrays Solomon as an exemplary king who kept the kingdom of Israel unified despite centrifugal forces that threatened that unity. In addition, Solomon faced no international political or military challenges. Israel simply basked in the glory of its world-renowned ruler. Like 1 Kings, 2 Chronicles sees Solomon's building of the temple as his most significant achievement, but unlike 1 Kings, 2 Chronicles includes nothing that can tarnish Solomon's reputation.

Solomon's Path to Kingship

Both Kings and Chronicles acknowledge that Solomon's path to kingship differed from that of Saul and David. Both Solomon's predecessors were designated as kings by the prophet Samuel, who acted in God's name. In both cases, prophetic designation was followed by popular acclamation. First Kings describes Solomon's accession as engineered by his mother Bathsheba and her allies Zadok the priest, Nathan the prophet, and Benaiah, the commander of David's bodyguards. Bathsheba was able to convince David to name her son Solomon king even though Adonijah, David's eldest surviving son, had already made his claim on the throne (1 Kgs 1). Solomon consolidates this hold on the throne by executing or exiling those who opposed his accession (1 Kgs 2:19–35). Solomon, then, was not designated as king by a prophet but by David.

Chronicles likewise asserts that David, not a prophet, named Solomon as his successor. Also, Chronicles omits any mention of the palace intrigue played by Bathsheba and her allies, but has David assert that God had chosen Solomon to be king in his place (1 Chr 29:1). Following their prophetic designation, both Saul and David were confirmed as king by popular acclamation. Chronicles does note that the "whole assembly" made Solomon king and anointed him as prince (1 Chr 29:22b). In 1 Kings 1:32–40, the number of those who acclaim Solomon as king is limited to Zadok, Nathan, Benaiah, and David's bodyguards. For Chronicles, dynastic succession was a legitimate path to kingship.

Solomon's Achievements

The story of Solomon's reign as told in Kings has been the basis of the traditional view of Solomon as a wise, wealthy, and successful ruler of an Israelite empire that stretched from the "Euphrates to the land of the Philistines, even to the border of Egypt" (1 Kgs 4:21).[17] Still, that story considers Solomon's most outstanding achievement to have been the building of a temple for YHWH in Jerusalem. Solomon appears to be an ideal king who is led astray only toward the end of his life by his foreign wives. First Kings does not contain overt, explicit criticisms of Solomon, but the careful reader and attentive hearer will note that Solomon's reign is not all that it appeared to be. There are hints of Solomon's deficiencies throughout his story in Kings.

The first hint of problems to come appears in the opening verse of 1 Kings 3:1: "Solomon made a marriage alliance with Pharaoh, king of Egypt; he took Pharaoh's daughter and brought her into the city of David." Deuteronomy 7:3–4 explicitly forbids marriage to non-Israelite spouses since this could lead to idolatry and apostasy. That is precisely what happened in Solomon's case. First Kings 3 also tells the story of Solomon's visit to the high place at Gibeon (vv. 4–15). Though the tent of meeting, the ark of the covenant, and the altar built by David are in Jerusalem, Solomon chooses to go to a high place to encounter God. Again, this is a harbinger of bad things to come, since most of Solomon's successors countenanced or even promoted worship at high places, disregarding the unique status of Jerusalem and its temple.

The account of Solomon's visit to Gibeon has him asking for wisdom to be a good king. God grants Solomon not only wisdom but also incomparable "riches and honor" (1 Kgs 3:13). That same story serves to provide legitimation for the path to kingship that he took. Kings depicts the pilgrimage as a personal act of piety while Chronicles presents Israel's leadership as accompanying Solomon (1 Kgs 3:4; 2 Chr 1:2). According to Kings, Solomon goes to Gibeon because it was "a principal high place," while Chronicles implies that the king's pilgrimage goes to Gibeon because "the tent of meeting" was there. This structure was built by Moses in the wilderness; Chronicles saw it as a predecessor of the temple that Solomon was to build. Chronicles does not wish to call attention to Solomon's visit to a "high place."

First Kings asserts that Solomon's encounter with God took place during a dream, but Chronicles never uses the term *dream* anywhere—perhaps because the author did not regard dreams as a legitimate form of divine-human communication. In Kings, God appears to Solomon in his dream at Gibeon and promises to grant whatever Solomon requests. The king asks for a "listening heart" with which to judge his people. God grants the king's request but promises to grant him "riches and glory" as well. Chronicles abbreviates the story as found in Kings and shifts the emphasis from Solomon's wisdom to Solomon's wealth (2 Chr 1:13–18). Also, according to Chronicles it is David who asks God to grant Solomon wisdom so that he would observe the Torah and enjoy success (1 Chr 22:12–13). Kings follows the story of the Gibeon encounter with a story to illustrate how Solomon employed the wisdom God had given him in settling the dispute between two prostitutes who both claimed to be the mother of the same infant

(1 Kgs 3:16–18). Chronicles follows up its version of the Gibeon encounter by having Solomon use his vast wealth to finance the building of the temple.

Before taking up Solomon's temple building project, 1 Kings describes other manifestations of Solomon's wisdom as a king. First Kings 4 focuses on the steps that Solomon took to provide his kingdom with an efficient administration. After listing the kingdom's principal administrators (1 Kgs 4:1–6), Kings names Solomon's representatives in the regions north of Jerusalem and Judah. These twelve regions were responsible for the support of the central administration of the kingdom. The regional division of the rest of the kingdom ignored the tribal territories. Apparently, Solomon's tribe of Judah was not part of this system. These policies likely engendered hard feelings among his subjects. First Kings 4 goes on to set Solomon within an international context, claiming that he dominated an area that extended from the Euphrates River in Mesopotamia to the border of Egypt (v. 24), that Israel lived in peace and prosperity during his reign (v. 25), and that he was well known in the world as a composer of songs and proverbs as well as for his knowledge of the world of nature (vv. 29–32).

Chronicles spends no time in providing details of Solomon's administrative policies or of his international reputation. After describing Solomon's wealth, which he garnered in part from his trade in horses and chariots (2 Chr 1:14–17), Chronicles moves immediately to the preparations the king makes for the construction of the temple in Jerusalem, leaving the impression that the reason Solomon became king was for that purpose.

The Temple

Both 1 Kings and 2 Chronicles present the building of the temple in Jerusalem as the high point of Solomon's reign. There were several Yahwistic temples or at least altars before Solomon's temple: Shiloh, Dan, Bethel, Beersheba, and Gilgal. But in Kings and Chronicles *the* temple of YHWH was in Jerusalem. First Kings 5 and 2 Chronicles 2 begin the account of the temple's construction with an exchange of letters between Solomon and the king of Tyre, who was an ally of David. Though Chronicles abbreviates the letters as found in 1 Kings, the thrust of the two accounts is similar. Chronicles, however, does have Solomon informing Huram (Hiram) of the reasons for having a temple built: the temple will be the setting for regular cultic services (2 Chr 2:4–5). Both Chronicles and Kings mention the conscription of laborers for the project. A particular concern of Chronicles are the artisans needed for the fine work, mentioning Huram-abi by name. Kings emphasizes the steep price that Israel had to pay to make the project possible. In addition to the forced labor, there were payments of great sums of grain and oil and twenty Galilean cities ceded to Tyre in payment for the cypress and cedar timber used in the construction of the temple (1 Kgs 9:11).

First Kings 5 assumes the temple-building prerogative and responsibility of ancient Near Eastern kings. In verse 3 Solomon explains that circumstances prevented David from exercising that prerogative. David had to deal with hostile nations that surrounded his kingdom. Because these circumstances have changed and Solomon does not have to face any military threats, he can build the temple. Chronicles, having dealt with this issue in 1 Chronicles 22:7–10, does not rehearse it here; rather, Chronicles asserts that the temple is necessary for a well-ordered, regular liturgical life. Such an approach fits well into circumstances and concerns of the Jewish community in Yehud. The implication is that building of the Second Temple is not a byproduct of Persian hegemony. It is an expression of the Jews' commitment to offer proper worship, at the proper time, in the proper place to YHWH, their ancestral Deity.

After dealing with the preparations for the temple's construction, both 1 Kings 6—7 and 2 Chronicles 3—4 describe the building and its furnishings. What appears to be surprising is Chronicles' relative lack of interest in these matters. After all, the construction of a temple has been the focus of Chronicles' treatment of David and Solomon, but this concern apparently did not transfer to an interest in the physical aspects of the building and its accoutrements used in the cult. The one exception is Chronicles' emphasis on the gold used to embellish the temple that 2 Chronicles mentions ten times in chapters 3—4. First Kings mentions the temple's gold nine times in chapters 6—7, although the passage in 1 Kings is fifty verses longer than the parallel text in Chronicles.

Although Kings and Chronicles agree that the building project began in the fourth year of Solomon's reign (1 Kgs 6:1; 2 Chr

3:2), only Chronicles mentions the site where the temple was to be built: "Solomon began to build the house of YHWH in Jerusalem on Mount Moriah, where YHWH had appeared to his father David, at the place that David had designated, on the threshing floor of Ornan the Jebusite" (2 Chr 3:1). This exemplifies a fundamental concern of Chronicles: to show continuity with the past as the way to legitimate institutions of the present. The rebuilt temple stands in the same place as Solomon's structure and enjoys the same connection with ancient traditions and therefore is an expression of authentic Israelite religion. The parallel passage in 1 Kings does not name the site on which the temple was to be built. The Deuteronomic formula suggests that the temple will be built on "the place that the LORD will choose" (Deut 12:14) without naming the precise location.

Both Kings and Chronicles devote considerable attention to the dedication of the temple, displaying a greater interest in the temple's dedication than in its construction (1 Kgs 8:1—9:8; 2 Chr 5:2—7:22). Chronicles appropriates the account in 1 Kings with just a few omissions and additions. The account in Kings contains little narrative. It is made up of oratory by Solomon. It is Solomon's dedicatory prayer that reveals the attitude of Kings toward the temple. Its characterization of the temple as "a house for YHWH's *name*." The Deuteronomic formula has a certain demythologizing function that is underscored in Solomon's prayer at the temple's dedication: "Will God indeed dwell on the earth? Even heaven and the highest heaven cannot contain you, much less this house that I have built" (1 Kgs 8:27). For Kings the temple is not the dwelling place of God, because God dwells in the heavens. The temple is the place for God's throne, for the ark, and for God's name (1 Kgs 8:13, 21, 27, 48). The temple also has a more humanistic function as it provides for worshipers a place to pray to the God who dwells in the heavens.

Solomon's prayer is framed by reports of the fantastic number of animal sacrifices that were part of the dedication ceremony (1 Kgs 8:1–5, 62–65). Within that frame, there is a second frame that sees the temple as the fulfillment of God's promises to David (1 Kgs 8:14–21) and to Israel through Moses (1 Kgs 8:54–61). The prayer proper begins with a petition for the endurance of the Davidic dynasty that recognizes the conditional nature of the promises of an eternal dynasty to David (1 Kgs 8:22–30). This petition is the last time that 1 Kings 8 shows any concern for the fate of the Davidic dynasty. The emphasis in the rest of the prayer shifts to the destiny of the people of Israel. This shift points to the new significance that the Kings gives to the temple as a place of prayer for all Israel and indeed for all peoples (1 Kgs 8:30, 41). The core of Solomon's prayer (1 Kgs 8:31–51) is made up of seven petitions. These petitions conceive of the temple as a place where Israelites and Gentiles alike gather to offer their prayers to God whose dwelling place is in the heavens (1 Kgs 8:30, 32, 34, 36, 39, 43, 45, 48). The repeated assertion of the heavens as God's dwelling place reinforces the relative significance that Kings gives to the temple. Those making petitions do not even need to be in the temple precincts; they need only pray toward the temple (1 Kgs 8:43).

Three of the petitions (1 Kgs 8:33–34, 44–45, 46–51) speak about Israel's defeat and exile, clearly laying the blame for these on the sins of the people. The petitions ask for forgiveness and restoration but make no mention of the Davidic dynasty. The petitions do speak of calamities that befall the people of Israel because of their sins, but the petitions go beyond sin and judgment and focus on repentance, prayer, and forgiveness. The destruction of Solomon's temple by the Babylonians in 587 BCE led to the conclusion that although the temple was holy, it was not immune to the effects of divine judgment on the sins of Judah's people and especially of its kings. The worship of Yhwh that took place in the temple did not ensure its survival. Like the other institutions of Judah, the temple too collapsed under the weight of Judah's infidelity. The ambivalent attitude of Kings toward the temple prepared the adherents of the ancestral religion of the Jews for a world without a temple and so contributed to the survival of Judaism.

In its version of Solomon's prayer, Chronicles omits Kings' references to the ark of the covenant and to Moses (1 Kgs 8:21 and 53), but it does insert citations from Psalm 132:1, 8–10 (2 Chr 6:41–42). These texts recall David's concern for the ark and the promise made to David of an eternal dynasty. These citations are examples of the preeminence Chronicles gives to Davidic tradition.

The principal difference between Solomon's prayer in Kings and in Chronicles is evident in the verses that conclude that prayer:

1 KINGS 8:52-53 (NRSV)	2 CHRONICLES 6:41-42 (NABRE)
"Let your eyes be open to the plea of your servant, and to the plea of your people Israel, listening to them whenever they call to you. For you have separated them from among all the peoples of the earth, to be your heritage, just as you promised through Moses, your servant, when you brought our ancestors out of Egypt, O Lord God."	And now: "Arise, LORD God, come to your resting place, you and your majestic ark. Your priests, LORD God, will be clothed with salvation, your faithful ones rejoice in good things. LORD God, do not reject the plea of your anointed, remember the devotion of David, your servant."

The prayer's ending in Kings serves to underscore the priority of God's actions in securing Israel's future. God is then responsible for Israel, since at the exodus Israel became God's people. Chronicles does not view the exodus as the once-and-for-all event that made the people of Israel the people of God. Chronicles replaces the conclusion to Solomon's prayer in 1 Kings 8 with a citation of Psalm 132:8–10. The psalm serves to connect the prayer with the act with which the dedication ceremony began, namely, the transfer of the ark to the temple. It may also reflect the experience of temple service in Chronicles' time when psalms were integral to temple worship. Most significantly, Chronicles' version of the prayer's conclusion alters its tone. Solomon's prayer focuses on sin, repentance, and forgiveness. The conclusion in Kings asks God to hear the people's plea for forgiveness. Chronicles' conclusion uses words like "salvation" and "rejoice," clearly changing the mood at the end of the prayer. The NRSV renders the final phrase of Chronicles' conclusion to Solomon's prayer as "your steadfast love for your servant David." The Hebrew phrase (ləhasdê dāwîd) is better translated as "the devotion of David" (NABRE). Rather than a call for the restoration of the Davidic dynasty as implied by the NRSV, this phrase serves to recall all that David did to make the temple and its rituals a reality.

Kings and Chronicles conclude their respective accounts of the temple's dedication differently. Kings has Solomon speak a word of blessing upon the people attending the ceremonies (1 Kgs 8:54–61). The king begins by asserting that God has kept every promise made to Israel and repeating the exhortation to keep the commandments as the most appropriate way to respond to God's fidelity. Chronicles does not include this blessing but does reproduce Kings' account of the concluding festivities (1 Kgs 8:62–66; 2 Chr 7:1–11) and the account of God's appearance to Solomon (1 Kgs 9:1–9; 2 Chr 7:12–22). Chronicles' account of the concluding ceremonies is much more dramatic than Kings' straightforward listing of the number of sacrifices offered. Chronicles has fire coming down from heaven to consume the sacrifices, leading the people to fall on their faces as they praise God. Kings is less interested in describing a dramatic scene and more concerned with calling Israel to obedience to the commandments. Chronicles reflects Kings' concern with obedience in the words that God speaks to Solomon. Both accounts underscore the choice that Israel is to make. It can choose the way of repentance and prayer that will lead to forgiveness and restoration or the people can choose idolatry and disobedience. The result of the latter will be exile from the land promised to Israel's ancestors. Both texts agree that Israel's future is in the hands of the people. The choices they make can lead to peace and prosperity in the land promised to their ancestors or they can lead to exile from the land. In the latter case, the temple just dedicated will not be a testament to Israel's commitment to God but a witness to the ungratefulness of a people who have chosen to forsake their ancestral Deity.

In both Kings and Chronicles the building of the temple did not have only religious implications for the Solomonic kingdom. There was also an important political objective: the consolidation of the Israelite state with its capital in Jerusalem. That this city provides the central location for the worship of Israel's patron Deity was a significant elevation of its status. This city, which did not enjoy a lengthy Israelite pedigree, became the nation's capital. The kings that will follow Solomon on the throne of David will be judged by their actions to maintain the centralization of Yahwistic worship in Jerusalem and, by implication, the unique status of Jerusalem. Those kings who promote or even tolerate worship at "high places" are considered to have failed in their responsibility as kings.

The Rest of Solomon's Story

Kings and Chronicles agree that Solomon was a very wealthy person and energetic builder, that he had significant international political and commercial contacts, and that at first he fulfilled his religious duties. Kings gives an account of Solomon's reign following the dedication of the temple in 1 Kings 9:10—11:40, and 2 Chronicles 8—9 reproduces most of what is found in 1 Kings, except for chapter 11, which describes the negative features of Solomon's rule. Both Kings and Chronicles note that Solomon used forced labor for his building projects, although Chronicles is careful to assert that Solomon did not employ Israelites in his forced labor gangs (1 Kgs 9:15; 2 Chr 8:9).

Perhaps the most familiar story of the latter part of Solomon's reign is the visit of the Queen of Sheba (1 Kgs 10:1–43; 2 Chr 9:1–31). Though her name is not given in the story, she is clearly its principal character. The story serves to underscore Solomon's reputation for wisdom, but the queen is the one who does almost all the talking in the episode. She gives Solomon an enormous amount of gold, and the king responds by ensuring that every desire of hers is met.

Kings does not hesitate to include the negative aspects of Solomon's reign that Chronicles chooses to ignore. First Kings 11 provides the details of the darker side of Solomon's reign, and Chronicles does not include anything from this text in his description of Solomon's reign. According to Kings, the most serious of Solomon's failings is his relationships with foreign women. He married the daughter of Pharaoh and many other foreign princesses. His harem was enormous, with three hundred wives and seven hundred concubines. Chronicles mentions only two wives: the daughter of Pharaoh and the Ammonite woman Naamah, who is the mother of Rehoboam, Solomon's successor (2 Chr 12:2). Kings asserts that Solomon's relationships with non-Israelite women led him into idolatry. He even built shrines for foreign gods of his wives. Idolatry was Solomon's undoing since it led God to raise opposition to him. Solomon had to deal with incursions by Hadad, an Edomite whom the Egyptians supported, and by Razon from Aram (1 Kgs 11:14–25).

According to Kings, the most serious threat to Solomon's rule came from a member of his administration (1 Kgs 11:26–40). Jeroboam from Ephraim was responsible for the forced labor gangs that worked on Solomon's building projects. These forced laborers came from "the house of Joseph," the tribes of Ephraim and Manasseh, the two largest of the northern tribes. The prophet

Ahijah from Shiloh supported Jeroboam's plan to lead a rebellion against Solomon and assume control of the larger portion of Solomon's kingdom. Jeroboam fled to Egypt to avoid Solomon's reaction to his rebellion. Solomon's mistreatment of the northern tribes along with his marriage to foreign women led to his apostasy and made this wisest and wealthiest of kings into a fool who managed to set the stage for the end of Davidic rule over all the tribes except for Judah.

Kings concludes its account of Solomon's reign by indicting the king as responsible for the dismemberment of the kingdom given him by David. Again, what began with such promise ends in disaster. What happened to the wise and just king of 1 Kings 3—4 and the pious king of 1 Kings 7—9? In the end, the wise and just king becomes a tyrant, enslaving his own people, and the pious king becomes an idolater. The pattern of Israel's first two kings is repeated in the life of its third king. What is most tragic in Kings' story of Israel's first three kings is that this pattern will be repeated in the life of the people as a whole.

Although Chronicles ends the story of Solomon by itemizing the luxury goods that were the evidence of Solomon's wealth and by noting the extent of Solomon's empire (2 Chr 9:25–28), Kings lists the threats to Solomon's rule (1 Kgs 11:23–40). Kings thus shows that Solomon's life followed the pattern of his two predecessors: what began with such promise, in the end, was a grave disappointment. The reigns of Saul, David, and Solomon presaged Kings' depiction of the Israelite monarchy as a failed institution. Saul commits suicide. David is a doddering old man, manipulated by his wife and courtiers. Solomon becomes an idolater beset by external and internal opponents.

For Chronicles the reason for the monarchy's existence was to ensure that Israel's ancestral Deity would be worshiped in a temple that was to be built in Jerusalem. That goal was achieved because David devoted his reign to preparing for the construction of the temple. He assembled the material for its construction and organized its cultic personnel. Solomon had the temple built and dedicated to the worship of the LORD. For Chronicles this is all that matters. David and Solomon were not failures; they fulfilled their responsibilities as kings to ensure that Israel would be in a position to worship in the most appropriate way. Chronicles was written for a subject people who had little economic power and even less political self-determination. Yehud was a small part of the vast Persian Empire. But its identity was not determined by political or economic power, but by the fulfillment of its commitment to serve YHWH alone. This was possible because the temple had been rebuilt, providing a setting for the people to worship the God of their ancestors.

CONCLUSION

Kings and Chronicles have different takes on Israel's first three kings. Though each used the stories of Saul, David, and Solomon to tell its respective version of their stories, their respective takes on the beginning of Israel's monarchy clearly differ. For Samuel and Kings, the reigns of Israel's first three kings are harbingers of the disasters that eventually befell Israel. For Chronicles, the achievements of David and Solomon provide a pattern for the people of Yehud. Samuel/Kings was trying to make sense of the collapse of the Kingdom of Judah and the end of the Davidic dynasty. Its story of Israel's early kings gives its readers/hearers hints about what is to come. The reigns of the first three kings of Israel begin with great promise. Each king has significant achievements, but in the end, each disappoints. Chronicles chooses to leave behind most of the disappointments and focuses on what David and Solomon have accomplished—especially in the realm of the proper worship of YHWH in the proper place, the temple of Jerusalem. Chronicles attempts to give meaning and purpose to the lives of the Jews living in Yehud. Chronicles finds that meaning and purpose in the worship of YHWH, the ancestral God of the Jews. David and Solomon, who devote all their talent and energy to the project of building a temple for YHWH in Jerusalem, are exemplars for the Jewish community of Yehud.

Chapter Three

The Two Israelite Kingdoms

THE BEGINNINGS

The Succession to Solomon

The events surrounding the succession to Solomon were a watershed in the biblical stories of ancient Israel's monarchy. The Book of Judges recounts tensions among the Israelite tribes and the Philistine threat to their continued control over the land of Canaan. These led the elders of Israel to press for the establishment of a centralized political and military system under the control of a king "like all the other nations." Saul, the first king of Israel, tried to counter the Philistine threat, but he committed suicide following a disastrous military defeat (1 Sam 31:1–7). David, his successor, neutralized the Philistines but was not able to overcome opposition to his succession to the throne by the Benjaminites, who considered him a usurper. David had to deal with internal threats to his rule. He faced three revolts—one led by one of his own sons. Solomon was able to end internal opposition and firmly establish the dominance of the Davidic dynasty. His reign was marked by peace, which led Chronicles to provide an explanation for Solomon's name as a prophecy of his reign (see 1 Chr 22:9). With Solomon's death came momentous changes for Israel and the Davidic dynasty.

Kings asserts that Solomon ruled over a kingdom that extended from the Euphrates to the border of Egypt (1 Kgs 4:21). Rehoboam, Solomon's son and successor, was unable to maintain control of that kingdom. Within a short time, the kingdom of David and Solomon devolved into two smaller states: The Kingdom of Judah comprised the tribe of Judah and Simeon, although the tribe of Judah had already absorbed the tribe of Simeon. The Kingdom of Israel included the territories of the northern tribes. Who was responsible for the breakup of the Davidic-Solomonic kingdom? What brought about the division of that kingdom? What is the significance of the rise of the two Israelite states? Kings and Chronicles give contrasting answers to these questions.

For Kings, the responsibility for the division of the Davidic-Solomonic kingdom falls principally upon Solomon. What had been a glorious time for Israel during the early years of Solomon's reign changed dramatically in his final years. First Kings 11 tells of the people of "the house of Joseph" being turned into slaves working on Solomon's extensive building projects.[1] Solomon had to face military incursions from Edom in the south and Aram in the north, threatening his control of Israelite territory. Worst of all, Solomon's marriages to foreign women led him to idolatry. The severing of Solomon's kingdom was endorsed by the prophet Ahijah, speaking to Jeroboam, the leader of the rebellion:

> Thus says the LORD, the God of Israel, "See, I am about to tear the kingdom from the hand of Solomon, and will give you ten tribes. One tribe will remain his, for the sake of my servant David and for the sake of Jerusalem, the city that I have chosen out of all the tribes of Israel. This is because he has forsaken me, worshiped Astarte the goddess of the Sidonians, Chemosh the god of Moab, and Milcom the god of the Ammonites, and has not walked in my ways." (1 Kgs 11:31–33)

The threat to the Davidic dynasty was a real one, despite the promises of an eternal dynasty made to David. There is a precedent in 1 Samuel for the revocation of promises made by God. First Samuel 2:27–36 recounts the promise of an eternal priestly dynasty for the house of Eli along with the revocation of that promise because of the behavior of Eli's sons. What God did once God can do again. For Kings then, the breakup of the Davidic-Solomonic kingdom was the divine response to Solomon's idolatry. The emergence of the Kingdom of Israel was one result of Solomon's infidelity. Kings also notes that if Jeroboam, who led the revolt against the house of David, kept the commandments, then God would promise him an "enduring house" like that of David (1 Kgs 11:38). The house of Jeroboam, however, was extinguished with the assassination of Nadab, Jeroboam's son and successor, along with the entire royal house because of Jeroboam's infidelity (1 Kgs 15:25–30). Chronicles does not mention Nadab, although Baasha, who assassinated Nadab, does merit inclusion in Chronicles only because Baasha and Asa of Judah were engaged in a dispute over their common border (2 Chr 16:1–2).

Chronicles has an entirely different take on the succession to Solomon and the subsequent events that led to emergence of the Kingdom of Israel. Chronicles makes no mention of Solomon's forced labor practices nor his descent into idolatry. The end of the Davidic-Solomonic kingdom was not the consequence of divine judgment on Solomon's infidelities. It was the result of a rebellion led by Jeroboam against the young Rehoboam before the new king could settle into his role as his father's legitimate successor. For Chronicles, then, the Kingdom of Israel was not divinely sanctioned. It should not have been established, since the kingdom was given to David and his successors forever by "a covenant of salt" (2 Chr 13:5).

The Shechem Assembly

Rehoboam came to the throne by dynastic succession. There was no prophetic designation or popular acclamation leading to his accession. Kings depicts Rehoboam as making his way to Shechem to secure popular support for his rule (1 Kgs 2:1–20).[2] The people came to David at Hebron to offer him the throne (2 Sam 5:2). David's grandson had to go to Shechem to seek popular approval. How times had changed! Kings implies that the dynasty was in trouble with the people of Israel. Jeroboam, newly returned from asylum in Egypt, led the people in requesting that Rehoboam lighten the economic burden imposed upon them by Solomon.

Rehoboam first consulted his advisors who were holdovers from Solomon times. They advised him to do as the people requested. Rehoboam disregarded their counsel and chose to act on the advice of the young men who grew up with him in Jerusalem. They favored suppressing the independence of the tribes in favor of the centralization that was characteristic of an absolutist monarchy.

The reaction of the tribal assembly was swift and decisive to Rehoboam's refusal to meet the assembly's demands. The elders from the northern tribes recognized that the centralization favored by the young men was a departure from traditional patterns and would severely compromise the independence of the tribes. Some of the northerners were not content with voicing their opposition to the economic policies of the new king. They assassinated the royal official who oversaw the forced labor gangs and broke with the Davidic dynasty, forcing Rehoboam to flee to the safety of Jerusalem. Only the tribe of Judah remained loyal; all the other tribes offered their allegiance to Jeroboam. Rehoboam sought to bring the northern tribes under his rule by military force, but "the man of God" Shemaiah asserted that God had forbidden such action. The account of the Shechem assembly in Kings suggests that the breakup of the Davidic-Solomonic kingdom was the fulfillment of Ahijah's prophecy to Jeroboam (1 Kgs 11:29–33; 12:18–19). Chronicles essentially tells the same story. While Chronicles notes that the result of the Shechem assembly fulfilled the word of the Lord spoken through Ahijah, the prophecy itself with its anti-Solomonic thrust is nowhere cited. Both Kings (1 Kgs 12:19) and Chronicles (2 Chr 10:19) characterize the results of the Shechem assembly as a "rebellion against the house of David," though Kings suggests that it was Solomon's behavior and Rehoboam's intransigence that led to the rebellion. Chronicles would later blame Jeroboam and other "worthless scoundrels" for taking advantage of Rehoboam's youth and inexperience to foment the rebellion (2 Chr 13:6–7).

For Kings, the events surrounding the succession to Solomon and the Shechem assembly that led to the division of the Davidic-Solomonic kingdom were the direct result of Solomon's failure to maintain his commitment to YHWH. Solomon's infidelity was so serious that it compromised the promises made to David through the prophet Nathan (2 Sam 7). That promise was not rescinded entirely. For the sake of God's promise to David, the dynasty would continue to rule in Jerusalem, but over a greatly diminished realm (1 Kgs 11:13). Still, Kings does foresee circumstances that could result in the nullification of the promises made to David. Chronicles makes no such implication and regards the establishment of the Kingdom of Israel as the result of a rebellion led by Jeroboam and, therefore, an illegitimate usurpation of the rights of the Davidic dynasty. Chronicles also notes that Rehoboam sought to crush the rebellion by military force but was dissuaded from doing so by Shemaiah, "the man of God," who announced that God had forbidden such an internecine conflict (2 Chr 11:1–4).

Rehoboam and Judah

Chronicles asserts that Rehoboam proved himself to be a pious and able king for the first three years of his reign over Judah (2 Chr 11:17). He welcomed priests and Levites who migrated to Judah because of the cultic innovations of Jeroboam. He obeyed "the man of God" Shemaiah, who told him not to attack his fellow Israelites in the north (1 Kgs 11:4). Nevertheless, Rehoboam did build a string of fortresses that protected the approaches to Judah, and he strengthened the defenses of several towns in Judah and Benjamin.

Chronicles noted that once Rehoboam secured his position as king, his behavior changed. He led his people in disregarding "the law of YHWH" (2 Chr 12:1). When Egypt, under Pharaoh Shishak,[3] began a raiding expedition against Judah that threatened Jerusalem, Rehoboam and his generals repented. Jerusalem was spared, although the Egyptians emptied the temple's treasury. Kings mentions the Egyptian raid (1 Kgs 14:25–28) but without the elaboration found in the account in Chronicles (2 Chr 12:1–12). The account in Chronicles underscores the value of repentance, which can avert the full effects of disregarding the Torah. Kings does not devote much attention to Rehoboam except to note that his reign was marked by the flourishing of non-Yahwistic cultic practices (1 Kgs 14:21–24). Kings pays much more attention to Jeroboam and the beginnings of the Kingdom of Israel.

Jeroboam and the Northern Tribes

The participants in the Shechem assembly from the northern tribes not only refused to endorse Rehoboam as king, but they also offered the throne to Jeroboam. The only tribe that remained loyal to Rehoboam was Judah—Rehoboam's own tribe. Jeroboam made Shechem his capital, later relocating to Penuel.[4] To discourage pilgrimage to Jerusalem that could have induced people to remain loyal to the Davidic dynasty, Jeroboam built shrines to YHWH at the northern and southern extremities of his kingdom. Kings describes these shrines at Dan and Bethel, their priests, worship, and feasts as nothing less than acts of idolatry (1 Kgs 12:26–33). A more benign interpretation has Jeroboam responding to the more conservative Yahwists in the north by choosing sites that have a history connected with the tribes' worship of YHWH. Bethel was probably a pre-Israelite shrine that became associated with the traditions about Jacob (see Gen 28:10–19). Similarly, Dan, because of its proximity to Mount Hermon, which the Canaanites considered a sacred mountain, was a pre-Israelite center of worship. It came into the Israelite orbit when the tribe of Dan settled in the region (Judg 18).[5] Jerusalem has no such pedigree, having become part of Judah only since the time of David (2 Sam 5:6–12). Similarly, the golden calves that Jeroboam had set up in his temples at Dan and Bethel were likely alternatives to the cherubim of the Jerusalem temple (1 Kgs 6:23–28; 8:6–7). Still the choice of golden calves was an unfortunate one since bulls were associated with the worship of Baal. Chronicles makes no mention of what Kings calls "the sin of Jeroboam,"[6] ignoring Jeroboam except to mention the border war with Abijah (Kings refers to this king as Abijam) of Judah. Kings, on the other hand, devotes significant attention to Jeroboam following the Shechem assembly.

Kings tells the story of Jeroboam's encounter with an unnamed "man of God" near the altar of Jeroboam's shrine at Bethel.[7] The man of God announces the destruction of the altar by the Judahite king Josiah.[8] When Jeroboam attempts to have the man of God arrested, the king's hand withers. It is restored at Jeroboam's request and at the prayer of his antagonist. Though the man of God was invited to share the king's table, he refuses because of God's command that he not eat or drink anything in Bethel. The man of God goes on his way (1 Kgs 13:1–10).

The story of Jeroboam's encounter with the man of God is followed by the story of that man of God's encounter with an unnamed "old prophet in Bethel" (1 Kgs 13:11–34). The old prophet persuades the man of God to eat with him despite the command that the man of God neither eat nor drink in Bethel. When the man of God eats with the old prophet, the latter turns on him and reproves him for disobeying God's command not to eat or drink in Bethel. As the man of God is on his way back to Judah, a lion kills him. The old prophet finds his body and buries it. The prophet then affirms that the words spoken by the man of God against Bethel will find fulfillment. Kings' use of this prophetic legend about the man of God from Judah and his encounter with Rehoboam and the prophet from Bethel serves one of the basic purposes of Kings' storytelling: to turn the past into a sermon. Kings is concerned about impressing upon the people of Judah the importance of obeying the word of God to the letter. The man of God from Judah allowed himself to be persuaded to do otherwise and he came to a tragic end. If there is anything that Kings wants those who read or hear this work to understand, it is that disobedience has consequences. This lesson is repeated several times in Kings. Still, it is important to note the reverse, namely that obedience also has its consequences. Kings' readers know the consequences that the people of Judah faced because of their infidelity. If there will be any future for Judah, it will come about as the people take responsibility for their future by choosing the way of obedience to the written authoritative Torah.

Kings' story of Jeroboam takes on a tragic note with the story of Jeroboam's son Abijah (1 Kgs 14:1–20). Abijah becomes seriously ill, so Jeroboam sends his wife incognito to the prophet Ahijah at Shiloh to inquire about their son's fate. The blind prophet recognizes the voice of Jeroboam's wife and uses her inquiry as an opportunity to announce the fall of the house of Jeroboam (1 Kgs 14:10b–11). The prophet's oracle is a reversal of Nathan's prophecy regarding David's dynasty. Jeroboam was succeeded by his son Nadab, who reigned for only two years before he was assassinated along with the rest of Jeroboam's family, fulfilling Ahijah's prophecy (1 Kgs 15:26–30). Ahijah's blunt and graphic words are occasioned by the cultic sins of king and people. Jeroboam's wife says nothing and returns to Tirzah.[9] Her son dies upon her arrival. His death is a harbinger of what lies ahead for Jeroboam's dynasty. Chronicles makes no mention of this episode in accord with its tendency to ignore the Kingdom of Israel and its kings except when they have some dealings with the Kingdom of Judah. By the time Chronicles was written, the Kingdom of Israel had passed into the pages of history more than three hundred years earlier. The territory of the former kingdom was home to the Samaritans, whom the Jews did not consider to be authentic Israelites (2 Kgs 17:23–34). Reflecting a serious growing rift between the Samaritans and Jews, which became worse due to religious and political considerations, Chronicles does not share Kings' view of the Samaritans as inauthentic Israelites.

Abijah's Speech (2 Chr 13:2–20)

Kings has little to say about the three-year reign of Rehoboam's son and successor Abijam (called Abijah in Chronicles),[10] except to say that the war between Israel and Judah that began following Rehoboam's accession continued into Abijam's reign (1 Kgs 15:6). Chronicles uses this war as the backdrop for a speech by Abijah that is given in a most improbable setting: Abijah addresses Jeroboam's army as the battle between Israel and Judah is about to begin. Though Abijah is outnumbered two to one, he is confident of victory because of the promises made to David and the legitimacy of the cult of YHWH as practiced in Judah. Kings recounts no such speech and says nothing about the outcome of the war. Chronicles asserts that Jeroboam died in that war, being struck down by God (2 Chr 13:20). Kings says nothing about the circumstances of Jeroboam's death, though it notes that he reigned for twenty-two years and was succeeded by Nadab (1 Kgs 15:25).

Abijah's speech is a composition by Chronicles. It serves to articulate Chronicles' theology.[11] Abijah declares that the Kingdom of Israel has its origin in an unlawful rebellion against the inexperienced Rehoboam. Jeroboam and the northern tribes were guilty of a gross violation on the rights of the Davidic dynasty, which had been chosen by God to rule. The defeat of Jeroboam's army is foreordained because of the cultic irregularities introduced by Jeroboam. Judah, by way of contrast, has legitimate priests and Levites presiding over the cult of YHWH in accord with traditional patterns of Yahwistic worship. Jeroboam's innovations are not merely illegitimate but are idolatrous.

There have been suggestions that Abijah's speech is a plea by Chronicles for a reunification of the northern and southern tribes. On the one hand, that seems unlikely since Chronicles appears to have written off the Kingdom of Israel. This kingdom and its rulers are all but ignored in Chronicles except when Judah and its kings have contact with the north. On the other hand, Chronicles still regards the people of the Northern Kingdom as Israelites though they have abandoned their ancestral religion in favor of an ersatz Yahwism designed by Jeroboam to give legitimacy to his rule. Gary Knoppers suggested that Abijah's speech serves to make the conflict between north and south into "Yahweh's war against Israel."[12]

Abijah's speech serves to turn one of the incessant border wars between Israel and Judah into something more: a conflict between tradition and innovation. From Chronicles' perspective, history has proven that any departure from traditional patterns of worship is tantamount to an abandonment of God (2 Chr 13:10). For Chronicles, the pattern of worship followed in the Second Temple is in continuity with the traditions of the past. It is this continuity that gives Yehud's worship legitimacy. Jeroboam's abandonment of traditional patterns of worship shows most clearly that his kingdom is illegitimate.

A Permanent Separation

Judah's victory, which Ahijah predicted, allowed Abijam to take ten miles of territory north of Jerusalem as far as Bethel. Kings mentions the war, claiming that it continued throughout Abijam's three-year reign (1 Kgs 15:6). The Abijam of Kings is not the pious Abijah of Chronicles. Abijam managed to survive the pressures brought to bear by the incursions of the Israelite forces only because of David's fidelity to YHWH.

Kings has the sinful Abijam succeeded by the pious Asa, who reigned for forty-one years. He took decisive action against idolatry—even removing his mother Maacah from her position as *gǝbîrâ*[13] because of her patronage of the Asherah cult (1 Kgs

15:13). Asa adorned the temple with his votive offerings. His one failure was his tolerance of worship at "high places" (Hebrew: *bāmôt*).[14] These were rural shrines at which sacrificial offerings were made, detracting from the temple's unique status. The high places were also centers of idolatrous worship. The border war with Israel continued in Asa's reign. Baasha of Israel captured the town of Ramah, which was six miles north of Jerusalem, which he fortified. This led Asa to forge an alliance with Aram. With Aram's army harassing Israel from the north, Baasha was forced to withdraw from Ramah. Asa was then able to move the border deeper into Benjaminite territory.

Chronicles expands on Kings' treatment of Asa by highlighting his building activity and his expansion of Judah's military. The latter enabled Asa to defeat a much larger invading force from Ethiopia.[15] Upon his return to Jerusalem, Asa is met by the prophet Azariah, who warns the king to remain loyal to God. The prophet reminds the king of what happened when the Israelites abandoned God in the past. Asa acts on the prophetic warning by initiating a renewal of the covenant (2 Chr 15:9–12). Chronicles then rehearses the Deuteronomic account of Asa's reign except to note that Asa did indeed remove the high places (1 Kgs 15:14; 2 Chr 14:3).

Though Kings depicts Asa as a "good king," Chronicles paints a dark picture of Asa's final years (2 Chr 16:1–14). The seer Hanani criticized Asa for a lack of faith in YHWH's commitment to Judah because he sought help from Aram during the war with Israel. The prophet asserted that, as a punishment, Asa would have to deal with a continuing series of wars during the remaining years of his reign. Asa, in turn, imprisoned Hanani and began persecuting some of his own people—probably those who supported the seer. During the last year of Asa's reign, the king suffered from an unspecified disease in his feet, but he refused to seek help from God. Despite the king's action against Hanani and his supporters, Asa was honored in death as his body was laid on a perfumed bier and a "great fire" was lit in his honor.

With the death of Rehoboam and his successors Abijam (Abijah) and Asa, and the death of Jeroboam and his successor Nadab, the rift between Judah and the other tribes became permanent. There were two Israelite kingdoms in place of the Davidic-

Solomonic kingdom, which would never be reconstituted, though the prophets Jeremiah (Jer 3:18) and Ezekiel (Ezek 37:16–17) held out hope that the separation would end one day. Once Chronicles describes the separation and its immediate aftermath, it ignores the Kingdom of Israel for the most part. Chronicles focuses its attention on Judah and Jerusalem—with special attention to the temple and its personnel. For Chronicles, Judah's future will be secure if the people of Judah worship YHWH, their ancestral Deity, in the temple in accord with the rituals and personnel that David prepared for with great care. The fate of the Kingdom of Israel did not concern Chronicles. It was part of a past that was the result of a rebellion against the Davidic dynasty, idolatry, and illicit patterns of worship. Still, Chronicles regarded the people of the Kingdom of Israel as true Israelites, pointing to Chronicles' notion that a united Israel—north and south—remained the ideal.

For Kings, the rebellion that led to the establishment of the Kingdom of Israel with its two cult centers at Dan and Bethel was a rebellion against YHWH, who promised that David's kingdom would last forever, and who chose Solomon to build the temple in Jerusalem. Kings reported the fall of the Kingdom of Israel, the exile of its people, and the importation of a foreign population into its territory (2 Kgs 17). This led to the characterization of the Samaritans as non-Israelite people who practice a syncretistic cult at an inappropriate place with cultic personnel who did not enjoy a Levitical origin. Kings chooses to tell the story of the ill-fated Kingdom of Israel to underscore the consequences of idolatry, the rejection of the unique status of the Jerusalem temple, and the abandonment of the Davidic dynasty. Kings does not gloat over the fate of the Kingdom of Israel because it warns its readers/hearers that a similar fate awaits the Kingdom of Judah (2 Kgs 17:19–20). The religious and political institutions of both kingdoms failed to maintain their people's loyalty to YHWH, their ancestral Deity.

EXCURSUS: THE *Gəbîrâ*

The Hebrew word *gəbîrâ* appears several times in Kings and Chronicles to designate a woman who held a position of power and prestige in the royal court of Judah. The title *gəbîrâ* is used to speak of only one royal woman from the Kingdom of Israel. Second Kings 10:13 speaks of the "sons of the *gəbîrâ*." The context makes it clear that the *gəbîrâ* in question is Jezebel. The nature of that position has been the subject of several recent studies.[16] When this word appears in Kings and Chronicles, both the NRSV and NABRE translate *gəbîrâ* as "queen mother" (1 Kgs 15:13; 2 Kgs 10:13; 2 Chr 15:16). This assumes that the mother of the reigning king bore this title. This has led some commentators to apply this title to mothers of Judean kings, whether or not the biblical text gives them the title. A case in point is Bathsheba, the mother of Solomon. Neither Kings nor Chronicles refers to Bathsheba as a *gəbîrâ*, though several scholars do not hesitate to do so.[17]

A philological analysis of the word is the first step in clarifying the identity and role of the *gəbîrâ*. The semantic field of the Hebrew root *gbr* includes the notion of power, strength, and dignity. The verb *gābar* means "to be strong," "to rule," "to exercise power." *Gĕbîr*, a masculine equivalent of *gəbîrâ*, appears in the blessing that Isaac confers on Jacob (Gen 27:29, 37). The feminine form *gəbîrâ* occurs only fifteen times in the Old Testament. In Genesis it is used to speak of Sarah as the mistress of Abraham's household (Gen 16:4, 8, 9). It also is used in several contexts to refer to the mistress of a household (Ps 123:2; Prov 30:23; Isa 24:2; 2 Kgs 5:3). In 1 Kings 11:19, it refers to the Pharaoh's wife.[18] In Isaiah 47:7, Babylon speaks of itself as *gəbîrâ* over nations. In none of these occurrences is the notion of motherhood implied.

There are only two instances where the mother of a Judean king is identified as a *gəbîrâ*: Maacha, the mother of Asa (1 Kgs 15:2, 10, 13), and Nehushta, the mother of Jehoiachin (Jer 13:18; 29:2). Scholars have extrapolated from these two instances that there was some sort of an official position in Judah's royal court for the mother of the reigning king. Still, the evidence to support this hypothesis is slim indeed.

To make up for the lack of information from the Bible about the identity and role of the *gəbîrâ*, scholars have turned to cross-cultural comparisons. Niels-Erik Andreasen points to a position among the West African Ashanti comparable to his conception of the role of the *gəbîrâ* in Judah's political system.[19] Marcin Sosik finds examples of women in ancient Near Eastern societies playing a role similar to the one he posits for the *gəbîrâ*.[20] The problem with these comparisons is that they assume there was such a position in the Judean royal court and that position was held by the mother of the reigning king. Why does Kings give this title to just one mother of the nineteen kings of Judah from Rehoboam to Zedekiah?

Neither Kings nor Chronicles gives the title of *malkâ* (queen) to either the wife or mother of the reigning king as might be expected.[21] This was part of a general pattern of minimizing the role and status of women in Judah's political system. In Kings, followed by Chronicles, the account of each Judean king's reign is preceded by an introductory formula that gives the king's age at accession, the length of his reign, his mother's name, and a preliminary evaluation of the king's religious behavior. However, none of the kings' mothers is given the title *gəbîrâ* when her name is given in the introductory formula. Is this part of the pattern of minimizing women's role in governance?

First Kings 15:13 and 2 Chronicles 15:16 mention that Asa removed his mother Maacha from the position of *gəbîrâ* because of her promotion of the cult of Asherah. This action was part of Asa's religious reform. Susan Ackerman suggests that the worship of Asherah was part of ancient Israel's cult and that the *gəbîrâ*'s responsibility was the promotion of that cult. Asa sought to end the cult of Asherah in Judah by stripping his mother of the title and status of a *gəbîrâ*. This effectively put an end to his mother's role as patron of that cult. But Asa's reform did not outlive him, requiring another reform of the cult by Hezekiah and Josiah (2 Kgs 23:4, 6). Ackerman also suggests that the worship of both YHWH and Asherah in the temple of Jerusalem was the norm, and that the importance of the king's mother flowed from her role in promoting the cult of Asherah.[22] The only other mother of a Judean king that probably bore the title of *gəbîrâ* is Nehushta, Jehoiachin's mother (Jer 29:2). Her name is probably derived from *nāḥāš* (serpent); one epithet of Asherah is "serpent lady."[23] It is likely that Kings suppresses the use of the title *gəbîrâ* except in the case of Maacha because of its association with an idolatrous pattern of worship. Maacha's title is stripped from her by her reforming son Asa. From the perspective of Kings, any use of the title *gəbîrâ* is a reminder of Judah's unfortunate past, in which Asherah was worshiped alongside YHWH.

Imbued with the exclusivism of Deuteronomy (Deut 6:4), Kings wishes to speak of the unfortunate past of Judah's cult in the most general terms.

In conclusion, it should be obvious that "queen mother" is a misleading translation of the Hebrew word *gəbîrâ*. Neither Kings nor Chronicles refers to either the wife or mother of the king as "queen." Also, the semantic field of the word *gəbîrâ* does not include motherhood. Ralph Klein suggests "great lady" as a preferable alternative.[24] Next, the biblical text does not provide information regarding the status and responsibility of the *gəbîrâ*, though there appears to be some connection of the *gəbîrâ* with the cult of Asherah. This is clear in the case of Maacha, the mother of Asa, and possible in the case of Nahshta, the mother of Jehoia-chin. There were powerful and influential women in Judah's royal family. Bathsheba and Athaliah are the best examples. Both were mothers of kings, but the biblical text calls neither of them a *gəbîrâ*. The identity, role, and status of the *gəbîrâ* remain one of the Bible's mysteries.

THE RISE OF THE KINGDOM OF ISRAEL

The picture Kings paints of the beginnings of the Kingdom of Israel is fraught with political instability. No one dynasty was able to establish itself over the Kingdom of Israel as did the Davidic dynasty in Judah. There were serious rivalries among the tribes that made up the Northern Kingdom. Each tribe guarded its independence while seeking preeminence over the others. This was a prescription for instability. Jeroboam was an Ephraimite (1 Kgs 11:26). He was succeeded by his son Nabab, who managed to reign for only two years before he was assassinated by Baasha of the tribe of Issachar. Baasha took the added step of killing all the members of the house of Jeroboam to eliminate all rival claimants for the throne of Israel. Kings ignores the rivalries among the northern tribes and asserts that the fall of Jeroboam's short-lived dynasty was the fulfillment of a prophecy spoken by the prophet Ahijah against the house of Jeroboam for the sin of idolatry (1 Kgs

15:29–30; 14:7–14). Kings considered the worship that took place at Dan and Bethel, the two royal shrines of the Northern Kingdom, to be idolatrous. The accession of Omri put a temporary end to the political instability of the Kingdom of Israel, making it possible for Israel to become a military and economic power in the southern Levant. Kings pays little attention to this. Instead Kings focuses its attention on the religious failings of the Kingdom of Israel and its rulers.

Baasha

Baasha assassinated Nadab, Jeroboam's son and successor, who reigned for just two years. In an attempt to forestall revenge for this act of rebellion and regicide, Baasha had the entire house of Jeroboam killed. Baasha was introduced into the story of the two Israelite kingdoms in connection with the border war with King Asa of Judah (1 Kgs 15:16–25). The war was over the control of trade routes in the central highlands. Asa succeeded in gaining control of the disputed region by inducing Ben Hadad, the king of Aram, to attack Baasha from the north, forcing him to abandon his war with Judah in the south. Chronicles also provides a similar account of the war between Baasha and Asa. Chronicles follows its account with a critique of Asa's political strategy in securing Ben Hadad as an ally in the war with Israel. The seer Hanani condemns Asa for turning to politics and diplomacy instead of relying on God's help as he did in an earlier war with Ethiopia and Libya (2 Chr 14:7–18; 16:7–9). This criticism enraged Asa, and he imprisoned Hanani. Kings does not include Hanani's condemnation of Asa. Kings' account of this war is followed by focus on the Kingdom of Israel and its first kings.

Baasha located his capital at Tirzah. He did so to place a distance between himself and the traditional tribal power center of Shechem. The fledgling monarchy in the north was still in its formative period, and Baasha was prudent to keep away from potential opposition. Tirzah was located in the territory of Manasseh. The town was well watered by several springs and was on the main road to the Jordan Valley. The city's name is the Hebrew word for "beauty." The Song of Solomon compares its beauty to that of Jerusalem (Song 6:4). It was a rural, unfortified settlement without monumental architecture, fortifications, or administrative centers.[25] Excavations revealed striking differences between the dwellings of the poor and the much larger houses of the wealthy, indicating the disparity between social and economic classes in the period of the Israelite monarchy. The town was surrounded by small farms.

Kings considers Baasha no better than Jeroboam and recounts the prophet Jehu's oracle against Baasha and his house (1 Kgs 16:1–4). Baasha ruled for twenty-four years and died a natural death, unlike his predecessor. He was succeeded by his son Elah, who reigned for only two years before being assassinated by Zimri, one of his generals. To consolidate his rule, Zimri had every male from among Elah's relatives and friends killed. Again, Kings asserts that the end of Elah and the house of Baasha was the consequence of the idolatry practiced in the Kingdom of Israel at Dan and Bethel, ignoring the political instability that was endemic to the Kingdom of Israel.

Zimri

Zimri had reigned for only seven days when Omri, the commander of Israel's army, moved against him because of his assassination of Elah. Zimri sought the safety of the royal palace in Tirzah, and so Omri besieged the palace. When Zimri saw that he could not withstand Omri's attack, he committed suicide. Again, Kings blames Zimri's unfortunate end on his support for Israel's idolatrous cult (1 Kgs 16:19). Following the fall of Tirzah and the death of Zimri there was a four-year civil war over the succession, pitting Omri against Tibni. The text of 1 Kings 16:21–22 does not mention any fighting between supporters of the two rivals. Still, it is hard to imagine how the rivalry between Omri and Tibni played out over four years without some armed conflict between their respective supporters. Tibni's death ended the conflict. Except for Jeroboam's twenty-two-year reign and Baasha's twenty-four-year reign, both of which ended with a peaceful death, the succession to the throne of Israel was tumultuous with two assassinations, one suicide, and a civil war. Kings blames the cult of YHWH as practiced in the northern shrines at Dan and Bethel as the reason for the kingdom's difficulties, but the antidynastic tendencies of the north almost guaranteed that succession would not go smoothly.

In the south, the Davidic dynasty was in control: Abijam succeeded Rehoboam, and Asa succeeded Abijam.

Omri and His Dynasty

Chronicles mentions Omri only once, incorrectly identifying
him as the father of Athaliah (2 Chr 22:2).[26] Kings devotes only
five verses to Omri's reign (1 Kgs 16:24–28). Kings gives no personal information about Omri. It does not mention his tribe nor
his parents' names. This has led some to suggest that Omri was a
foreign mercenary who rose to prominence in the army of Israel.[27]
With the support of his troops, he was able eventually to rise to
assume the throne of Israel. There is, however, no direct evidence
in the text of Kings that Omri was a foreigner.

Kings says almost nothing about what Omri did following
the conclusion of the civil war with Tibni. It does note that Omri
purchased land on which he built his capital (1 Kgs 16:24). At the
beginning of his reign, Omri resided at Tirzah. He knew how vul-
nerable it was to attack. He began to fortify it, but after two years
he abandoned the town to build his capital on the land that he
had purchased—land on which no town had previously been built.
The site was well chosen. It was easily defensible and was adjacent
to an important north-south trade route. It was royal property that
was not part of any tribal holding. Samaria,[28] the city that Omri
built, served as the capital of the Kingdom of Israel until the fall
of the kingdom.

More than any of his predecessors Omri was responsible for
forging the northern tribes into a genuine national state. He came
to the throne about fifty years after the Shechem assembly that led
to the northern tribes' refusal of allegiance to the Davidic dynasty.
He brought an end to a period of assassinations and usurpations
and began a dynasty that included four kings, who ruled the Kingdom of Israel for thirty-four years. At about the same time that
Omri came to the throne, the Kingdom of Aram with its capital
at Damascus was coming into prominence. Aram would become
Israel's chief rival in the north of the Levant. Ashur-nasir-pal
ascended the throne of Assyria three years before Omri became
king. Assyria began a period of expansion in the west and would
prove to be an even greater threat to Israel than would Aram.

Omri began an expansionist program of his own, subjecting Moab to his rule, as memorialized on the Moabite Stone: "Omri was king of Israel, and he oppressed Moab for a long time."[29]

Omri solidified Israel's position in the southern Levant by political marriages that served to make allies of his neighbors. It is likely that Omri was on friendly terms with Asa of Judah, ending the rivalry between Judah and Israel. He had his son Ahab marry the Phoenician princess Jezebel. This ensured good relations with the Phoenicians to the north. He also sought to mend fences with Judah by having his granddaughter Athaliah marry Joram, the heir to the throne. Though this marriage took place after Omri's death, he certainly encouraged it. The alliance with Judah served to support Israel in the face of threats from Aram. Omri sought to reduce tensions within his kingdom by treating his Canaanite subjects on a par with his Israelite subjects by not only allowing the practice of Canaanite religion, but encouraging it. This policy, however, backfired because of the fierce opposition of Yahwists like the prophets Elijah and Elisha. The Omride dynasty eventually ended during a violent revolution led by militant supporters of traditional Israelite religion.

Omri turned the fledgling Kingdom of Israel into a genuine national state with a strong and efficient administrative apparatus, a wise foreign policy, and a tolerant domestic policy. It is not an exaggeration to claim that Omri was the real founder of the Kingdom of Israel. He established its first real dynasty. That Kings pays him scant attention testifies to the ideological bent of the Book of Kings. Omri continued to support the type of Yahwistic cult that Jeroboam established, and which Kings considered illegitimate. He tolerated and even encouraged Canaanite religious practices. In the mind of Kings this was enough to merit condemnation: "Omri did what was evil in the sight of the LORD; he did more evil than all who were before him" (1 Kgs 16:25). Chronicles mentions Omri only once (2 Chr 22:2). Kings ends its brief treatment of Omri by noting his death and his burial in Samaria.

Ahab

The summary of Ahab's reign in 1 Kings 16:29–33 provides some basic information: Ahab succeeded his father Omri and ruled the Kingdom of Israel for twenty-two years. He was married to Jezebel,[30] the daughter of Ethbaal, the king of Sidon. Kings accuses Ahab of promoting and participating in the worship of Baal. This is a more serious offense than those of his predecessors. They promoted the worship of YHWH directed by an illegitimate priesthood in Dan and Bethel. Ahab compounded "the sin of Jeroboam" by building a temple for Baal in Samaria. The prophet Elijah vehemently opposed Ahab's policy of promoting the cult of Baal. Kings intertwines the stories of Ahab and Elijah to draw a clear contrast between the royal establishment with its readiness to compromise, and those like Elijah, who called for Israel to serve YHWH alone. Elijah's name (My God is YHWH) corresponds to the stance he took in the conflict between the adherents of Baalistic religion and the adherents of traditional Yahwism. The introduction to Ahab's reign serves to identify the issue that Elijah will confront in his prophetic ministry: the problem of the cult of Baal.

In telling the story of Ahab's reign, Kings marginalizes elements of the story that are not in accord with its negative view of Ahab. It mentions Ahab's ivory palace because it underscores the opulence of his lifestyle.[31] Ahab transformed his kingdom into a military power in the region and formed a coalition of states to stand up to Assyrian expansionism in the region.[32] These projects were made possible because of the increase of trade, economic prosperity, and material culture in Israel during Ahab's reign. Also, under Ahab the Kingdom of Israel became a formidable military power. Ahab was a leader of an alliance of kingdoms in the Levant that opposed Assyrian expansionism in the region. Israel contributed chariot forces under the command of Ahab that helped secure a victory of the alliance over the Assyrians at Qarqar in 853 BCE.[33] The Bible does not mention the alliance's victory, which temporarily halted Assyrian expansion into the Levant. The conflict that concerned Kings was that between Baal and YHWH, which was played out in the conflict between Ahab and Elijah.

The conflict between king and prophet is set within a period of drought. Israel did not have a river system comparable to Egypt's Nile and Mesopotamia's Tigris and Euphrates to support agriculture. Farmers in the southern Levant were almost completely dependent on rain to provide moisture for their crops. When rainfall was insufficient, famine was a distinct possibility—especially when rainfall was insufficient in consecutive years. While Ahab built a shrine to Baal, the storm god who brings rain, in Samaria (1 Kgs 16:31), Elijah informs Ahab that YHWH, the God of Israel, has decreed a drought that will last several years—certainly an ironic twist (1 Kgs 17:1). The drought is prompted by Ahab's support for the cult of Baal.

To forestall Ahab's certain revenge against Elijah, YHWH then orders the prophet to cross the Jordan to the Wadi Cherith, where he will find water and where the ravens will feed him.[34] Eventually the wadi dries up, and God instructs Elijah to travel northwest to Zarephath, a town on the Mediterranean coast near Tyre and Sidon. Zarephath, too, is suffering from the drought. Another ironic twist: Baal could not prevent the drought even in his own territory (Phoenicia). Elijah meets a widow with a son. She has almost nothing to share with the prophet, but nonetheless she offers him what little she has. Miraculously her food supply is not diminished while she feeds the prophet. While Elijah is still with the widow and her son, the boy dies, but in answer to the prophet's prayer, "the life of the child came into him again" (1 Kgs 17:22). This led the Canaanite woman to recognize Elijah as a prophet sent by God. In view of what follows, this is another ironic twist since Ahab does not believe Elijah to be a prophet but calls him a "troubler of Israel" (1 Kgs 18:17).

The conflict between Baal and YHWH for the loyalty of the Israelites is played out in a contest between 450 prophets of Baal and the solitary prophet of YHWH, Elijah, on Mount Carmel, which is along the Mediterranean coast south of the region of Tyre (1 Kgs 18:20–40). Elijah and YHWH were victorious over Baal and his prophets. Elijah was able to induce YHWH to consume the sacrifice the prophet placed on the altar he built, while the entries of Baal's prophets had no effect. The Israelites who witnessed this contest shouted, "YHWH indeed is God!" (1 Kgs 18:39). Elijah had the prophets of Baal executed and informed Ahab that the drought is over and that the rains will come (1 Kgs 18:41–46).

Ahab and Elijah make their way to the town of Jezreel located twenty-five miles southeast of Mount Carmel. The king informs his wife of what Elijah did to the prophets of Baal. Jezebel is furious and promises revenge, and so Elijah flees to Beer-sheba, about ninety miles south of Jezreel (1 Kgs 19:1–3). From there

Elijah goes to Horeb (Deuteronomy's name for Mount Sinai). The prophet is weary from his attempts to evade Jezebel's vengeance. At Horeb, he has an encounter with the Divine, who speaks to him in a barely audible voice, instructing the prophet to go to "the wilderness of Damascus"[35] in order to anoint Hazael king of Aram, Jehu as king of Israel, and Elisha as Elijah's successor. Elijah finds Elisha plowing and induces Elisha to follow him.

The Elijah stories are interrupted by a story about a war between Ahab of Israel and Ben-hadad of Aram. An unnamed prophet assures Ahab that he will be victorious (1 Kgs 20:13), but Ahab is not convinced. Ben-hadad does not give up following his defeat in the first battle of the war. The Aramean scouts sent out by Ben-hadad suggest luring the Israelite army out of the hills into a valley where the Aramean army could be more effective. Another unnamed "man of God" assures Ahab of victory (1 Kgs 20:28). The Israelite army is successful again. Ben-hadad flees the battlefield but is captured. He convinces Ahab not only to spare his life but to conclude a treaty with him. The unnamed prophet denounces Ahab's decision to let Ben-hadad go after concluding a treaty with him (2 Kgs 20:42). The king did not appreciate the prophet's criticism and returns to Samaria unhappy despite his victories over Aram.

The account of Ahab's conflicts with Aram is interrupted by the story of Naboth's vineyard (1 Kgs 21:1–29). The setting for the story is Jezreel. The town's name ("May God make fruitful") suggests that it was known for the fertility of its soil. The town was located at the eastern end of the Jezreel Valley, breadbasket of the region. Ahab maintained a residence in the town. He had a small vegetable garden near his palace, which he tended for recreation. He wanted to expand his garden but was unable to do so because Naboth's vineyard abutted it. Ahab proposed purchasing the vineyard from Naboth. In the short term the sale would have enriched Naboth, but in the long term it would have reduced his heirs to poverty since they would have had no land from which to derive their support. In an agricultural economy, land provides the means of production, and those without land are poor unless they have some other source of income. Naboth wisely refused to sell.

Ahab was disappointed, but he recognized that Naboth was within his rights as he sought to preserve the patriarchal system of inheritance for his family. What he received from his ancestors he will leave for his heirs. The king's wife Jezebel came from a country in which the land belonged to the king, who was free to grant that land to whomsoever he wished. Jezebel asks Ahab, "Do you now govern Israel?" (1 Kgs 21:7a). Jezebel hatches a plot with the cooperation of compliant Israelite elders and Naboth's own neighbors to have Naboth tried and executed for treason with his property being forfeit to the crown. Elijah curses Ahab, his dynasty, and Jezebel because of the judicial murder of Naboth (1 Kgs 21:20–24). In an editorial aside, Kings accuses Ahab of unprecedented acts of idolatry that were encouraged by Jezebel (1 Kgs 21:25–26). There is a connection between Baalism and the absolutist form of monarchy favored by Jezebel, since it provides support for a hierarchical social and political system. Yahwism supports a familial approach to monarchy in which the king is considered a brother to his subjects (see Deut 17:20).

In a surprise ending to the Naboth story, Ahab repents of his crimes, and so the curse is suspended because of Ahab's contrition. It will be carried out during the reign of Joram, Ahab's son. This is reminiscent of the fallout from David's adultery with Bathsheba and his complicity in the death of her husband, Uriah. The prophet Nathan pronounces a curse upon David and his house (2 Sam 12:7–12). David repents and his life is spared, though that of his infant son borne to him by Bathsheba is taken. In both cases, the life of a sinful king is spared because of the king's repentance. For the books' hearers/readers, this is a subtle but clear suggestion that the people of Judah may be spared if they repent. The tragic reality was that despite the prophets sent to them, the people did not repent, and so they have to face the real possibility that God will annul the promises made to their ancestors.

The story of Ahab ends with a strange prophetic encounter that took place when Ahab made plans to reignite the conflict with Aram.[36] To prepare for the renewal of hostilities Ahab asked Jehoshaphat of Judah to join forces with him. At first Jehoshaphat seemed agreeable, but he asked that Ahab "inquire first for the word of YHWH" (1 Kgs 22:5). In a bit of an overkill, Ahab produced four hundred prophets who affirmed that God was going to grant Ahab victory over Aram. Jehoshaphat probably assumed that the four hundred prophets were court prophets, who would as such be expected to speak words of support for the king. The reluctant Jehoshaphat requests an independent prophetic voice. Ahab then summons Micaiah ben Imlah, though he warns Jehoshaphat that Micaiah never prophesies anything favorable about him. Surprisingly, Micaiah does announce that God will grant the king victory over Aram. The king then forces the truth from Micaiah. The prophet announces that Israel will be defeated and the king killed in battle. Micaiah further explains the positive response given by the four hundred prophets as the result of a "lying spirit" that Yhwh had put into the mouths of those prophets in order to encourage Ahab to embark on a course of action that will lead to his death (1 Kgs 22:19–23). Micaiah then is sent to prison until the king should return safely, which would prove that Yhwh did not speak through him.

Ahab and Jehoshaphat go into battle, though Ahab is disguised. The Arameans pursue Jehoshaphat, thinking that he is the king of Israel. When the Arameans realize that Jehoshaphat is not whom they were seeking, they break off the chase. An arrow strikes Ahab and he bleeds to death. His body is brought to Samaria for burial. Kings refers readers to the "annals of the kings of Israel" for information about Ahab's achievements as a builder.

First Kings 22 reflects Kings' equivocal attitude toward prophets and the institution of prophecy. On the one hand, Kings illustrates how Elijah's prophecy concerning Ahab's death was fulfilled. The king's blood was licked up by dogs just as the prophet asserted it would be (1 Kgs 22:38; see 21:19). On the other hand, the story of the four hundred prophets shows that even genuine prophecy is an unreliable guide to the future, since God can place a "lying spirit" into prophets to induce actions that are detrimental to those seeking guidance from a prophet. Those four hundred prophets did not intend to deceive Ahab but were led to do so by Yhwh (1 Kgs 22:2–28). How is it possible, then, to have confidence when one is inquiring of a prophet for a word from Yhwh?

One goal of Kings is to affirm that the written, authoritative Torah is the one infallible guide for Israel's life (see 2 Kgs 22—23). Kings does not reject prophecy as such but asserts that it has its limitations. The prophets did not prevent the disasters that fell on the two Israelite kingdoms and will not be able to effect a restoration. Only obedience to the Torah is the kind of response that God expects of Israel. That obedience leads to blessing on Israel's life and makes possible Israel's future.

Ahaziah

Ahab was succeeded by his son Ahaziah, who reigned for less than two years. Kings dismisses him as an idolater—no better than his father (1 Kgs 22:51–53), and Chronicles all but ignores him except to note that his joint commercial enterprise with Judah failed, according to a prophetic word from Eliezer, because the king of Judah allied himself with the idolater Ahaziah (2 Chr 20:35–37). Ahaziah suffered a serious fall in his palace in Samaria. He then sent a delegation to Ekron, a Philistine village near the border with Israel. The delegates were to consult with Baal-zebul about the king's prospects for recovery. This, of course, angered Elijah who condemned Ahaziah for his disloyalty to Israel's God. Elijah convinced the delegation to return to Samaria. Ahaziah sent three other delegations, two of which were consumed by fire from heaven before they could complete their task. The leader of the third delegation asked Elijah to spare their lives. The prophet then confronted Ahaziah directly and informed him that he would die shortly because of his idolatry (2 Kgs 1:2–16). Ahaziah died childless and was succeeded by his brother Jehoram.

Jehoram (Joram)[37]

Kings' treatment of Jehoram of Israel is scattered across 2 Kings 1:17 to 9:26. Also treated in this section of 2 Kings are the Judahite king Jehoram, the prophets Elijah and Elisha, and wars with Moab and Aram.[38] Kings states that Jehoram of Israel reigned in Samaria for twelve years. Like all his predecessors, he supported the shrines at Dan and Bethel originally established by Jeroboam. Similarly, like the other kings of the Omride dynasty, Jehoram made allowances for his Canaanite subjects to worship as they desired. This, of course, enraged Yahwists like Elijah and gained for Jehoram the reputation as an idolater. Kings, however, does credit Jehoram for removing a cultic pillar of Baal originally erected by Ahab (2 Kgs 3:2), though he maintained the temple of Baal in Samaria. With the death of Ahab, Jezebel acquired the position of the *gəbîrâ*—the only queen of Israel to bear this title in Kings (see 2 Kgs 10:13). With this position, Jezebel could ensure that the worshipers of Baal would be undisturbed and even supported.

Jehoram had good relations with the Kingdom of Judah. His aunt, Athaliah, married into the Judahite royal family (2 Kgs 8:26). This served Jehoram well as he had to deal with the growing power of Moab. Second Kings 3:4–27 states Jehoram was allied with the kings of Judah and Edom in the campaign against Moab.[39] The coalition was unsuccessful since Moab did manage to wrest itself from Israelite control (*ANET*, 320–21).[40] According to Kings, Jehoram led the Israelite army against Hazael at Ramoth-gilead (2 Kgs 8:28–29; 9:14–15). Jehoram was wounded in battle. During his recuperation in Samaria, his army mutinied and acclaimed their general Jehu as king after he was anointed by a disciple of Elisha (2 Kgs 9:1–14). This act led to the death of Jehoram and the end of the Omride dynasty.

The end of the Omride dynasty was a serious blow to the prospects for the future of the Kingdom of Israel. It would never reach the heights of military, political, and economic power as it enjoyed during the reigns of the Omride kings. The Books of Kings had no use for these kings because they maintained the shrines at Dan and Bethel. While these were Yahwistic shrines, they were served by priests whom Kings considered illegitimate and, more importantly, were not the places that God chose to make God's name dwell. In addition to this "sin of Jeroboam," the Omride kings promoted the worship of Baal. To be fair, Omri and the other kings of his dynasty were simply allowing their Canaanite subjects to worship their ancestral patron deities. Tensions between the Israelite and Canaanite subjects of the kingdom rose to an unhealthy level with the marriage of Ahab and the Tyrian princess Jezebel. Although this marriage made sense from political and economic perspectives, it upset the homeostasis of the kingdom. Jezebel's promotion of the worship of Baal aroused the anger of committed Yahwists such as Elijah and Elisha. Tensions rose to such a level that Jehu's revolt was all but inevitable. The level of violence that accompanied this revolt is evidence of the high level of opposition to the Omrides that developed among the Yahwist population of the kingdom—opposition encouraged by their prophets.

Chronicles and the Rise of Israel

Chronicles ignores the kings of Israel unless the kings of Judah are involved with them in some way. It mentions Jeroboam in connection with the breakup of the Davidic-Solomonic kingdom and with the border wars that he had with Judah. Chronicles makes note of the border conflicts between Asa of Judah and Baasha of Israel. Ignoring Elah, Zimri, and Omri, Chronicles next mentions Ahab because of the connection with Jehoshaphat, reproducing 1 Kings 22:1–40 with only minimal changes in 2 Chronicles 18:1–34. After Chronicles mentions Ahab's death, attention then centers on Jehoshaphat. The only time Chronicles mentions Ahaziah is to note the failure of the joint maritime commercial venture that he and Jehoshaphat attempted. Chronicles ignores Jehoram of Israel.

During the Omride period the Kingdom of Israel reached its apogee. But in the eyes of Chronicles the Kingdom of Israel should not have existed. It was born of a revolt against the House of David. Its priesthood and its temples at Dan and Bethel were illegitimate. Its kings not only tolerated but promoted the worship of Baal. There is little from the story of the Kingdom of Israel that needs to be remembered. Its fate was foreordained by its rejection of the Davidic dynasty and the temple of Jerusalem. For Chronicles, the rise of the Kingdom of Israel is best left in the past. Also, Chronicles is only interested in the past insofar as it has relevance for the future of Judah. That future is tied up with the worship of YHWH in Jerusalem, which is the site of the only legitimate temple. By the time Chronicles is written, the Second Temple has been in existence for more than one hundred years. Chronicles wishes to show the continuity of that Second Temple with the cult of YHWH as established by David and Solomon. The Kingdom of Israel has no part to play in this scheme. Its kings established and maintained a cult of YHWH that lacked continuity with that established by David and Solomon. Its temples and priesthood were illegitimate.

There was no place for the former Kingdom of Israel in the future that Chronicles could see.

THE RISE OF THE KINGDOM OF JUDAH

Second Samuel 2:1–4 notes that David ruled as king over Judah in Hebron for seven years before the elders of Israel asked that he add the territory of the northern tribes to his realm (see also 1 Chr 11:1–3). David's reign was marked by three revolts against his rule, but, in the end, he was able to hand on his kingdom intact to his son Solomon. The union of Judah with the northern tribes, however, ended following Solomon's death. After the breakup of the Davidic-Solomonic kingdom, the first kings of Israel and Judah were occupied with a series of border wars before matters settled down after Asa's victory over Baasha. With the end of those wars, Judah was able to come into its own politically and militarily under Jehoshaphat. Both stories of the Israelite kingdoms depict Jehoshaphat in favorable terms, though Chronicles (17:1—20:37) expands on the attention Kings devotes to him. The Kingdom of Judah will reach its highwater mark with the reign of Uzziah. Kings and Chronicles, however, find fault with Uzziah's conduct in the religious realm.

Jehoshaphat

Jehoshaphat was a contemporary of three kings of Omri's dynasty: Ahab, Ahaziah, and Joram. He recognized that it was to Judah's advantage to maintain good relations with the Kingdom of Israel (1 Kgs 22:45) since it was more powerful economically and militarily than the Kingdom of Judah. This new, positive relationship between Israel and Judah was cemented by the marriage of Joram, Jehoshaphat's son and heir, to Athaliah, a member of the family of Omri (2 Kgs 8:18). Judah's alliance with Israel brought economic and military advantages to both kingdoms. Jehoshaphat's twenty-five-year reign was an era of prosperity for Judah.

Kings depicts Jehoshaphat as one of Judah's "good kings." Although he tolerated worship on the high places (1 Kgs 22:42b), he expelled the male prostitutes from the temple (1 Kgs 22:46). Without getting into specifics, Kings notes that Jehoshaphat "waged war" (1 Kgs 22:45)—despite the reluctance he showed when Ahab asked him to join in his war against Aram. Jehoshaphat failed in his attempts to engage in maritime commerce. Ahaziah of Israel invited Jehoshaphat to participate in Israel's commercial enterprises, but Jehoshaphat declined the offer.

Jehoshaphat supported the military adventures of the Omrides, though the Kingdom of Judah was the junior partner in any alliance with the Kingdom of Israel. Jehoshaphat lent support to the Omrides because it was to Judah's benefit to maintain good relations with the wealthier and more powerful neighbor to the north. When Ahab sought to reclaim the fortress at Ramoth-Gilead, Jehoshaphat was his ally, albeit a reluctant one (1 Kgs 22:1–38). Jehoshaphat also lent support to Israel's campaign against Moab (2 Kgs 3:4–37). In both cases, the outcome of these wars mattered more to Israel than to Judah.

Chronicles paints a much more flattering portrait of Jehoshaphat. Second Chronicles devotes four chapters to him, emphasizing his fidelity to YHWH and his antipathy toward the worship of Baal (2 Chr 17:1—20:37), as well as his removal of the high places and Asherahs (2 Chr 17:6). Chronicles suggests this loyalty to YHWH led to military victories over the Moabites, Ammonites, and Edomites (2 Chr 20:1–30). Chronicles claims that Jehoshaphat's army did not have to engage the enemy. Prayer and fasting induced YHWH to ensure Judah's victory. Chronicles reproduces Kings' account of the Judean-Israelite coalition that took Ramoth-Gilead from the Arameans, but it reports that the prophet Jehu objected to Jehoshaphat's allying himself with the evil Ahab (2 Chr 19:2–3). Chronicles notes that the prophet Eliezer cited Jehoshaphat's association with Ahab's son Ahaziah as the reason his seaborne commercial enterprises failed (2 Chr 20:35–37).

For Chronicles a most significant of Jehoshaphat's achievements was his reform of Judah's judicial system (2 Chr 19:5–11). This reform plus his construction of forts and store cities (2 Chr 17:12) and his attention to Judah's military preparedness (2 Chr 17:14–19) suggest that Jehoshaphat can be credited with turning

Judah into a full-fledged national state—something recognized by the Philistines, who paid him tribute (2 Chr 17:11). For Chronicles, Jehoshaphat's achievements were the consequence of his commitment to Yhwh. Chronicles, however, is not entirely consistent in its portrait of Jehoshaphat. Second Chronicles both praises the king for eliminating the "high places" (17:6) and faults him for failing to do so (20:33).

It is clear in both Kings and Chronicles that the reign of Jehoshaphat constitutes a new page in the stories of the two Israelite kingdoms. The border wars between the two kingdoms were over (1 Kgs 22:45); nonetheless, the prophet Jehu condemned Judah's alliance with the Kingdom of Israel (2 Chr 19:1–3). Jehoshaphat should be acknowledged as the founder of the Kingdom of Judah, just as Omri was the founder of the Kingdom of Israel. Both Omri and Jehoshaphat turned small, insignificant Levantine chiefdoms into genuine national states that became important military and commercial forces in the region. Jehoshaphat was respected by Judah's neighbors, and his army was a force to be reckoned with. Though Kings suggests that Israel held the dominant position, Chronicles notes that Jehoshaphat took actions to redress this inequality.

Chronicles holds Jehoshaphat in much higher esteem than does Kings, which provides just a brief eleven-verse summary of his twenty-five-year reign (1 Kgs 22:41–51). Kings notes that Jehoshaphat did "what was right in the sight of the Lord," though the high places remained throughout his reign (1 Kgs 22:42–43). Chronicles devotes four chapters to Jehoshaphat (2 Chr 17—20), crediting him with removing the high places and the asherahs.[41] A particular emphasis is the king's dispatch of royal officials, Levites, and priests to instruct people, using the "book of the law" (2 Chr 17:9). Chronicles also reports Jehoshaphat's judicial reform. Because of his policies of military preparedness, Judah was able to repulse attacks from the Transjordanian kingdoms (2 Chr 20:1–4, 20–30). Chronicles, however, suggests that Jehoshaphat's victories were the result of support from Elijah's and the king's assembling the people of Judah in the temple for prayer (2 Chr 20:5–19).

Chronicles' portrait of Jehoshaphat depicts him as an ideal king: pious, wise, devoted to the welfare of his people, and committed to Yhwh. He enjoyed wealth, prosperity, and international renown: "Jehoshaphat had great riches and honor" (2 Chr 18:1). This is Chronicles' way of affirming that the people in the Second Temple period ought to follow Jehoshaphat's lead since fidelity to YHWH has its rewards.

Jehoram (Joram)

Jehoram (2 Kgs 8:16–24) succeeded his father Jehoshaphat. Though Kings does mention Jehoram's age at his accession and the length of his reign, it does not give the name of his mother. This omission is most unusual. The only other time such an omission occurs is in the introduction to the reign of Ahaz. Kings numbers Jehoram among Judah's "bad kings," but notes that no evil came upon Judah as a result, owing to the promises made to David (2 Kgs 8:18–19). Jehoram was married to Athaliah, the daughter of Ahab of Israel and his wife Jezebel. The marriage helped cement the good relations between the two Israelite kingdoms. Kings reproves Jehoram for behavior like that of the kings of Israel, but without specifying the exact nature of his failures. Kings asserts that Jehoram had to deal with serious external and internal problems. The Edomites rebelled against Judah's rule over their homeland. They defeated Judah's army, freeing themselves from Judean domination. Kings dismisses Joram's reign of eight years with just nine verses (2 Kgs 8:16–24).

Chronicles devotes an entire chapter to Jehoram (2 Chr 21), portraying him as a fratricidal, sinful, and incapable king. To cement his hold on the throne, he killed his six brothers along with other princes. He promoted the high places, leading the people of Judah into idolatry comparable to that of the Kingdom of Israel under Ahab. The prophet Elijah[42] announced that the people of his kingdom would experience a "great plague" and that he himself would suffer a debilitating illness that would eventually kill him. The "great plague" turned out to be a raid by the Philistines and their allies. Jehoram did suffer a terribly painful illness that led to his death. Chronicles notes that Jehoram died "unloved" after an eight-year reign. No special rites marked his passing, and he was not buried with the other kings of Judah, though Kings has Jehoram buried among his ancestors (2 Chr 21:20; 2 Kgs 8:24).

Ahaziah[43]

Jehoram of Judah was succeeded by his ill-fated son Ahaziah, who was king for little more than one year. Chronicles notes that Ahaziah was Jehoram's youngest son. His older brothers died in a battle during their father's war with the Arabian allies of the Philistines (2 Chr 22:1). References to Ahaziah are scatted throughout 2 Kgs 8—11, while 2 Chronicles tells his story in 22:1–2, 6–11. Ahaziah's mother was an Omride, and so it is easy to explain his cooperation with Joram of Israel against the Arameans (2 Kgs 8:28). When Joram was wounded in battle and was recuperating in Jezreel, Ahaziah came to visit him there (2 Kgs 9:15–16). Ahaziah found himself in the middle of a military coup led by Jehu against Joram. Ahaziah fled south to Beth-haggan[44] on his way to the safety of Jerusalem. Jehu's forces caught up with Ahaziah and inflicted a grave wound on the king. Ahaziah made it as far as Megiddo, where he died. His body was brought to Jerusalem, where he was buried. That Ahaziah was Joram's in-law and ally no doubt led Jehu to have him killed along with Joram. Jehu also had other members of the Judean royal family who had been visiting in the north killed as well (2 Kgs 10:12–14). Second Chronicles 22:9 offers a different account of Ahaziah's death. That text has Jehu finding Ahaziah hiding in Samaria and kills him. Ahaziah was buried in Samaria rather than in Jerusalem.

Kings accuses Ahaziah of being as guilty of idolatry as were his in-laws, the Omrides of the Kingdom of Israel, implying that his mother Athaliah was responsible for leading Ahaziah into idolatry (2 Kgs 8:26–27). Second Chronicles 22:3, however, states explicitly that Athaliah encouraged her son's apostasy. Ahaziah's death gave his mother Athaliah the opportunity to seize the throne for herself, inaugurating a unique episode in the story of the two Israelite kingdoms: a woman from the Omride dynasty of Israel ascended David's throne.

Athaliah

Athaliah's seizure of power in Jerusalem almost brought the Davidic dynasty to a premature end. She must have had a position of status, influence, and power in the royal court since she was able to take advantage of the chaos that followed Jehu's assassination of Ahaziah and many members of the Judean royal family. Her status allowed her to marshal the forces necessary to take control of the situation. Like several monarchs of the Kingdom of Israel who took the throne by violence, Athaliah moved to eliminate all potential rivals—among whom were her own grandchildren (1 Kgs 15:29; 16:11; 2 Kgs 10:17). Athaliah nearly succeeded in bringing the Davidic dynasty to an end. Second Kings notes that Joash, a grandson of Athaliah, was spirited away and hidden in the residential precincts of the temple by Jehosheba, Ahaziah's sister (2 Kgs 11:2). Second Chronicles 22:11 adds the note that Jehosheba was the wife of Jehoiada, the temple's chief priest, which explains the reason the temple precincts became Joash's place of refuge.

Neither Kings nor Chronicles describes Athaliah's reign, though both mention the destruction of a temple of Baal immediately following her assassination (2 Kgs 11:18; 2 Chr 24:17). It is likely then that Athaliah had such a temple erected in Jerusalem. Apparently, there were those in Judah's capital city who supported Athaliah's rule. Included among them would have been a Canaanite segment of the city's population and foreign mercenaries whose values were not shaped by Israelite traditions.

Both Kings (2 Kgs 11:4–16) and Chronicles (2 Chr 23:1–15) tell the story of Athaliah's fall. Although Chronicles provides more details, both describe a plot led by Jehoiada, the high priest, who enlists some foreign mercenaries and native Judahites and Levites in the coup to replace the queen with her grandson Joash, the son of Ahaziah, who was assassinated during the Jehu revolt. The conservative, rural population of Judah supported the move against Athaliah and the destruction of the Baal temple, while "the city was quiet" (2 Kgs 11:20; 2 Chr 23:21). When Athaliah came upon the coup's participants gathered in the temple to acclaim Joash as king, she exclaimed, "Treason! Treason!" (2 Kgs 11:14; 2 Chr 23:13), the only words the storytellers give her to say. Athaliah was taken back to the palace where she was killed, ending the reign of the only woman to rule as queen in either of the two Israelite kingdoms.[45] Though Athaliah promoted the worship of Baal, her name contains a Yahwistic theophoric element. She is the first woman in the biblical narratives to have such a name. This detail adds to the paradox Kings describes.

Immediately following Athaliah's death, the priest Jehoiada, the leader of the coup, attempted to restore Judah's commitment to YHWH by making a covenant between God, the king, and the people. A second covenant between king and people affirms their support for the legitimate Davidic king (2 Kgs 11:17). Chronicles omits the mention of the covenant between king and people, replacing it with a covenant between Jehoiada and people (2 Chr 23:16). This reflects the reality of the fourth century BCE, the period of Chronicles' composition. The Davidic dynasty had not been restored and the high priest was the de facto ruler of the Jewish community.

Neither Kings nor Chronicles explicitly finds fault with Athaliah because she was a woman who usurped a position that properly belonged to a man. Both stories blamed her for promoting the worship of Baal in place of YHWH. Second Kings accuses her of leading her husband, Joram (8:18), and her son Ahaziah (8:26–27) into idolatry. Chronicles, too, notes her evil influence on his son (2 Chr 22:3). Chronicles adds the accusation that she allowed the temple of YHWH in Jerusalem to fall into ruin, while favoring the cult of Baal (2 Chr 24:7). The concern of both stories is not so much Athaliah's political moves, as much as it is her actions in the religious sphere. In telling the story of the coup that replaced her with Joash, Kings emphasizes the legitimacy of Joash as his father's successor. Chronicles, however, focuses on the role of the Levites during the popular revolution in opposition to Athaliah's rule. With her death, the last of the Omrides is gone. This dynasty had a profound effect on both Israelite kingdoms. Despite their success in the realm of politics, Kings and Chronicles maintain that the members of this dynasty were not loyal to YHWH alone.

Joash (Jehoash)

The precise chronology of the monarchic period in Israel and Judah is a matter of dispute. Still, it is clear that attributing a forty-year reign to Joash (2 Kgs 12:1; MT v. 2) is based on ideology rather than history. Joash represents the restoration of the Davidic dynasty. He "did what was right in the sight of YHWH," though worship at the high places continued (2 Kgs 12:3–4). A forty-year reign made readers think of the reigns of David and Solomon, who each reigned for forty years. Kings implies that, with Joash on the throne of David, things returned to the way they should have been, with the priest Jehoiada being credited with guiding the young king.

Both Chronicles and Kings devote most of their story of Joash's reign to his efforts at putting the temple in good financial shape. This allowed for repairs on the temple to proceed as needed.[46] Underlying the story of Joash's overseeing the fiscal health of the temple may be conflict over control of funds. Joash takes matters into his hands and his actions eliminate any problems (2 Kgs 22:3–7, 9). According to Chronicles, it was Jehoiada who kept Joash moving in the right direction. Once Jehoiada died, Joash fell under the influence of Judah's elite, and the king soon abandoned the temple of YHWH and fell into idolatry. When prophets including Jehoiada's son Zechariah announced divine judgment on Joash's apostasy, the elites of the kingdom had the son of Joash's trusted protector and wise advisor stoned (2 Chr 24:17–22). This is an example of Chronicles' underscoring the importance of priestly leadership for Judah.

Although Kings does not include the account of Joash's apostasy and the consequent prophetic condemnation, it does tell the story of what Chronicles presents as the divine judgment on Joash's actions: the conflict with Aram. In the ninth century, Aram dominated the other national states in the Levant. Aram was threatening to take Jerusalem. A first step was to capture Gath, originally a Philistine city that came under Israelite control once the Philistine threat was checked. Gath was located on a road that passed through the Elah Valley and Bethlehem. Once the Arameans took that city, Joash had no choice but to pay an enormous indemnity to Hazael, the Aramean king. Once this indemnity was paid, Hazael withdrew. Joash's inability to counter the Aramean threat without payment of tribute emboldened the Judeans who opposed his rule, and Joash was assassinated (2 Kgs 11:18–22). Chronicles, however, asserts that the Aramean victory over Judah was God's judgment on Judah for its apostasy. According to Chronicles, Joash's own courtiers assassinated him because of the king's command to have the prophet Zechariah killed (2 Chr 24:23–27).

The story of Joash in Kings is another example of a king who started out well but ended badly—a pattern found in the stories of Saul, David, and Solomon. Joash did not live up to the expectations of those loyal to YHWH and the Davidic dynasty. Once Jehoiada died, the voice of Yahwistic tradition was silenced and Joash listened to that of Judah's elites, who led the king into idolatry. This made the king's eventual downfall inevitable.

Amaziah

Joash was succeeded by his son Amaziah, whose reign followed an arc similar to his father's. Kings speaks well of Amaziah but notes that he did not measure up to the standard set by David, and that he allowed worship at the high places to continue. He started out well enough by restraining his impulses, as a son who had witnessed the murder of his father. Amaziah had his father's assassins executed but spared their families in accord with the principle found in "the book of the law of Moses" that children not pay the penalty for their parents' sins (2 Kgs 14:6; see Deut 24:14).

Kings notes Amaziah's successful campaign against Edom (2 Kgs 14:7) with the capture of Sela, a site located in the vicinity of the Nabatean city of Petra, though the exact location is a matter of some discussion.[47] Amaziah makes a claim of ownership by renaming the city Joktheel ("God subdued"), ascribing the victory over the Edomites to God. Chronicles embellishes the one verse that Kings devoted to the war with Edom. In addition to his own troops, Amaziah employed mercenaries from Israel, for which he was criticized by an unnamed "man of God" from Judah. These mercenaries then were denied their opportunity to share in the booty that victory brought. In their anger, they raided the Judean countryside to make up for their loss. Chronicles also notes that Amaziah captured the idols of Edom and set them up "as his gods" (2 Chr 25:14). An unnamed prophet announced that this apostasy would end with the king's destruction.

Flush with victory over Edom, Amaziah challenges Joash, king of Israel, to battle, ending the rapprochement with Israel. Joash tries to dissuade Amaziah by recounting a fable to him that identified Israel as a cedar of Lebanon and Judah as a thistle of Lebanon. Amaziah would not be dissuaded and was soundly defeated. Joash captured Amaziah at Beth-shemesh, a town along the western base of the central highlands eighteen miles west of

Jerusalem. Joash dismantled some of Jerusalem's defenses and took some booty from both temple and palace. He also rounded up some hostages and took them back with him to Samaria (2 Kgs 14:9–14).

Despite his humiliating defeat by Joash of Israel, Amaziah held on to his throne for fifteen additional years and outlived his rival from Israel. With no explanation given, Kings reports that Amaziah was assassinated by some of his courtiers just as his father was. Amaziah was succeeded by his son Azariah.

Azariah (Uzziah)

Azariah is the name of Amaziah's son and successor in 2 Kings 15:1–7. Chronicles knows him as Uzziah (2 Chr 26:1–23).[48] Kings' account of Azariah's reign is formulaic, noting the length of his reign, his mother's name, and that he was a good king except for his tolerance of the high places. The only unusual note concerns the leprosy with which the king was afflicted, causing him to live apart and to have his son Jotham act as his regent. Unfortunately, Kings offers little information about the reign of one of Judah's most successful monarchs. Second Chronicles offers a more detailed account of Uzziah's reign.

Uzziah was a contemporary of Jeroboam II. Both kings exercised economic, political, and military power that allowed their respective kingdoms to be in control of their own destinies without interference from other states in the Levant. Uzziah could not expand Judah northward because of Jeroboam, so he turned his attention to the south, west, and east. He began by retaking the port city of Elath and the southern tip of the Negev. This made Judah a player in the important Red Sea commerce by facilitating trade with Arabia. He then turned to Philistine territory, bringing several Philistine city-states into Judah's orbit. Finally, he ventured into the Transjordan, forcing the Ammonites to pay him tribute. He upgraded Jerusalem's defenses and built a string of fortresses in the south to provide long-range protection for his capital.[49] Among his most notable achievements was the formation of a large standing army,[50] which he outfitted with weapons and siege engines. All these efforts did not go unnoticed—even the Egyptians were impressed (2 Chr 26:8, 15b).

Agriculture was the basis of Judah's economy. Chronicles characterizes Uzziah as a lover of "the soil" (2 Chr 26:10b), suggesting that the king promoted Judean agriculture. The king himself raised cattle, cultivated grains, grapes, and vegetables. His support of agriculture was a major contribution to the prosperity of eighth-century Judah. Chronicles concludes its profile of Uzziah by dealing with the religious aspects of his life, focusing on the reason for his leprosy. In the early years of his reign, Uzziah benefited from the counsel of an otherwise unknown individual named Zechariah. In his later years, the king's achievements engendered an arrogance that led to his fall. Uzziah decided to exercise the role that every other ancient Near Eastern king enjoyed: to serve as the chief priest to the nation's patron Deity. In ancient Israel, the role of king and priest became separate. Uzziah, nonetheless, chose to act as priest by offering incense in the temple (2 Chr 26:16), which the text characterizes as an example of his arrogance. The chief priest Azariah, along with eighty other priests of the temple, reprimanded Uzziah for exercising a function that properly belonged to them. When Azariah and the others noticed a leprous lesion on the king's forehead, they ushered him out of the temple (2 Chr 26:19–20). The king's leprosy made it impossible for him to exercise the ceremonial aspects of his position, so his son Jotham acted in his stead, though it is likely that Uzziah continued to shape Judah's public policy. But even in death, Uzziah was buried apart from his ancestors in a field next to the royal cemetery. He was succeeded by his son Jotham.

Chronicles credits the Prophet Isaiah with producing an account of Uzziah's reign (2 Chr 26:22), but no such account has survived. The Prophet's temple vision (Isa 6:1–13) is dated to the year of Uzziah's death. Amos 1:1 and Zechariah 14:5 mention that a very destructive earthquake took place during Uzziah's reign. Finally, the superscriptions in both Amos (1:1) and Hosea (1:1) mention Uzziah. Both Kings and Chronicles assert that Uzziah reigned for fifty-two years (2 Kgs 15:7; 2 Chr 26:3). That is probably an exaggeration. He did, of course, share responsibilities with his son Jotham for part of his reign because of his leprosy. It is not an exaggeration to conclude that Uzziah was a most capable and accomplished monarch. Under his leadership Judah rose to a level that made it a genuine regional power. It was strong politically, economically, and militarily to the point that no other nation in the region could challenge it successfully. Judah maintained that position throughout his reign—a remarkable achievement.[51] That Kings all but ignores Uzziah underscores its genuine interests. The Book of Kings is not interested in providing a record of the past achievements of Judah's rulers; rather, its principal goal is to persuade its hearers and readers that the people of Judah had control of their future but chose to act against their own best interests. The story of Uzziah's reign was only tangential to that purpose. Chronicles, however, does describe Uzziah's achievements but suggests that, in the end, these achievements and the king's international reputation did not work to his benefit. He died as a leper because of his attempt to violate the norms prescribed for authentic worship of YHWH. Chronicles saw Judah's future as bound up with the worship of Judah's ancestral Deity, but the conduct of that worship was the prerogative of the priests—not even a king could ignore that.

CONCLUSION

The reign of Uzziah was the highwater mark of the Davidic dynasty. After the dismantling of the Davidic-Solomonic kingdom upon Solomon's death, the two Israelite kingdoms were involved in a series of conflicts over their borders. Jehoshaphat sought to have a more positive relationship with the Kingdom of Israel and the two Israelite kingdoms became allies. This new relationship was sealed by the marriage of Jehoshaphat's heir to the daughter of Ahab, king of Israel. When Judah was on the track of peace with prosperity, fallout from the Jehu revolution in Israel nearly brought an end to the Davidic dynasty. One Judean prince managed to survive Athaliah's murderous rampage. Joash began the return of the Davidic dynasty. His grandson Uzziah was perhaps the greatest king of Judah. Kings and Chronicles, however, found Uzziah wanting from a religious perspective. For Kings, Uzziah's principal failure was his toleration of the high places; for Chronicles it was his usurpation of the prerogatives of the priests.

Uzziah bequeathed to his son Jotham a kingdom that was secure, prosperous, and at peace. For the rest of Judah's story as told in both Kings and Chronicles, Judah will have to deal with the rise of the neo-Assyrian and then the neo-Babylonian kingdoms. The pressure brought to bear on Judah by these two Mesopotamian kingdoms will reveal Judah's weaknesses. Its freedom to control its own destiny will gradually diminish until it is lost entirely. Kings and Chronicles will tell their story under the specter of the Mesopotamian kingdoms' rise and Judah's inevitable fall.

The kings of the Omride dynasty transformed the Kingdom of Israel from a small and insignificant Levantine state into a major commercial and military power in the region—certainly overshadowing the Kingdom of Judah. The kings of that dynasty ruled for almost half a century, providing the kingdom with stability that made its rise to power possible. None of this was worth mentioning according to the biblical stories of the Kingdom of Israel. Kings dismisses Omri's reign in four verses. His son Ahab receives more attention, but his achievements are underplayed or disregarded entirely. For the Book of Kings, the Omrides, like all the monarchs of the Northern Kingdom, were guilty of promoting and practicing idolatry. They were the patrons of the temples at Dan and Bethel, which Kings regarded as venues for idolatry since authentic Yahwistic worship could only take place at the temple of Jerusalem. Kings also regarded the polity of the Northern Kingdom an affront to YHWH, who chose David and his descendants as the legitimate rulers of God's people. Chronicles all but ignores the Omrides.

Both biblical stories of the rise and fall of the two Israelite kingdoms shape their respective stories by their theological perspectives. Both consider Ahab to have compromised the ancestral religion of ancient Israel. The policy of the Omrides was to tolerate the religious beliefs and practices of both their Israelite and Canaanite subjects. Kings and Chronicles consider this policy tantamount to the promotion of idolatry, and they condemned the Omrides accordingly. In their view, fidelity to YHWH alone trumps any economic, political, and military achievements.

Chapter Four

The Decline and Collapse of the Two Kingdoms

THE ROLE OF THE PROPHETS

Prophets have a significant role in stories of the rise and fall of the Israelite kingdoms in both Samuel/Kings and Chronicles. This is not surprising since prophecy was a powerful force in ancient Israelite society and culture. This is evident not only from the role of prophets in biblical narratives but also from the collection of prophetic oracles that have survived in the second division of the rabbinic canon, known as the Latter Prophets: Isaiah, Jeremiah, Ezekiel, and the Twelve. People consulted prophets about problematic situations that they faced, seeking the prophets' advice about the course of action they should take in perplexing circumstances.

Divination

The people of ancient Israel also consulted diviners in order to learn what the future held in store for their personal and national lives. Diviners used various techniques to answer people's queries. The use of divinatory practices assumes that deities provide information about the future through phenomena in the material world. The diviner is a specialist in recognizing and interpreting these phenomena.[1] Divination was popular in the ancient Near East generally and in Israel in particular. Isaiah testifies to the popularity of divination as he decries the practice of consulting spirits and mediums (Isa 8:19–20).[2] Deuteronomy prohibits several forms of divination (Deut 18:9–14). Although Deuteronomy implies that divination does work, it insists that the use of divination is forbidden to Israel.[3] Both Samuel/Kings and Chronicles see the use of divination as something to be avoided. For example, both see Saul's downfall connected with his seeking to consult the spirit of the dead Samuel (1 Sam 28:3–5; 1 Chr 10:13). Similarly, both stories note that Manasseh of Judah practiced divination, for which he is condemned (2 Kgs 21:6; 2 Chr 33:6).

There are two problems with divination that led to its rejection by staunch Yahwists like the circles responsible for Samuel/Kings and Chronicles. First, when the interpretation of an omen by a diviner comes true, the temptation to serve other gods follows (Deut 13:3–4). The way for Israel to secure a future marked by the blessing of prosperity and peace is to observe YHWH's commandments (Deut 13:5). A second problem with divination is its connection with the use of apotropaic rituals.[4] A negative omen often led to the use of some ritual activity that supposedly would lead to a reversal of the consequences of a negative omen. For example, in the listing of forbidden divinatory techniques in Deuteronomy, there is the prohibition of making a son or daughter "pass through fire," that is, be sacrificed (18:10). Second Kings 17:17 also associates child sacrifice with divination. Both Ahaz (2 Kgs 16:3) and Manasseh (2 Kgs 21:6; 2 Chr 33:6) are condemned for employing such rituals in the crises they faced. The use of apotropaic rituals assumes that the Deity is really indifferent regarding the inquirer's fate. If one says the right prayer or offers the right sacrifice, one can manipulate the Deity to be more favorably disposed to the inquirer. Such assumptions run contrary to Israel's understanding of YHWH who cannot be manipulated.

Prophets and Prophecy

Instead of using divination, Israel was to inquire of a prophet concerning the future. David consults the prophet Nathan concerning his intention to build a temple to house "the ark of God" (2 Sam 7:1–3). When the king of Israel asked Jehoshaphat of Judah to join him in a campaign to recover Ramoth-gilead from the Arameans, Jehoshaphat requests that a prophet be consulted. The king of Israel accommodates Jehoshaphat by assembling four hundred prophets for the consultation (1 Kgs 20:1–6). When Josiah wishes to determine what action he should take with regard to the law-book found during repair work in the temple, he ordered his advisors to "go, inquire of YHWH," so they consult with the prophet Huldah (2 Kgs 22:11–13). In prophecy, then, YHWH communicates through human beings rather than through omens that are ambiguous and require interpretation. Ancient Israel's prophets were the means of divine-human communication.

The legitimate prophets were part of ancient Israel's religious leadership; their specific area of concern was the "word" (Jer 18:18), which they received from YHWH, and which they were to speak to kings, priests, and the people at large. The books that preserve the oracles of the prophets depict them as attempting to preserve the distinctive elements of Israelite religion—especially the requirement that Israel serve YHWH alone. Also, prophets serve as intermediaries between God and people, communicating the divine will in specific circumstances. For example, Isaiah offers words of support to Hezekiah during the crisis caused by Sennacherib's incursion into Judah (2 Kgs 18:20–28). Prophets, then, have a well-established role in ancient Israelite society. It is not surprising that stories of the two Israelite kingdoms do take notice of the activities of some of ancient Israel's prophets. Stories about prophetic activities in both Samuel/Kings and Chronicles suggest that a significant social location of such activity is the royal court. Prophets offer kings advice in times of crisis (2 Kgs 19). They speak words of both encouragement (2 Sam 7:1–17) and criticism (1 Kgs 17—19). They take part in political activities (1 Kgs 1; 2 Kgs 9). The stories in both Samuel/Kings and Chronicles depict the prophets as operating on a national level for the most part, though Elijah and Elisha interact with ordinary folk (e.g., 1 Kgs 17:8–24; 2 Kgs 4). Although the principal focus of both stories of the Israelite kingdoms is on kings and their activities, the role of prophets is not ignored. In fact, it appears that prophecy and monarchy were symbiotic institutions in ancient Israel.

The theological assumptions behind the portrait of prophetic activity in both Samuel/Kings and Chronicles are that God can determine events in this world and that human beings can influence the way that God acts through repentance, that is, responding to the message the prophets deliver. The prophets call for loyalty and obedience to YHWH. The result of that obedience will be prosperity and peace. Disobedience and disloyalty will bring divine judgment, and with it, disaster and ultimately the loss of the land. This perspective is most clearly stated in 2 Kings 17, which describes the reasons for the fall of the Kingdom of Israel. Among these was the people's failure to listen to the warnings God sent through the prophets (v. 13).

Samuel/Kings

Saul's rise to kingship took place in the midst of prophetic activity (1 Sam 10). The prophet Samuel, who acts as the leader of a prophetic band (1 Sam 19:20), recognizes Saul as the individual chosen by God to be Israel's king. During his encounter with Samuel, Saul himself is drawn into the ecstatic activities of the prophetic bands supervised by Samuel. Eventually, there is a break in the relationship between Samuel and Saul that leads Samuel to seek out another to serve as Israel's king (1 Sam 13:7b–15a; 15:1–15; 16:1–13). Samuel anoints David as the divinely designated king of Israel. Two prophets were part of David's entourage: Gad (1 Sam 13:5) and Nathan (2 Sam 7:2). Nathan set in motion the plans to have Solomon succeed David (1 Kgs 1:11–14). Ahijah predicts the dissolution of the Davidic-Solomonic state (1 Kgs 11:29–32). Jehu, son of Hanani, announces the end of the house of Baasha (1 Kgs 16:7, 12).

The stories of Elijah and Elisha add another dimension to the portrait of the prophet. Both are staunch Yahwists who do not hesitate to criticize and condemn kings for promoting the worship of Baal. Stories about these two prophets include the healing of lepers, the miraculous multiplication of food, and the raising of the dead.[5] Elijah defeats the prophets of Baal who were supported by Jezebel. Elisha foments the Jehu revolution that brings an end to the Omride dynasty (2 Kgs 9:4–10). The prophet Jonah predicts Jeroboam II's success in regaining territory lost to Aram

(2 Kgs 14:23–25). Isaiah serves as a counselor to Hezekiah during the Assyrian crisis (2 Kgs 19:1–7), and Huldah authenticates the lawbook found in the temple (2 Kgs 22:14).

Prophets deal not only with the national sphere, but also with personal issues with a few kings. Nathan accuses David of murder and adultery in the Bathsheba incident. David acknowledges his guilt and his life is spared, though the infant son of Bathsheba dies shortly after birth (2 Sam 12:1–19). Similarly, Elijah announces divine judgment on Ahab because of the Naboth incident. Ahab repented after hearing Elijah's word of judgment, and his life was spared (1 Kgs 21:17–28). These two kings and their response to the word of God given through the prophet are an example to all Israelites. If one listens to the words of the prophets and repents, there is hope that one can escape judgment.

The Deuteronomic test to identify an authentic prophet involves the fulfillment of the prophetic words (Deut 18:21–22). Kings calls attention to this fulfillment. It sees the exile of the priest Abiathar by Solomon as the fulfillment of the prophecy by the unnamed "man of God" concerning the fall of the house of Eli (1 Sam 2:27–36; 1 Kgs 2:26–27) and that of the prophet Ahijah concerning the dissolution of the Davidic-Solomonic kingdom (1 Kgs 11:26–40; 12:15). This concern about the fulfillment of prophecy stands in marked contrast to Nathan's oracle about the promise to David of an eternal dynasty. With the death of Jehoiachin (2 Kgs 25:30), that promise is voided. This is an example of the subordination of the prophetic word to the Torah. Despite the promise Nathan made to David, the Judahite state and its Davidic dynasty came to an inglorious end because of the failure of king and people to serve Yhwh alone (2 Kgs 23:26–27).

There are two episodes in Kings that reflect the unique perspective of Samuel/Kings on the institution of prophecy. The first is the story of Micaiah ben Imlah (1 Kgs 22; see above, ch. 3, p. 106–7 for a summary of this episode). The story of Ahab's consultation with prophets suggests that the prophetic word is unreliable since the prophet may be under the influence of a "lying spirit" without realizing. The prophetic word may give a positive reply to an inquiry when this reply only leads to actions that are harmful to the person making the inquiry. What then is the value of inquiring a "word from Yhwh" from a prophet? Kings resolves this dilemma in 2 Kings 17 as it gives the reason for the fall of the Kingdom of Israel: "Yet the LORD warned Israel and Judah by every prophet and every seer, saying, 'Turn from your evil ways and keep my commandments and my statutes, in accordance with all the law that I commanded your ancestors and that I sent to you by my servants the prophets'" (2 Kgs 17:13). This passage effectively transforms the prophets from messengers who make known the "word of YHWH" to Israel to teachers of the law. The law embodies God's will for Israel. The prophetic word is subordinated to the word found in the Torah. This solves the problem of prophetic conflict, in other words, when prophets give competing messages.[6] For Samuel/Kings the prophets fulfill their commission from God if they teach the people of Israel the Torah, which is the fundamental expression of the divine will.

Though prophets and prophecy are important components of Israelite society and religion, Deuteronomy seeks to regulate this institution because unregulated it could lead to undermining Israel's commitment to YHWH alone (Deut 13:1–5; 18:15–22). Samuel/Kings takes an additional step by subordinating prophecy to the Torah and making prophets teachers of Torah. The effect is to keep prophecy fully within the Yahwistic camp. Prophets and prophecy were a significant part of Israel's past. In the end, however, they proved unable to maintain the people's loyalty to YHWH. It is the Torah that binds the people to YHWH. The written, authoritative law is the key to Israel's future. While the two kingdoms have experienced the consequences of ignoring and violating that law by serving other gods, the surviving remnant of the Kingdom of Judah has the opportunity to experience the blessings of peace and prosperity that come with obedience.

Chronicles

Gary Knoppers maintained that the depiction of prophets and prophecy in Samuel/Kings was a major influence on Chronicles.[7] Every prophet mentioned by name in Samuel and Kings also appears in Chronicles except for Elisha. In addition, Chronicles reproduces five prophetic speeches from Samuel/Kings.[8] This points to the interest of Chronicles in prophetic activity. But Chronicles also introduces new stories about prophets not found in Kings. For example, 2 Chronicles 21:12–15 gives the text of a letter that Elijah was to have sent to Jehoram, the successor of the pious Jehoshaphat. In that letter Elijah excoriates Jehoram for his infidelity, which was just like that of Ahab of Israel, and for the murder of his brothers that brought him to the throne of Judah. Elijah announces divine judgment that will come in the form of a plague upon the king's family and upon the people of Judah. The king himself is to die of a disease of the bowels. This letter has no parallel in Kings, which confines Elijah's ministry to the Kingdom of Israel. Also, Chronicles does not rehearse the stories of Elijah's miracles or his conflict with the prophets of Baal and the Northern Kingdom's royal family. The context for these stories of Elijah is the Kingdom of Israel, which Chronicles virtually ignores. In the episode of Elijah's letter to Jehoram, Chronicles introduced the idea that prophecy can take a written, as well as an oral, form. The prophet's word is not confined to prophetic speech.

The Prophet Isaiah appears in both Kings and Chronicles. In Kings, Isaiah has an important role in supporting Hezekiah during the time of the Assyrian siege of Jerusalem. The Prophet also comforts Hezekiah when he thought he was dying (see 2 Kgs 19—20). In Chronicles, Isaiah's role is greatly diminished. Second Chronicles 32:30 notes that Isaiah joined Hezekiah in prayer during the siege of Jerusalem. Both 2 Chronicles 26:22 and 32:32 suggest that Isaiah kept the written record of the reigns of Uzziah and Hezekiah. These three verses constitute all that Chronicles relates about Isaiah.

There are several prophets mentioned by name in Chronicles that do not appear in Samuel/Kings.[9] The most notable of this group is Jeremiah.[10] Chronicles mentions that the prophet offered a lament for the fallen king Josiah though the prophet's words are not recorded (2 Chr 35:25). In assessing Zedekiah's reign, Chronicles notes that the king failed "to humble himself before the prophet Jeremiah" (2 Chr 36:12). In offering an explanation for the exile, Chronicles 36:21 conflates the prophecies of exile in Jeremiah (Jer 25:11–12; 29:10) with those in Leviticus (Lev 26:34–35, 43) to assert that the forced migration of the Judeans allowed the land to have its Sabbath rest while the people are in Babylon and their land remains untilled. Finally, Chronicles introduces the decree of Cyrus by noting that the end of the exile will serve to fulfill Jeremiah's prophecy about the length of Judah's exile (2 Chr 36:22). Although Chronicles mentions Jeremiah, it does not contain any of the prophet's words as such. Still, the remembrance of Jeremiah's prophecies frame the story of Judah's exile in Chronicles (2 Chr 36:12, 22).

Chronicles contains some prophetic speeches, though these are likely compositions by Chronicles, revealing its theological agenda. These prophetic speeches have no counterparts in Samuel/Kings. Shemaiah's address to Rehoboam and his officers (2 Chr 12:1–11) asserts that the success of Pharaoh Shishak's raid into Judah is a direct consequence of the abandonment of YHWH by both king and people. When Rehoboam and his officers repent, Shemaiah announces that Judah's defeat will not be total—Judah, though devastated, will survive. In a similar situation during the reign of Asa, the prophet Azariah cites historical precedent and assures Asa that YHWH will not abandon him if the king is faithful to the responsibility of ridding Judah of all forms of idolatry and illegitimate worship. However, if Asa forsakes YHWH, then YHWH will forsake him (2 Chr 15:1–7). Chronicles' point in both prophetic speeches is clear: infidelity brings judgment; repentance brings restoration.

A unique feature of Chronicles' idea of the prophet is the repeated reference to the prophet as a keeper of royal records. At the conclusion of the Chronicles' treatment of an individual king, the reader/hearer is referred to written records maintained by prophets. For example, Chronicles maintains that written records of David's reign were maintained by the prophets Samuel, Nathan, and Gad (1 Chr 29:29). Those of Solomon were kept by Nathan, Ahijah, and Iddo (2 Chr 9:29). The prophets Shemaiah and Iddo kept the records of Rehoboam's reign (2 Chr 12:15). Iddo also kept the records of Abijah's reign (2 Chr 13:22). The prophet Jehu recorded the acts of Jehoshaphat. The Prophet Isaiah was responsible for the records of two kings: Uzziah (2 Chr 26:22) and Hezekiah (2 Chr 32:32). This reflects Chronicles' broader conception of prophetic activity. Its expression involves writing as well as speaking. By way of contrast, Samuel/Kings does not portray the prophets as recorders of royal activities; rather, they convey verbal messages from God to kings.

Gary Knoppers identified another aspect of prophetic activity unique to Chronicles: several individuals whom he characterizes as ad hoc prophets.[11] Among those who engage in prophetic activity on a temporary basis are Zechariah son of Jehoiada (2 Chr 24:20–22), Jehziel the Levite (2 Chr 20:14–15), and Eliezer ben Dodavehu (2 Chr 20:37). Chronicles suggests, then, that individuals who are not prophets may engage in prophetic activity as the need arises. Knoppers included two foreign kings among the ad hoc prophets. The first is Necho, who delivers a message from God to Josiah (2 Chr 35:20–22), and Cyrus who asserts that God directed him to build a temple in Jerusalem (2 Chr 36:22–23). Chronicles expands the notion of prophetic activity by including those who engage in prophetic activity on a temporary basis along with those who are prophets by vocation, implying that the latter group does not have exclusive access to revelation.

Chronicles depicts the prophets as occupying a significant place in the Israelite kingdoms. The task given by God to the prophets is to convey messages to king and people. The thrust of these messages was the need to remain committed to YHWH alone by avoiding idolatry. Chronicles asserts the fall of Judah was caused by the people's failure to treat the prophets and messengers from God with respect and respond appropriately to the message they conveyed (2 Chr 36:15–16).[12]

Conclusion

Samuel/Kings and Chronicles provide ample evidence that prophecy was a powerful force in ancient Israelite society and religion. The two stories of the rise and fall of the Israelite kingdoms both point to the repeated failures of king and people to heed the word of God as communicated to them by prophets as among the causes for the fall of first the Kingdom of Israel and then the Kingdom of Judah. There are some differences between the ways Samuel/Kings and Chronicles describe prophecy and prophets, but there is no fundamental difference in their description of the prophets' message. Prophets call for commitment to YHWH alone, as evidenced by the avoidance of idolatry and by obedience to God's commandments.

The kings of Israel and Judah, who were the frequent object of prophetic criticism, believed themselves compelled to act in terms of military, political, and economic realities as they tried to maintain the existence of their small kingdoms, competing with their neighbors for control of the limited resources of the southern Levant. The kings' task became more complicated with the resurgence of the powerful and expansionist Mesopotamian kingdoms. In the face of these realities, the prophetic message remained remarkably constant: loyalty to Y HWH will bring reward, and disloyalty will bring judgment. Samuel/Kings depicts the prophets as fighting a losing battle. In the end, the prophets were unable to persuade the kings and people of either kingdom of the need to serve Y HWH alone. The most they were able to accomplish was to announce the consequences of infidelity. For the most part, Chronicles follows suit. It, too, is compelled to relate the failure of prophets to maintain the loyalty of the kings and people of Judah to their ancestral Deity.

The reconstituted people of God following the return from exile chose to see prophets and prophecy as part of their past but not part of their future: "On that day the prophets will be ashamed, every one, of their visions when they prophesy...but each of them will say, 'I am no prophet'" (Zech 13:4–5).

Samuel/Kings, though it portrays prophets as God's messengers, kingmakers, and miracle workers, finally is content to present them simply as teachers of Torah (2 Kgs 17:13; 21:10–11). It is the written, authoritative law that points the way to the future. Chronicles comes from a time when prophets and their activity were part of Judah's collective memory. Chronicles honors that memory but finds the foundation of Judah's life with God in the temple and its rituals. Yehud is a temple state. It is politically impotent and economically dependent, but its temple in Jerusalem is the dwelling place of God on earth, where God's people come to offer the service of their worship. In offering Y HWH that service, the people of God find their identity and destiny.

THE FALL OF THE KINGDOM OF ISRAEL

The Omride dynasty marked the highpoint of the Kingdom of Israel's standing among the states of the Levant. Jehu, after leading a religiously inspired revolt against the Omride dynasty, founded a dynasty of his own that postponed the inevitable fall of the Northern Kingdom. The end of the Kingdom of Israel came quickly following the assassination of Zechariah, the last king of the Jehu dynasty. The kings that followed Zechariah had to face the might of the militaristic and expansionist Assyrian Empire. The Kingdom of Israel was not politically or militarily up to the task. Given this fact, coupled with divisive internal religious and economic issues that plagued the kingdom, it is surprising that it managed to last as long as it did. Its collapse was quick and decisive. Once the Kingdom of Israel fell, its territory was absorbed into the Assyrian provincial system and was not recovered until the Hasmonean kings succeeded in extending their realm north in the second century BCE.

Jehu's Revolt and Dynasty

The Kingdom of Israel began its downward spiral because of a serious internal conflict. There was growing dissatisfaction with the Omride kings, especially among the kingdom's Israelite citizens. The wide berth that the Omrides gave to their Canaanite subjects—especially when it came to the worship of Baal—grated on the YHWH worshipers in the kingdom. Toleration morphed into the promotion of the Baal cult during Ahab's reign because of Jezebel's patronage. Another source of discontent was the almost constant warfare during Ahab's reign—something that continued under his son Joram. Omri fought the Moabite kingdom and subdued it. Ahab fought Ben-hadad of Aram, but then the two became allies when the Assyrians began incursions into the Levant. The peasants, who had to fill the ranks of the army and support its campaigns, felt the economic crunch that comes with war. These pent-up religious and economic tensions burst forth in a revolt that took the form of a coup d'état led by Jehu, a general in the Israelite army.

Second Kings treats Jehu's revolt at length (2 Kgs 9:1—10:31). Though Chronicles tends to ignore goings on in the Kingdom of Israel, Jehu's revolt could not be ignored because of its repercussions in the Kingdom of Judah. Chronicles notes that Jehu killed King Ahaziah of Judah, who had the misfortune of being in Samaria visiting the wounded Joram, when Jehu's revolt broke out. Ahaziah simply got caught up in the general bloodletting that was the hallmark of that revolt (2 Chr 22:7–9).

According to 2 Kings, it was the prophet Elisha who set the stage for the revolt by having one of his followers anoint Jehu as king (2 Kgs 9:1–3), providing Jehu with prophetic designation and the consequent legitimation.[13] With Joram recuperating in Jezreel from the wound he received in battle with the Arameans, Jehu left the Israelite camp at Ramoth-Gilead and headed to Jezreel. He met Joram at the field of Naboth and killed him there. Kings notes that Joram's death was the fulfillment of the curse that Elijah put on Ahab because of the murder of Naboth (2 Kgs 9:26; see 1 Kgs 18:22). Ahaziah of Judah immediately left Jezreel, but he too was assassinated, dying at Megiddo (2 Kgs 9:27). Jehu returned to Jezreel and had Jezebel killed. Again, 2 Kings points out that this was in accord with a prophecy uttered by Elijah (2 Kgs 9:36–37; 1 Kgs 21:23). More killings followed as Jehu consolidated his position by having anyone who had any connection with Joram killed. When a delegation came from Judah to visit "the sons of the king" and "the sons of the gəbîrâ" (2 Kgs 10:13), Jehu had them executed.[14] Finally, Jehu had the worshipers of Baal massacred as they gathered in the temple of Baal in Samaria. The revolt was a very bloody affair, the memory of which did not fade even after a hundred years (see Hos 1:4).

Though Jehu suppressed the worship of Baal in Israel, he did not escape criticism from 2 Kings, because he continued to use the temples at Dan and Bethel for Yahwistic worship. Still, 2 Kings 10:30 suggests that the five-king dynasty established by Jehu was the reward for his actions against "the house of Ahab" (2 Kgs 10:30; 15:12). Jehu presided over an Israel weakened by internal dissension and years of war. This led to the loss of territory east of the Jordan River. Jehu's revolt also had consequences in the political realm. With the assassination of Jezebel, who was the daughter of the king of Tyre, Israel's alliance with Tyre came to an end. Similarly, the assassination of Amaziah ended the alliance with Judah. Moreover, Jehu's purge of Israel's political leaders left the country without an experienced bureaucracy. Hazael of Aram took full advantage of Israel's weakness to strip away more Israelite territory, leaving Israel as little more than a dependency of

Aram. Jehu's seventeen-year reign began a five-king dynasty that ruled Israel for 102 years—the longest of any of the dynasties that ruled the Northern Kingdom.

Second Kings relates a curious episode during the reign of Jehoahaz, Jehu's son and successor. Kings takes note of the continuing problem the Kingdom of Israel faced from the Kingdom of Aram and asserts that Jehoahaz asked YHWH for relief. With a depleted military force, Israel was virtually defenseless. Surprisingly, that relief did come in the form of an unidentified "savior" who provided temporary relief from Aramaean oppression (2 Kgs 13:5). Despite this, Israel continued to worship YHWH at Dan and Bethel, which Kings considered a sinful disregarding of the divine will since Jerusalem was the place God chose. Jehoahaz did provide Israel with a measure of stability during his twenty-eight-year reign despite the problems with Aram.

Israel's fortunes improved under Jehoash, the son and successor of Jehoahaz. Jehoash was able to recover much of the lost Transjordanian territories (2 Kgs 13:25). Kings mentions a war with King Amaziah of Judah but fails to explain the cause of that conflict. Chronicles supplies an explanation. Amaziah hired mercenaries from Israel to supplement his own forces but did not use them in his war with Edom. He did not need them so he simply dismissed them without payment. On their way back to Israel, the mercenaries plundered some Judahite towns to compensate themselves. This led Amaziah to declare war on Israel. Jehoash, however, inflicted a serious defeat on Amaziah at Beth-shemesh, a town about eighteen miles west of Jerusalem. Jehoash captured Amaziah and took him to Jerusalem, where he proceeded to take down a portion of the city's wall, take some hostages, and confiscate gold from the temple before returning to Samaria (2 Kgs 14:1–22). After a reign of sixteen years, Jehoash was succeeded by his son Jeroboam II.

Biblical historians and commentators have usually described the forty-one-year reign of Jeroboam II as a time of peace and prosperity. Reconstructing Jeroboam's reign[15] is difficult because of a lack of historical sources. The archaeological record, however, does not support the view that Jeroboam's reign was particularly grand or splendid. While the elite were able to live in luxury (see

Amos 4:1–4), the kingdom's agrarian economy stagnated.[16] The bulk of Israel's population continued to live on a subsistence level.

Kings restricts its comments on Jeroboam to a few verses (2 Kgs 14:23–29), and Chronicles all but ignores him except for a cryptic reference in 1 Chronicles 5:7. Most of what Kings says about Jeroboam II are formulaic statements made of several kings of Israel. There are, however, two surprising features of Kings' treatment of Jeroboam. The first is the note that he was able to extend his kingdom's territory into the Transjordan (v. 25), and the second, that he captured Damascus and Hamath (v. 28). That assumes that Jeroboam would have been able to halt the Assyrian expansion in the region. As problematic as the claims for Jeroboam's military success are, even more difficult is the assertion that YHWH reversed Israel's fortunes through Jeroboam according to the word of the prophet Jonah (vv. 25–26). Still, this was YHWH's final act of compassion toward the Kingdom of Israel.

The Collapse of the Kingdom of Israel

The downfall of the Northern Kingdom came quickly following the death of Jeroboam II. His son Zechariah reigned for just six months before being assassinated by Shallum, bringing an end to the dynasty of Jehu (2 Kgs 15:10). Second Kings 15:12 reckons that Zechariah's assassination by Shallum fulfills YHWH's promise to Jehu that his dynasty would last for four generations (2 Kgs 10:30). Shallum managed to occupy the throne for just one month before being assassinated by Menahem (2 Kgs 15:15). The people of Tiphsah opposed Menahem's usurpation, so he sacked the town and the neighboring region, employing gruesome, terroristic tactics (2 Kgs 15:16). Menachem reigned over the Kingdom of Israel for ten years. During that time, he had to deal with the Assyrian threat led by Tiglath-pileser III, whom the Bible knows as Pul (see 2 Kgs 15:19). First Chronicles 5:2 mentions the name of Tiglath-pilneser (*sic*) in addition to Pul, apparently thinking these were two separate individuals. Tiglath-pileser seized the Assyrian throne during a civil war. After consolidating his position, he turned his attention to the west, with Egypt as the ultimate prize. To guard his lines of communication, he had to subdue the small states in the Levant, so he began his Egyptian campaign. The Assyrian army was a formidable force, and cities like Damascus and Tyre paid tribute to Tiglath-pileser to avoid destruction. Second Kings affirms that the Kingdom of Israel was among those paying a heavy indemnity to the Assyrians (2 Kgs 15:20). To pay this tribute, Menahem had to levy tax on his subjects, but Menahem's submission prevented war with the Assyrians.

Menahem was succeeded by his son Pekahiah. This was the last peaceful succession to the throne of Israel. The last two kings, Pekah and Hoshea, took the throne after assassinating their predecessors. Kings' account of Pekahiah's reign simply strings together the type of expressions that are the usual critiques of the kings of Israel (2 Kgs 15:23–24). It is likely that Pekahiah continued his father's policy of submission to Assyria. After all, that policy prevented Assyrian military action. Pekah, an officer in Israel's army, thought he could do better. He was supported by men from Gilead. They overthrew Pekahiah and had him killed (2 Kgs 15:25–26). Pekah began building an anti-Assyrian coalition. Rezin, the king of Aram, became Pekah's coalition partner. They approached King Ahaz of Judah to join them. When Ahaz refused, Rezin and Pekah invaded Judah and planned to depose Ahaz and replace him with a more pliant ruler. The coalition was short-lived. Tiglath-pileser invaded Israel and captured several cities (2 Kgs 15:29). Pekah was assassinated by Hoshea. The Assyrians also moved against Damascus, the capital of Aram, and had Rezin killed. This ended the anti-Assyrian coalition. The Prophet Isaiah foresaw its demise (Isa 7:7–9).

Hoshea reinstituted the policy of submission to Assyria and managed to rule Israel for nine years. His fatal mistake was to begin secret negotiations with Egypt to conclude an anti-Assyrian pact. Evidently, Hoshea thought Egypt would help maintain Israel as a buffer against Assyria. This was a serious miscalculation. When Hoshea withheld the payment of tribute, the Assyrians under their new king Shalmaneser V captured Samaria, deposed Hoshea, and led the people of the city into exile.[17] Hoshea was imprisoned but his final fate is unknown. In evaluating the last ruler of the Kingdom of Israel, Kings is not as harsh as with other kings of the Northern Kingdom—probably because of the anti-Assyrian stance the king took at the end of his reign (2 Kgs 17:2).

The fall of Samaria and the forced migration of its people marked the end of the Kingdom of Israel. Second Kings, then, offers a theological reflection on the fall of the city and the end of the kingdom, beginning with the words, "This occurred because the people of Israel sinned against YHWH their God" (2 Kgs 17:7–23). Kings does make some specific accusations: idolatry and worship at "high places," ignoring the prophets, failure to observe the terms of the covenant, the worship of Baal, and the use of divination and apotropaic rituals such as child sacrifice (2 Kgs 17:18). These offenses led to Israel's dispossession of, and exile from, the promised land, leaving only Judah in possession of its inheritance. Second Kings notes that the people of Judah were no more faithful to their ancestral religion and would come to share the fate of the Kingdom of Israel (2 Kgs 17:19–20).

Second Kings's story of the Northern Kingdom's fall has a ring of inevitability about it. Toward the end of the reign of Jeroboam I, the prophet Ahijah utters this oracle about the future of the Kingdom of Israel: "The LORD will strike Israel, as a reed is shaken in the water; he will root up Israel out of this good land...because of the sins of Jeroboam, which he sinned and which he caused Israel to commit" (1 Kgs 14:15, 16). The phrase "the sin(s) of Jeroboam" appears twelve more times as Kings asserts that Jeroboam's successors all maintained the temples of Dan and Bethel with their golden calves, leading to the eventual fall of the Kingdom of Israel because of its illegitimate cult. In addition, 2 Kings accuses the people of the Northern Kingdom of a variety of idolatrous practices (2 Kgs 17:10–12, 16–17).

Following the fall of Samaria, Kings notes that in accord with prophetic warnings, the people of Israel were taken from their homeland and sent off to Mesopotamia to live in exile (2 Kgs 17:23). The Assyrians sought to pacify conquered peoples by exchanging populations of the nations under their hegemony. They brought in people from several areas in Mesopotamia to replace the exiles of Israel. This new population did not worship YHWH or observe the law of the God of the territory of the former Kingdom of Israel, which, according to Kings, led to predation by lions because God's protection of Samaria's population was no longer operative. This forced the Assyrians to bring in an Israelite priest who taught them "how they should worship YHWH" (2 Kgs 17:28). The new inhabitants of the land did come to worship YHWH, but they also continued to worship the gods of their respective homelands and failed to live according to the Torah (2 Kgs 17:29–41). These editorial observations reflected the views of the returnees from the Judean exile in Babylon in the latter part of the sixth century BCE. They regarded the people who lived in the territory of the former Kingdom of Israel as descendants of Mesopotamian peoples brought in to repopulate the north after the forced migration of the Israelites to the east. Furthermore, they practiced a syncretistic religion— not authentic Yahwism. Chronicles had no such views, regarding the people who lived in the territory of the former Northern Kingdom as genuine Israelites.

Though Chronicles ignored the kings of Israel, it was certainly sympathetic to the people of the former Northern Kingdom. Not all the northerners followed Jeroboam's lead. Chronicles notes that some priests, Levites, and lay folk from the north sided with Rehoboam and worshiped in Jerusalem (2 Chr 11:16). It also asserts that the northerners regarded the people of Judah as their brothers and sisters (2 Chr 28:8, 11). Even some of Judah's "good kings" had positive connections with the Kingdom of Israel (2 Chr 15:8; 19:4; 30:10–11; 34:6, 21). Asa and Hezekiah made covenants with the people of the north (2 Chr 15:9–15; 31). When Josiah began the restoration of the temple of Jerusalem, people from the north supported his project financially (2 Chr 34:9). Chronicles devotes not a single verse to the fall of the Kingdom of Israel. The focus of Chronicles is on the continuity of restoration-period Judah with the worship of YHWH in the temple of Jerusalem. By the time Chronicles is written, more than three hundred years have passed since the fall of the Kingdom of Israel. For Chronicles, there was no point in rehearsing the tragic story of the Kingdom of Israel.

It is surprising that the Kingdom of Israel managed to survive as long as it did. In its approximately 210 years of existence, it was ruled by nineteen kings who came from five different dynasties. Ten kings inherited the throne, and seven took the throne after bloody coups. Stability was not much in evidence in the Northern Kingdom. Only two kings, Jeroboam I and Omri, enjoyed popular acclamation. Kings attempts to give some account of the Kingdom of Israel; Chronicles ignores it for the most part. The story of the Kingdom of Israel is a sad one. It ends with its territory absorbed by Assyria and many of its people forced to relocate at various places in Mesopotamia with a foreign population introduced into the Israelite homeland. The Hasmoneans were eventually successful in reclaiming most of the territory of the defunct Kingdom of Israel in the first century BCE. Unfortunately, there developed strong animosity between the people of Judah and the people who lived in the north, though they both claimed descent from Jacob, and both worshiped the same God and treasured the sacred text of the Torah. Old rivalries die hard.

THE FALL OF THE KINGDOM OF JUDAH

The Israelite kingdoms were able to chart their own destiny in the southern Levant because of the absence of any imperial power in the region from the thirteenth to the eighth century BCE. This changed when Tiglath-pileser III seized the throne of Assyria and assassinated the entire family of his predecessor, Ashur-nirari V. Tiglath-pileser III reorganized Assyria's military, political, and economic systems. Once the changes took effect, Assyria was in a position to make its presence felt in the ancient Near East. The real goal of Assyria's expansionism was Egypt because of its abundant natural and agricultural resources. Between Assyria and Egypt stood the small states of the southern Levant, including the two Israelite kingdoms. It was necessary to neutralize these states in order to protect the lines of communication between Assyria and its armies in the field. Tiglath-pileser began his incursions into the Levant in 740. Assyrian inscriptions claim that he received tribute from Menahem of Israel and Uzziah of Judah—details that the Bible does not mention. These incursions continued to occur in succeeding years, and their goal went beyond collecting tribute, to the incorporation of the territory of the Israelite kingdoms into the Assyrian provincial systems. Both Israelite kingdoms felt the pressure brought to bear on them by Tiglath-pileser III and his successors.

Eventually Assyria fell victim because of a succession of incompetent kings. The Babylonians took the opportunity to replace Assyria as the dominant power in the ancient Near East. By the time Babylon made its presence felt in the Levant, the Kingdom of Israel was no longer in existence. This section will examine the fall of Judah as reflected in 2 Kings and 2 Chronicles. It is a story of incompetent leadership, an unstable political system, and religious conflict at a time when Judah could not afford these problems. The Kingdom of Judah fell to the might of the Babylonians under their king Nebuchadnezzer, and the Davidic dynasty, which was to be eternal, came to an inglorious end—never to rise again.

Jotham

Jotham inherited a secure and prosperous Judah. He wisely followed the path blazed by his father, Uzziah. Chronicles describes his construction projects in Jerusalem and in rural areas, that is, the "hill country of Judah" (2 Chr 27:1–9). It tells of his subjugation of Ammon and lists the tribute the Ammonites presented to him. More importantly, Jotham, like his father, "did what was right in the sight of the LORD," but Chronicles adds that Jotham "did not invade the temple of the LORD," recognizing the limits of his prerogatives and those of the priests. Chronicles asserts that Jotham had a successful reign "because he ordered his ways before the LORD his God." Chronicles does introduce one ominous note in its story of Jotham's reign when it asserts that the people of Judah "still followed corrupt practices." Chronicles does not specify the specific ways that this corruption manifested itself. Still, it does alert the hearers and readers of Judah's story that things were not what they should be, despite how well Jotham fared as king.

The story of Jotham in Kings is largely formulaic, as was Kings' treatment of his father's reign (2 Kgs 15:32–38). Kings notes Jotham's age at his accession, the length of his reign, and his mother's name. It includes Jotham among Judah's "good kings," though he did tolerate worship at high places. He built the "Upper Gate" of the temple's inner court (also 2 Chr 27:3).[18]

The one ominous remark in Kings' story of Jotham concerns the intrusion of Aram and Israel in Judah's affairs (2 Kgs 15:37). Rezin king of Aram and Pekah king of Israel were trying to induce Jotham to join in an anti-Assyrian coalition. Assyria under Tiglath-pileser III became a militaristic, expansionist state intent on reviving the Assyrian Empire. The Assyrian army entered the Levant as early as 740 BCE, exacting tribute from both Aram and Israel. Rezin and Pekah recognized the seriousness of the threat posed by Assyria. The small national states of the Levant were able to establish themselves because of the absence of an imperial power with political and military power. The Assyrians were a threat to establish hegemony over the entire region. At first, the Assyrians were content with extracting tribute. Before matters deteriorated any further, Rezin and Pekah decided to withhold tribute and oppose Assyrian presence in the region. Jotham died after sixteen years on the throne, and before accepting the invitation of Rezin and Pekah to join them in their anti-Assyrian coalition. Without further explanation, Kings asserts that during Jotham's reign "YHWH began to send Rezin...and Pekah...against Judah" (2 Kgs 15:37). This brief comment marks the beginning of the end for Judah.

Ahaz

The twenty-year-old Ahaz came to the throne faced with having to decide either on joining the anti-Assyrian coalition or becoming an Assyrian vassal.[19] Rezin and Pekah did not wait for Ahaz's answer. They began a siege of Jerusalem. Ahaz believed he had no other choice but to seek Assyria's help against the coalition.[20] Ahaz cemented his relationship with Tiglath-pileser by paying a substantial tribute to him. The Assyrian king attacked Damascus, deporting many of its citizens and executing Rezin. This, of course, ended the threat from the coalition but began Judah's subjugation to the Assyrian Empire.

Ahaz considered his submission to Assyria as a recognition of a political reality, but Kings presents it as the action of an apostate. Kings considered Ahaz no better than the kings of Israel because he practiced child sacrifice like the nations[21] and he participated in worship at the high places (2 Kgs 16:2b–3). Kings offers additional evidence of Ahaz's apostasy by describing his voluntary introduction of an altar from Damascus into the Jerusalem temple following his visit with Tiglath-pileser (2 Kgs 16:10). Usually, Kings does not devote much attention to "bad kings," but it takes pains to describe the extent of Ahaz's apostasy, since Ahaz represents a most decisive step that will eventually lead to the end of Judah and the Davidic dynasty.

Chronicles itemizes Ahaz's misdeeds as Kings does, though its description of the consequences differs from that in Kings. For example, Kings notes that the anti-Assyrian coalition laid siege to Jerusalem but was unable to take the city. Chronicles, however, describes the fall of Jerusalem to Rezin and Pekah, the great loss of life that ensued—including that of the king's son and two of his principal advisors, the forced migration of thousands of Judeans, and the vast amount of plunder taken to Samaria. Chronicles reports that the prophet Oded from Samaria denounced the ferocity of the attack on Judah and the taking of hostages and plunder (2 Chr 28:8–15). Oded called upon Israel's army to release the hostages. The hostages were released, given clothes, sandals, food, and drink. They were even anointed with oil. With the weak carried on donkeys, the hostages were led to Jericho, where they were reunited with their families.[22] This is another instance of Chronicles' positive view of the people of Samaria. They are genuine Israelites who listen to the prophet sent to them, while 2 Kings 17:13–14 accuses the people of Samaria of not listening to the prophets.

Chronicles' treatment of Ahaz ends by noting that Ahaz's request for help from Assyria meant that Judah no longer was capable of independent action. Ahaz thought that he would receive help from Assyria but found himself to be just another subject of the Assyrian king. Ahaz opened the door for Assyria to exploit Judah. This experience did not induce Ahaz to repent, but to increase his acts of apostasy. He worshiped the gods of Damascus, destroyed the implements used in the temple, set up altars throughout Jerusalem, and established high places elsewhere in Judah.

Both Kings and Chronicles assert that Ahaz was buried in Jerusalem, with Chronicles adding the note that he was not, however, buried among the other kings of Israel. The amount of space devoted to describing Ahaz's acts of apostasy in both Kings and Chronicles underscores the role that Ahaz played in both stories. Ahaz's reign was a watershed in the story of Judah. Readers and hearers of these stories of Judah's kings recognize that Ahaz's misdeeds were unprecedented. YHWH drove out the nations from Canaan, and Ahaz decides to follow the religious practices of these nations, which makes his deeds unforgivable. The Kingdom of Judah and the Davidic dynasty are marked for destruction that will be fully unleashed in 587 BCE with the Babylonian sack of Jerusalem and destruction of the temple. Kings and Chronicles do not explicitly condemn the actions that proceed from the king's apostasy. Readers and hearers are left to draw the inescapable conclusion that the king's actions will end in a disaster that must come. This is especially clear in Kings. The story of Ahaz immediately precedes that of the fall of the Kingdom of Israel (2 Kgs 17), which stands as a harbinger of what lies ahead for Judah (2 Kgs 17:19–20). In Chronicles the story of Ahaz immediately precedes that of his son and successor Hezekiah, who initiated a reform—a short-lived one that was not extensive enough to halt Judah's march toward its destruction.

Hezekiah

The twenty-five-year-old Hezekiah, Ahaz's son and successor, had serious differences with his father regarding both religion and politics, as is clear from his efforts to reverse his father's policies in both areas. The new king ended worship at the high places, demolishing the accoutrements associated with that worship. He also destroyed a bronze serpent that was associated with Moses because it became a custom to offer incense to it.[23] Following this brief summation of Hezekiah's actions to end idolatry in Judah, Kings acclaims Hezekiah as a king without peer (2 Kgs 18:3–5).

The account of Hezekiah's actions in the religious sphere is much more detailed in Chronicles (2 Chr 29:20–36). Hezekiah initiated repairs on the temple during the first month of his reign. He called upon the Levites to take up the project of cleaning up the temple, ending years of neglect. Several Levitical families took up the challenge. The Jerusalem priests joined in the project, handing to the Levites all the refuse taken from the temple. The Levites deposited this refuse in the Kidron Valley east of the temple. The cleaning project was completed in sixteen days and was followed by sacrificial offerings that marked the temple's purification. The priests slaughtered the sacrificial animals, and the Levites provided music for the ritual according to the pattern set by David. The assembly of worshipers sang to the accompaniment of the instruments. After the sacrifices were offered, Hezekiah had the Levites

sing some of the psalms of David and Asaph. The animals brought
for sacrifice were so numerous that the Levites assisted the priests
in completing their duties. The service of YHWH was thus reestablished in the temple.

Hezekiah then decided to extend an invitation to the people
of Ephraim and Manasseh, the two most populous of the northern
tribes, to come to Jerusalem and join the people of Judah for the
celebration of the Passover. This was a bold and inspired attempt
to repair the centuries-old breach between Judah and the other
Israelite tribes. The Passover could not be celebrated at the prescribed time (the 14th of the first month of the year) because not
enough priests were available. The celebration was put off for one
month. Hezekiah sent messengers "from Dan to Beer-sheba" to
call people to Jerusalem for a Passover that was to be celebrated
in the prescribed manner after years of popular neglect of this
feast. The invitation to the northerners to join the people of Judah
in the celebration of the Passover expresses a major difference
between Kings and Chronicles regarding the people who lived in
the territory of the former Kingdom of Israel. Kings considered
these people to be the result of intermarriage with a foreign population introduced into the region by the Assyrians, in accord with
the Assyrian practice of pacification through exchange of populations (2 Kgs 17:24). For Chronicles, the people of the north are
authentic Israelites. Hezekiah goes as far as to alter the regulations
for Passover to make it possible for everyone to participate (2 Chr
30:2–3, 16–19). The participants in Hezekiah's Passover became
enthusiastic Yahwists because of their experience. They returned
to their homes in the north and destroyed idolatrous shrines and
the symbols of other gods (2 Chr 31:1). This episode shows the
power of worship to strengthen people's loyalty to YHWH.

Chronicles credits Hezekiah with reform of the temple personnel (2 Chr 31:2–4). The king reestablished the proper divisions
of priests and Levites and made provisions for their support. He
established a schedule for the priests and Levites to fulfill their
duties in the temple. The king supported the temple out of his personal wealth and ensured that the liturgical calendar was observed
as required by the "law of the LORD." The people responded to
Hezekiah's reform by bringing their tithes to the temple again,

which led to the construction of storerooms in the temple where the people's offerings could be kept.

Chronicles is effusive in its praise of Hezekiah for his initiatives in the religious sphere. After years of neglect while his father was king, Hezekiah had the temple cleansed and returned to its pristine shape. He ended worship at the high places and renewed the observance of the Passover, which celebrated the first of God's liberating deeds on behalf of Israel. Hezekiah did all this for no other motive than out of his commitment to God (2 Chr 31:21–22). Hezekiah's achievements in the political and military realm were much more modest than in the religious. This area is the major concern of Kings, which dedicates three chapters to Hezekiah's politics (2 Kgs 18:7—20:20), compared to Chronicles' single chapter (2 Chr 32:1–33). Hezekiah became king during the final years of the Assyrian king Sargon II. Sargon managed to piece together a large empire; keeping it together was another thing. He was kept busy putting down rebellions against his rule. The Levant was the setting for several revolts. Sargon claimed credit for ending the revolt led by Hoshea, king of Israel. Sargon's victory led to the end of the Kingdom of Israel and the incorporation of its territory into the Assyrian provincial system. Sargon died in battle while attempting to end the rebellion of the province of Tabal in central Anatolia. He was succeeded by his son Sennacherib. But transitions to new royal leadership hardly ever went smoothly in the ancient Near East. Periods of transition were often used as opportunities for subject people to proclaim their independence. From Babylon to Egypt, there were uprisings against Assyrian rule.

No doubt Hezekiah was preparing to claim Judah's independence during Sargon's final years. Preparations for a long siege included the digging of the Siloam tunnel to convey water from the Gihon Spring to a pool inside the city walls (2 Kgs 20:20; 2 Chr 32:30), and construction of barns to house livestock and store food (2 Chr 32:28–29). He also began work on the "Broad Wall" in the western part of a city.[24] It was a very wide casemate wall to protect the growing population of Jerusalem. He also reorganized Judah's army and refitted fortresses that protected the approaches to his capital (2 Chr 32:5–6).

The death of Sargon led to a period of unrest in the Assyrian Empire. Marduk-apla-iddina II of Babylon, whom 2 Kings 20:12

names Berodach-baladan and Isaiah 39:1 calls Merodach-baladan, took the opportunity of Sennacherib's accession to lead a revolt against Assyrian rule. He managed to detach southern Mesopotamia from Assyria's control for a few years before Sennacherib regained control of southern Mesopotamia, eventually destroying the city of Babylon in 689. Marduk-apla-iddina's initial success likely encouraged the Levantine states to withdraw their allegiance and tribute from Sennacherib. Hezekiah took the additional step of aligning himself with Egypt (2 Kgs 18:20–21) and Ethiopia (2 Kgs 19:9). Hezekiah attacked the Philistines, probably because they did not join the revolt against Assyria (2 Kgs 18:8). It appears that Marduk-apla-iddina tried to establish friendly relations with Judah, hoping to include Judah in the anti-Assyrian coalition—something that Isaiah opposed (2 Kgs 20:12–19).

With Sennacherib, Assyria reached the height of its political and military power—something Hezekiah failed to recognize: "[Hezekiah] rebelled against the king of Assyria and would not serve him" (2 Kgs 18:7b). This was a most serious misstep. Sennacherib could not ignore Hezekiah's actions, and so he took steps to make Hezekiah regret his failure to remain loyal. The result of Sennacherib's campaign in the Levant was disastrous for Judah. The Assyrian king attacked the wall cities of Judah (2 Kgs 18:13; 2 Chr 32:1), claiming to destroy forty-six of them and taking more than two hundred thousand captives (*ANET*, 287–88).

The last of Judah's cities to have been captured was Lachish.[25] From there Sennacherib sent a delegation to Jerusalem, demanding the city's surrender. The Assyrian king boasted that he had Hezekiah trapped in Jerusalem "like a caged bird." Sennacherib demanded and received a substantial tribute from Hezekiah (2 Kgs 18:14–16), though he failed to take Jerusalem itself. That Hezekiah paid tribute without Jerusalem being captured suggests the possibility that the text of Kings and the Assyrian chronicles that describe the resolution of the Judean revolt actually describe two separate invasions, with 2 Kings 18:17—19:36 providing details of a second campaign in Judah.[26] Resolving this question is the concern of historians. The theological significance of the story of Sennacherib and Hezekiah lies in the biblical account of Jerusalem's survival in the face of the otherwise catastrophic Assyrian incursion into Judah.

Second Kings provides a detailed description of Jerusalem's deliverance. The Prophet Isaiah plays a prominent role in that story. The Prophet instructs Hezekiah's messengers to tell the king not to be afraid of the Assyrian threat. Isaiah asserts that the king will withdraw, return to Assyria, and be assassinated there (2 Kgs 19:7). When Hezekiah does not surrender after Sennacherib's messengers informed him of the hopelessness of Jerusalem's situation, the Assyrian king sends another delegation to Hezekiah, reminding him of the fate of other kings who were in rebellion (2 Kgs 19:9–13). In his desperation, Hezekiah goes to the temple and prays for Jerusalem's deliverance. The Prophet then, speaking in God's name, reassures the king, "[Sennacherib] shall not come into this city....I will defend this city to save it, for my own sake and for the sake of my servant David" (2 Kgs 19:32–34). Kings concludes its story of Jerusalem's deliverance by telling of the decimation of the Assyrian army by "the angel of the LORD," the return of Sennacherib and the remnants of his army to Nineveh, and Sennacherib's assassination by two of his sons (2 Kgs 19:35–37). Two of Sennacherib's sons did, in fact, assassinate him, probably because Sennacherib passed over them in favor of Esarhaddon, a younger son. The assassination touched off a war over the succession between Ersarhaddon and his older brother Arda-Mulissu. Ersarhaddon prevailed. Jerusalem's deliverance raised a problem for later prophets such as Jeremiah because it engendered a belief in the city's invulnerability. People came to believe that the city would never fall to a conqueror since it was the city of God. The fall of Jerusalem to the Babylonians in 587 BCE put an end to such thinking.

The story of Hezekiah in Kings continues on a more personal note. Hezekiah fell seriously ill. The king went to the temple to pray for healing and was again assured by Isaiah that his prayer was granted. During Hezekiah's illness, a delegation from Babylon arrived, bringing good wishes for the king's recovery from the king of Babylon. Hezekiah gave the delegates a tour of his treasury. This gave Isaiah the occasion to prophesy that one day all Judah's treasure would be carried off to Babylon and that some of his descendants would become servants of the king of Babylon (2 Kgs 20:17–18). Hezekiah accepted the Prophet's word and was grateful that the rest of his reign would be peaceful.

Chronicles reprises the story of Hezekiah as found in Kings, though Chronicles expands the description of the king's liturgical reform. Kings devotes three verses to Hezekiah's reforms (2 Kgs 18:3–5), while Chronicles needs seventy-four verses to give its account (2 Chr 29:1—33:3.) Underscoring this aspect of Hezekiah's reign is of great significance because it serves to show that fidelity to the proper worship of YHWH in the proper place (the temple of Jerusalem), at the proper times, and led by the proper personnel is the way that the people of Yehud could secure their future. Kings shows more concern about eliminating the "high places" and ending the illegitimate worship taking place there. At the same time, however, the temple, its personnel, and its liturgy are not central to Kings, as is evident from the scant attention Kings gives to Hezekiah's cultic reforms. For Kings the temple is a place of prayer. Those offering prayers need not even be in the temple area. All one needs to do is pray in the direction of the temple (1 Kgs 8:41–42). For Kings, authentic worship of YHWH can take place in the land of exile. This is not so for Chronicles. The Diaspora is not the proper setting for the worship of YHWH. People living in exile—in the Diaspora—should return to Jerusalem and offer proper worship in the temple. Jerusalem is, then, the center of Jewish life (2 Chr 36:23).

Both Kings and Chronicles recognize the shift in Judah's fortunes that came with the rise of the neo-Assyrian Empire. From the perspective of political reality, the survival of Judah and the Davidic dynasty is no longer in the hands of the king and people of Judah. Judah's survival depends upon its ability to accommodate itself to Assyrian hegemony. Hezekiah tried to free Judah from Assyrian control and failed. That Judah survived his political and military miscalculation was a "miracle." Judah must now learn to live in the shadow of the militaristic and expansionist Mesopotamian empires. What complicated Judah's situation was the growing belief in Jerusalem's inviolability after Sennacherib's siege of the city was lifted. This belief prevented people from taking a prudent approach to the political and military might of the Mesopotamian empires. People who held on to this belief pressured the king to withhold tribute thus easing Judah's economic burden.

Manasseh

Hezekiah was succeeded by his son Manasseh, who had the longest reign (fifty-five years) of any Israelite or Judahite king. He was able to reign for so long because of his policy of submission to Assyrian hegemony, ignoring calls to assert Judah's independence. Manasseh realized that the wind blew from the east and he acted accordingly, even though it meant reversing his father's policies. Manasseh had little real choice, if he wished to remain on the throne and keep Judah at peace. At Manasseh's accession to the throne of David, Assyria was at the height of its political and military power. Any attempt to escape from the empire's orbit would have been suicidal. Manasseh submitted to reality. Assyrian documents always speak of him as a loyal vassal, even though Chronicles lists the actions taken by Manasseh to ensure Judah's military preparedness (2 Chr 33:14).[27]

Both Kings and Chronicles depict Manasseh as an apostate and provide a catalog of the king's evil deeds: the rebuilding of the high places dismantled by his father, the construction of altars to Baal and to other pagan deities, even in the temple, the erection of an asherah, his use of divination—including necromancy, the sacrificial offering of his own son,[28] and murder (2 Kgs 21:2–6, 16; 2 Chr 33:2–6). According to Kings, Manasseh's actions had a profoundly negative effect on Judah's commitment to Yʜwʜ and led to its ruin. Kings asserts that it was Manasseh who was responsible for Jerusalem's eventual fall (2 Kgs 21:11–15). Chronicles, however, does not follow Kings' lead on this score.

Chronicles depicts Manasseh as a contrite sinner. Without providing any explanation, Chronicles has the Assyrians arrest Manasseh, bind him in chains, and haul him off to Babylon.[29] While under arrest, he asks God to effect his freedom and reinstate him as king in Jerusalem. Chronicles asserts that God heard Manasseh's prayer and returned him to his throne, leading Manasseh to acknowledge that Yʜwʜ is God (2 Chr 33:12–13).[30] Of course, there have been debates about the historical value of this story of Manasseh's repentance, but as a story it presents Manasseh as a model for the Jewish people. The Books of Samuel and Kings present Saul, David, and Solomon as foreshadowing the fall of the two Israelite kingdoms. What began with such promise ends in disappointment. Chronicles portrays Manasseh, a most unlikely character, as calling the Jewish people to repentance leading to restoration. The story of Manasseh in Chronicles is an example of turning the past into a sermon. Chronicles' portrayal of Manasseh highlights a significant theological motif: repentance—a motif absent in Samuel/Kings' account of Manasseh's reign. For Chronicles, there is always the possibility of turning away from sin and turning toward God, if one so chooses. Chronicles blames the fall of Jerusalem not only on Manasseh, but also on Zedekiah, the priests, and people who failed to repent.[31]

After Manasseh returned to Jerusalem, according to Chronicles, he initiated a program of reform that appears to be focused on the temple, from which he purged all foreign idols (2 Chr 33:15). Worship on the high places continued to take place, though YHWH was the God worshiped there. The focus on the temple is what one can expect from Chronicles. Kings, however, does not tell of Manasseh's rehabilitation. Manasseh is a foil to his father Hezekiah and his grandson Josiah, both of whom Kings depicts as religious reformers. In both cases, however, their reforms did not outlive them, and Judah continued on its path toward total collapse. Manasseh is a convenient strawman for Kings. His behavior explains the catastrophe of Jerusalem's fall to Babylon. For Kings, Manasseh helps explain Judah's disastrous past, while for Chronicles Manasseh offers a model that can show the way to Judah's future. A "quest for the historical Manasseh" is not a concern for this book. The divergence between the way Kings and Chronicles depict this king is the result of the divergent goals of these works.

Amon

Amon was just twenty-two years old when he succeeded his father Manasseh as king of Judah. It is likely that he had older brothers who were passed over. This would have caused some friction in the court. Amon's older brothers and their supporters would have resented the placing of the young Amon on the throne by passing over his older and more experienced brothers. Of course, it is speculation to explain the opposition of unnamed royal officials to Amon (2 Kgs 21:23; 2 Chr 33:24). Kings and Chronicles devote little attention to Amon's brief two-year reign, offering little beyond the formulas that are used to describe Judah's "bad kings" (2 Kgs 21:19–22; 2 Chr 33:21–22) though Chronicles adds that Amon "did not humble himself before Y<small>HWH</small>, as his father Manasseh had humbled himself" (2 Chr 33:23). Amon is condemned because of his idolatry.

Amon's brief reign ends with his assassination by members of the Jerusalem bureaucracy. Neither Kings nor Chronicles offers even a hint of the assassins' motivation. It could have been political and economic. The royal officials may have opposed Amon's pro-Assyrian policies, which were an economic drain on Judah. It is also possible that religious zealots killed Amon because they had enough of the idolatry that was the royal policy for more than a half century. A third possibility is that it was the result of pent-up jealousy and resentment over Amon's succession to the throne. Amon's assassination is an indicator of the growing instability of the Judean state and monarchy.

Although the Jerusalem establishment was dissatisfied with Amon, Judah's more conservative rural gentry reacted against this threat to the dynasty.[32] They had the conspirators killed, and they then placed Josiah, Amon's eight-year-old son, on the throne, assuring the continuation of the Davidic line (2 Kgs 21:23–24; 2 Chr 33:24–25). Neither Kings nor Chronicles has any additional comments on Amon except to note his idolatry, but the attentive reader/hearer of these two stories cannot help but conclude that the Kingdom of Judah will share the fate of the Kingdom of Israel. Both have been unfaithful to their ancestral Deity. The Northern Kingdom no longer exists—its territory swallowed up by several Assyrian provinces, and its people living far from their ancestral homes. It is more than likely that the Kingdom of Judah will share that fate.

Josiah

After more than a half century in which the kings of Judah promoted and participated in idolatrous worship, there was a dramatic shift during the reign of Amon's son and successor Josiah, whom the conservative rural landowners of Judah placed on the throne. Josiah was a child of just eight years old when he became king. His thirty-one years on the throne witnessed a revival of Judah's commitment to Y<small>HWH</small>, its patron Deity. Both Kings and Chronicles credit Josiah with leading this revival, which also had important political consequences. It is important to remember that the line between religion and politics in the ancient Near East was not as sharply drawn as it is in modern secular states.

The story of Josiah's reign is framed by two tragic events: the assassination of his father Amon and Josiah's own untimely death in battle. The accounts in Kings and Chronicles of what occurred between these two events differ to some extent. Chronicles asserts that when Josiah was just sixteen years old, he began "to seek the God of his ancestor David" (2 Chr 34:3). After four years, the king's personal reformation led him to take action against the popular non-Yahwistic worship that flourished under his father and grandfather.[33] Josiah dismantled the high places, the asherahs, and the images used in idolatrous worship. He defiled the altars scattered around Judah by scattering the ashes of the priests who had once served at these altars. He did not confine these actions against non-Yahwistic cults in Judah but extended these activities into the territory of the former Kingdom of Israel—as far north as Galilee (2 Chr 34:6–7). Chronicles has Josiah's reform extend far into the north because Chronicles believed that the people of these territories were genuine Israelites who should be led back to the authentic worship of their ancestral Deity. Kings, too, has Josiah taking action against temples built by the kings of Israel at Bethel and other high places in Samaria (2 Kgs 23:15–20), though Kings has this take place eight years later.

This move into territory directly ruled by Assyria as part of its provincial system was possible because of unrest in Mesopotamia. There was conflict over the succession between two of Asshur-banipal's sons. While Assyria was dealing with internal matters, Babylon under Nabopolassar managed to free itself from Assyrian domination. At the same time, Josiah was able to make his presence felt in the territory of the former Kingdom of Israel. While there were political ramifications to Josiah's move, both Kings and Chronicles depict those moves as religious reform.

The Book of Kings makes it clear that Josiah's actions, both in Jerusalem and in the north, were the consequence of the finding of a "book of the law" in the course of repair work on the temple that Josiah mandated (2 Kgs 22:3–8; 2 Chr 34:14). One of the king's advisors read the book to the king, who was deeply moved by its contents because he feared the consequences of the failure of the kings and people to live in accord with its ideals and laws.

A question that has occupied readers of Kings centers on the identity of the lawbook found during the temple repairs. In 1805, Wilhelm M. L. de Wette, considered the first practitioner of critical biblical scholarship, suggested that the lawbook could have been the Book of Deuteronomy.[34] At one time, scholars tended to characterize the story of the book's discovery as narrated in Kings and Chronicles to be a "pious fraud."[35] Today, more than two hundred years after de Wette's *Dissertatio critica*, the scholarly consensus holds that what was found in the temple was some form of Deuteronomy.[36] Although the language of 2 Kings 23:3 is Deuteronomic, the principal concern of 2 Kings 22 is the authenticity of "this book that has been found" (2 Kgs 22:13)—not its identity.

Whether or not a book was actually found during repairs on the temple and whether the lawbook was Deuteronomy or some portion of it, it is clear that the story in Kings wants the reader/hearer to conclude that the book found in the temple was Deuteronomy. The ideals of that book are infused in the story of the two kingdoms—especially the demand that Israel worship Yhwh alone. Kings describes the failure and collapse of ancient Israel's political and religious institutions, including the monarchy, the national state, the temple and its priesthood, and prophecy.[37] All that is left to Judah is the written, authoritative law. Its discovery offers Judah a path toward restoration. Telling of the "lost" book's discovery serves to make plausible the book's association with Moses. This serves to provide the lawbook with authenticity and legitimacy.

As Kings tells the story of the book's discovery, Josiah wanted to be certain of the book's authenticity despite his initial response to hearing Hilkiah's reading of the book to him. The king "tore his garments" as a sign of sorrow and repentance. The king's advisors sought out a prophet for this task. The prophet whom they consulted was a woman named Huldah. Both Jeremiah (Jer 1:2) and Zephaniah (Zeph 1:1) were active during Josiah's reign, but Josiah's advisors sought the counsel of Huldah—perhaps because she was the wife of another royal official (2 Kgs 22:14), or she may have been a court prophet regularly consulted by the king and his advisors. In any case, there is no hint in the text that consulting a female prophet was anything extraordinary. Female prophets were known in the ancient Near East, though Huldah is the only female prophet mentioned in Kings.[38] As a prophet, Huldah is a person of authority. Her word serves to authenticate the lawbook.

Huldah responds to the query of Josiah's royal official with two oracles (2 Kgs 22:15–20). The first is a judgment oracle on Judah that asserts that Judah will feel the effect of the curses in the lawbook because of the people's idolatry. Speaking in God's name, Huldah exclaims that God's anger against Judah cannot be extinguished. The second oracle assures Josiah that he will be spared seeing Jerusalem's destruction, and that he will die in peace. Chronicles simply reproduces both oracles (2 Chr 34:23–28). In a departure from the usual presentation of prophets in Joshua–2 Kings, the prophetic word is not fulfilled completely. Josiah died in a battle at Megiddo. Though this death was tragic, it prevented him from witnessing the destruction of Jerusalem and the forced migration of its people to Babylon.

Both Kings and Chronicles follow up the story of the lawbook's discovery in the temple with their respective accounts of the reading of the lawbook to the people and the people's commitment to live in accordance with the laws found in the book (2 Kgs 22:1–3; 2 Chr 34:29–33). The story in Kings uses language typical of Deuteronomy, while Chronicles makes it clear that *all* Israel participated in the covenant renewal, promising to serve YHWH. Chronicles also adds the note that this commitment was kept during Josiah's lifetime. Kings describes the actions Josiah took in assuring that Israel would serve YHWH alone. Chronicles, however, presents the reform as already in progress when the lawbook was found. Josiah had already rid the temple of all the accoutrements associated with the worship of Baal and the host of heaven. He had the asherah destroyed and rid the temple area of the women devotees who served Asherah. He dismantled the high places. He also demolished the altars and shrines erected by his predecessors to serve the cults of the gods of Judah's neighbors. He dismantled the high places and brought their priests to Jerusalem. The closing of the rural shrines (high places) deprived the priests of these shrines of their income. Deuteronomy makes some provision for their support (Deut 18:6–8) and commends them to the charity of their fellow Israelites (Deut 14:27, 29). All this was accomplished before the finding of the lawbook, according to Chronicles.

Josiah's religious reform was actually two-pronged. He rid Jerusalem of foreign, idolatrous cults, and he centralized the worship of YHWH in Jerusalem. Both these actions had clear political overtones. The introduction of altars to the gods of foreign nations into the temple was likely the result of alliances made over the years by Josiah's predecessors to ensure good relations with Judah's neighbors. Ending worship at the high places and bringing their priests to Jerusalem served to heighten that city's status and to strengthen the people's loyalty to the dynasty. Josiah's "reform" needs to be seen against the backdrop of political events taking place in Assyria, whose control of the Levant was being compromised by the civil war in Assyria. This allowed Josiah to stake his claim to territories that were part of the former Kingdom of Israel by extending his reform to Bethel and other cities of Samaria (2 Kgs 23:15, 19; 2 Chr 34:6).

Kings and Chronicles present the celebration of the Passover by Josiah as the climax of his reforms, asserting that no such Passover was celebrated since the time of Samuel (2 Kgs 23:21–23; 2 Chr 35:1–29). Both stories fail to mention the Passover celebration that was an important component of Hezekiah's reform less than a century earlier. The Chronicles account of the Passover adds additional details to the Kings account by highlighting the role of priests and Levites. The celebration of the Passover served to appropriate the exodus traditions into Josiah's attempt to underscore the importance of Jerusalem and its temple in the development of Judah's religious identity. Chronicles casts the net wider, as it includes all Israel in the king's reform.

Kings maintains that no other king had been as committed to YHWH and as faithful to that commitment as had Josiah (2 Kgs 22:2; 23:25). At the same time, however, Kings notes that Josiah's fidelity was not enough to outweigh the effects of Manasseh's infidelity. Kings is aware that Josiah's reform did not outlive him. Second Kings 23:27 asserts that the Kingdom of Judah will share the fate of the Kingdom of Israel. Jerusalem, the city that God chose, will not escape the coming disaster (2 Kgs 23:26–27). Kings then describes Josiah's death in battle against Egypt at Megiddo. It does so without a word of explanation about the king's tragic death.

After Josiah's burial in Jerusalem, the members of Judah's rural aristocracy anoint Jehoahaz, Josiah's son, as king.

Chronicles attempts to explain the reason for Josiah's tragic death.[39] It portrays the Pharaoh Neco as warning Josiah not to interfere with his plans to wage war on "another kingdom." The pharaoh asserts that he is doing God's bidding. Indeed, Chronicles asserts that the warning Neco gives to Josiah came from "the mouth of God" (2 Chr 35:22). Josiah disregarded Neco's warning and attacked the Egyptians at Megiddo. Josiah was severely wounded and was taken to Jerusalem, where he died and was buried. Chronicles, nonetheless, concludes its treatment of Josiah by pointing to his "faithful deeds" done in accord to "what is written in the law of Yhwh" (2 Chr 35:26). The death of Josiah drove Judah into the maelstrom of ancient Near Eastern politics. Assyria's star was growing dimmer. Egypt used Assyria's near collapse as an opportunity to advance its own agenda. Babylon's star was rising on the horizon. In comparison with these powers, Judah was practically a political and military nonentity. Kings and Chronicles ignore these political realities as much as possible. Both stories see Judah's approaching fate as the consequence of failed leadership by Judah's kings and the people's penchant for idolatry.

The story of Josiah plays a pivotal role in the story of the Kingdom of Judah and its fall. It is like the eye of a hurricane that offers a brief respite in the midst of a most destructive storm. Both Kings and Chronicles have a favorable opinion of Josiah because of his efforts to rid Judah of idolatry and to bring about a renewal of Judah's commitment to Yhwh. In the end, Josiah's reforms did not outlive him. After his death, Judah again returned to a path that led it inevitably to its own death. The question that both Kings and Chronicles had to face was whether there was a future for the people of Judah after the death of its religious and political institutions that gave the people of Judah their identity.

Jehoahaz

The pace of Judah's journey to death picks up following Josiah's death. Judah's defeat by the Egyptians at Megiddo cost Judah not only its king, but also its independence. Judah became a vassal of Egypt, which wrested control of the Levant from the

Assyrians, whose empire was crumbling. Jehoahaz was the choice of the Judean rural aristocracy to succeed Josiah—he was not the choice of the Egyptians.[40] Those who placed Jehoahaz on the throne in place of his older half-brother Eliakim did so believing that he would continue the anti-Egyptian policy of his father Josiah. Evidently, so did the Egyptians, who deposed Jehoahaz after just three months on the throne. The Egyptians imprisoned Jehoahaz at Riblah, an Egyptian stronghold on the Orontes River in the northern portion of the Levant. Eventually Neco had Jehoahaz taken to Egypt, where he died. Kings numbers Jehoahaz among Judah's bad kings (2 Kgs 23:32) but provides no other details about his brief reign or his time as a hostage in Egypt. Chronicles follows the presentation in Kings, though it does not accuse Jehoahaz of having done evil in YHWH's sight, as Kings does.

Jehoahaz is the first in the succession of the last four kings to rule Judah. Their respective evaluations in 2 Kings are similar. The first part of those evaluations is similar to those of earlier "bad kings" of Judah: "he did what was evil in the sight of YHWH." The second part is unique to these four kings: "just as his ancestors had done" (2 Kgs 23:32). Second Kings tells the story of these last four kings of Judah quickly without much embellishment, leaving the hearer/reader with the impression that Judah is rushing toward its fate, and that these kings did nothing to prevent the coming disaster.

Jehoiakim

Jehoiakim was the last of three kings (Josiah, Jehoahaz, and Jehoiakim) who ruled in succession during a single year. Jehoiakim provided Judah with some breathing space by being a compliant vassal to the Egyptians, who set him on Judah's throne and gave him the name Jehoiakim to replace Eliakim, his given name. Jehoiakim's pro-Egyptian policy made it possible for him to rule for eleven years while Egypt controlled the Levant. The first challenge he faced was the payment of the heavy indemnity that Neco imposed upon Judah.[41] Jehoiakim passed on the burden to those who supported Jehoahaz's accession, the rural aristocracy.

Second Kings 24 begins by noting that Judah ceased being Egypt's vassal after Nebuchadnezzar, the king of Babylon, made his appearance in the Levant. Before he became king, Nebuchadnezzar led Babylonian forces to victory in two strategically important battles against the Egyptians—one at Carchemish in the north of Aram, and the second at Hamath, an Aramean fortress city on the Orontes River. Neither Kings nor Chronicles mentions these decisive Babylonian victories over the Egyptians, though 2 Kings 24:7 notes that the Egyptian presence in the Levant was ended by "the king of Babylon." Nabuchadnezzar made Jehoiakim a vassal of Babylon, but the Egyptians were down but not out. Neco managed to fight the Babylonians to a draw when they invaded Egypt. This apparent resurgence of Egypt led the pro-Egypt faction of Judah to support Jehoiakim's withholding the tribute paid to Babylon (2 Kgs 24:1b). This was a violation of Jehoiakim's duty as a vassal of Nebuchadnezzar. No doubt the Egyptians encouraged Jehoiakim to take this action. Nebuchadnezzar sent Babylonian forces stationed in Aram to deal with Judah (2 Kgs 24:2). They besieged Jerusalem, and Jehoiakim died shortly after the siege began.[42]

Jehoiakim's reign saw the end of Josiah's reform. Second Kings 23:37 states that the king did evil as his predecessors had done. The prophet Jeremiah spoke out against Jehoiakim, whom he regarded as a tyrant. The prophet criticized the king's luxurious lifestyle that was made possible by the king's oppression of the poor (Jer 22:15–17). The prophet contrasted Jehoiakim with Josiah. When the latter heard the word of God read to him from the scroll found in the temple, he tore his garments as a sign of his repentance, but Jehoiakim made no such gesture (2 Kgs 22:11; Jer 36:24). On the contrary, when Jehoiakim heard the word of God proclaimed to him from the scroll containing Jeremiah's oracles, he had the scroll burned. Josiah's repentance and reform bought the people Judah some time for their own repentance. Jehoiakim's actions sealed the nation's doom.[43]

Jehoiachin

Jehoiachin was only eighteen years old when he succeeded his father Jehoiakim (2 Kgs 24:18; 2 Chr 36:9 reads eight years old).[44] He came to the throne while Jerusalem was under siege because of Jehoiakim's ill-advised renunciation of his obligations as a vassal of Nebuchadnezzar. When the Babylonian king arrived to take charge of the siege, Jehoiachin thought it wiser to surrender, hoping for mercy from Nebuchadnezzar. The details given in the Babylonian Chronicles makes it possible to date the fall of Jerusalem to March 15/16, 597.[45] As expected, the Babylonian king deposed Jehoiachin, replacing him with his uncle Mattaniah, whom he gave the throne name Zedekiah (2 Kgs 24:17).[46] Jehoiachin was king for just three months (2 Kgs 24:8; 2 Chr 36:9 credits Jehoiachin with ten additional days).

Nebuchadnezzar allowed the Judean state and its native dynasty to continue its nominal existence. But to forestall any further rebellion from Judah, Nebuchadnezzar took Jehoiachin, most of his family, important military and political leaders, and artisans to Babylon as hostages. Second Kings asserts that the only people left in Judah were "the poorest people of the land" (2 Kgs 24:14). In addition to the hostages, the Babylonians confiscated valuables from both the palace and the temple. Chronicles adds nothing to the story of Jehoiachin as given in 2 Kings 24. It agrees with 2 Kings in its assessment of Jehoiachin's brief reign: "[Jehoiachin] did what was evil in the sight of YHWH" (2 Kgs 24:9; 2 Chr 36:9b).

Zedekiah

The last king of Judah was placed on David's throne by Nebuchadnezzar, the Babylonian king. The twenty-one-year-old Zedekiah found himself in a most difficult position. The Judean state and its Davidic dynasty were hanging by the slimmest of threads. Egypt and Babylon were locked in a conflict of empires with the small states of the Levant sandwiched between the two. Although these states were nominally in Babylon's orbit, Nebuchadnezzar found it difficult to keep the states of the Levant in line, since Egypt was actively encouraging them to free themselves from Babylonian hegemony. The Babylonian king also had to deal with a revolt in Babylon itself, limiting his ability to respond to rebellion elsewhere in his realm. The other Levantine states tried to persuade Zedekiah to join with them in rebelling against Nebuchadnezzar (Jer 27:1–11). In Judah there were pro-Babylonian and pro-Egyptian factions. Zedekiah was initially pro-Babylonian since he owed his throne to Babylon, but the king's advisors were pushing him toward Egypt. This led the pro-Babylonian Jeremiah to denounce the king's advisors, comparing them to rotten figs, unfit for eating (Jer 24:8–10). Among these advisors was the prophet Hananiah, who thought the fall of Jerusalem and the exile of Jehoiachin were just temporary setbacks. Hananiah asserted that the king and those who went into exile with him would return in two years (Jer 28:4). Jeremiah, however, advised the people of Judah to submit to the yoke of Babylon (28:14–17). Although the prophet had no use for the Judean political and religious establishment, he never condemned Zedekiah, though the prophet did consider him to be a weak and tragic king (Jer 36). Second Chronicles 36:12–14 does condemn Zedekiah for not taking Jeremiah's advice. Also condemned are the religious leadership and the people as a whole for their idolatry.

Although Zedekiah ruled for eleven years, neither Kings nor Chronicles has much to say about his reign before the siege of Jerusalem that brought an end to the Judean state and its Davidic dynasty. With the accession of a new pharaoh (Hophra/Apries) to the throne in Egypt, Zedekiah's advisors encouraged him to take the opportunity to seek Egypt's help in throwing off Babylonian domination of Judah (Ezek 17:15). When apprised of Zedekiah's disloyalty, Nebuchadnezzar acted quickly. He first neutralized Phoenicia before turning his attention to Judah. While the Babylonian king remained at his headquarters in Riblah, he sent his army south to Judah. Second Kings 25:1–21 describes the siege of Jerusalem, with 2 Chronicles 36:15–21 providing a shorter version of the story. Jeremiah tells of an advance of the Egyptian army into the region (Jer 37:5). Zedekiah convinced Jerusalem's aristocrats to free their slaves to help with the defense of the city. When the Babylonian forces lifted the siege in order to deal with the Egyptians, those slaves who were freed were taken back into slavery (Jer 24:8–10). Though neither Kings nor Chronicles reports this, the prophet's account shows how short-sighted and corrupt the Judean aristocracy was.

After the Babylonians dealt with the Egyptian threat, they returned to Jerusalem and quickly breached the city's wall. The fall of the city was just a matter of time. Zedekiah abandoned Jerusalem, fleeing toward the Arabah. The Arabah is that portion of the Great Rift Valley that lies below the Dead Sea and gradually ascends toward the Red Sea. It is a desert most inhospitable to human life. Presumably, Zedekiah thought that the Babylonians would hesitate to follow him there. Zedekiah's escort deserted, leaving him to be captured near Jericho. It is ironic that the Judean state comes to an end with the capture of its king at the very place where the Israelites won their first battle to take the land promised to their ancestors. The king's captors took him to Nebuchadnezzar at Riblah. The Babylonian king repaid Zedekiah's disloyalty in a most harsh fashion. He had him witness the execution of his sons before he was blinded. The erstwhile king of Judah was then taken to Babylon in chains. That is the last time Kings mentions Zedekiah by name. Presumably he died as an exile in Babylon.

Second Kings 25:8–21 describes the fate of Jerusalem, the temple, and Zedekiah's principal counselors. The Babylonians destroyed the temple, the palace, and the homes of the Jerusalem aristocracy. They led the people of the city—even those Judeans who changed sides and abandoned Zedekiah—into exile. The only people spared were a few of Judah's poorest farmers. The temple was stripped of anything of value. All worth saving from destruction was taken to Babylon. Members of the royal Judean court—Judah's principal religious and political leaders—were taken to Nebuchadnezzar. Because they promoted rebellion against Babylon, all were executed.

So ended the Kingdom of Judah, the Davidic dynasty, the temple and its priesthood, and the political and military establishment of Judah. All the institutions that gave the people of Judah their identity were gone. The ancestors of the people of Judah crossed the Jordan from the east to take control of the land promised to their ancestors. After the fall of Jerusalem, the people of Judah crossed the Jordan from the west as they were led to Babylon to live in exile from the land of Israel. The only people who remained were a few of the poorest farmers.

Second Chronicles 36:11–20a asserts that the fall of Jerusalem was due to the infidelity of king and people, while Kings does not assign blame because that already had been laid at the feet of Manasseh (2 Kgs 21:10–16). Chronicles asserts that infidelity in Judah was so pervasive that no remedy was possible. The fall of the kingdom, the destruction of the city, and the exile of its people was inevitable. Chronicles notes that the exile continued until the rise of the Kingdom of Persia (539 BCE). The length of the exile was determined by the prophecy of Jeremiah, who announced that the exile would give the land its sabbatical rest (Jer 25:11–12;

29:10), which it did not enjoy because of the people's failure to observe the command about the fallow year (Lev 26:34–35, 43).

Kings adds that, following the destruction of Jerusalem and the exile of its king, Nebuchadnezzar appointed Gedaliah to rule "over the people who remained in the land of Judah" (2 Kgs 25:22).[47] Gedaliah was the grandson of Shaphan, who was an advisor to Josiah. Evidently Gedaliah belonged to the pro-Babylon party that tried but failed to persuade Zedekiah to remain a compliant vassal of Nebuchadnezzar. Gedaliah made his headquarters Mizpah, a town eight miles northwest of the now-ruined capital Jerusalem.[48] Nebuchadnezzar gave him authority over the Judeans who were not sent into exile. Gedaliah belonged to a family that served in the administration of the kings of Judah, and his pro-Babylonian leaning made him an obvious choice to maintain order in what was left of the Kingdom of Judah. He tried to convince the last remnants of Judah's army to submit to political and military reality and return to their farms. Some did follow his advice (Jer 40:12), but there were some Judeans who thought of Gedaliah as a collaborator. Plots were hatched to move against Gedaliah. He was forewarned about them, but he chose to ignore these warnings. A member of the royal family, Ishmael son of Nethaniah, assassinated Gedaliah, who served for just two or three months. The assassins also murdered the Judeans and Babylonians who were part of Gedaliah's entourage. Jeremiah gives more information about the conspirators' actions (cf. Jer 41). According to the prophet, Ishmael seized the daughters of Zedekiah whom the Babylonians entrusted to Gedaliah's care. This may have been a claim to kingship on Ishmael's part.[49] Johanan ben Kareah, who tried to warn Gedaliah about the plot against him, caught up with Ishmael and killed him. The fallout from Gedaliah's assassination was the flight of as many Judeans as possible to Egypt in order to escape retaliation by the Babylonians (2 Kgs 25:26).

So ends the story of the Judean state and monarchy according to Kings. It ends with a self-inflicted blow delivered by a member of the royal family. Kings presents the monarchy as a failed institution that led Judah to an ignominious end. Kings gives no hint of any restoration, leading to the question so poignantly raised to God at the end of Lamentations: "Have you forgotten us completely?"

(Lam 5:20a). Chronicles, however, asserts that the period of exile was limited to seventy years (2 Chr 36:21).

CONCLUSION

The Kingdom of Judah survived for 136 years longer than the Kingdom of Israel. This is sometimes credited to the stability provided by the rule of a single dynasty over that kingdom's entire history, except for the seven-year rule of Athaliah of the Omride dynasty. Of the sixteen kings that ruled Judah from the time of Jehoshaphat to Zedekiah, five were assassinated, three died in exile, and one died in battle. There were periods of peace, but such times came at the cost of high tribute that had to be paid to foreign empires. Periods of war were more common because of conflicts among the national states of the southern Levant. The towns and cities of Judah had to face raids and punitive campaigns by Egypt, Assyria, and Babylon. It is a wonder that the Kingdom of Judah was able to survive as long as it did, given its internal political conflicts and the external military threats that the kingdom had to face.

The yardstick by which Kings and Chronicles measures the Kingdom of Israel is the loyalty of king and people to YHWH, their ancestral Deity. By this measure the Kingdom of Judah was an even greater failure than it was in the political and military sphere. The people of Judah, it appeared, were addicted to worship on the "high places" that were often the setting for rites connected with Baal and Asherah, YHWH's principal rivals. Most kings of Judah allowed the high places to remain in operation, and some kings actively promoted the rites that were celebrated at the high places. Kings and Chronicles both maintain that the proper place to conduct the authentic worship of YHWH is in the temple of Jerusalem under the direction of Levitical priests. Hezekiah and Josiah receive highest praise because they called the people of Judah to worship in the temple from which all pagan accoutrements had been removed. A few other kings get credit for renovating the temple, but most kings "did what was evil in the sight of YHWH." In the end, the Kingdom of Judah fell victim to its own religious failing—to its failure to worship YHWH alone in the place where YHWH chose to be worshiped.

Is the story of the Kingdom of Judah a tragic one? For Kings it is. What began with such promise, as the Israelite tribes crossed the Jordan and took possession of the land promised to their ancestors as an eternal inheritance, ends with the absorption of that land into the Babylonian provincial system, its people—with the exception of the poorest of the land—forced to migrate to Babylon with no clear indication of any future. The institutions that gave Judah and its people their identity are dead: the monarchy and dynasty, temple, and priesthood. The prophets are taken into exile as well. The only remnant of Judah's ancestral religious tradition available is the written authoritative Torah, but the story of the rise and fall of the Kingdom of Judah does not give the reader/hearer of the story any confidence that the people of Judah-in-exile will be able to transform the curse about which the Torah warns to the blessing that the Torah promises.

Chronicles makes its appearance some two hundred years after Samuel and Kings. Even if the fortunes of the people of Judah have not been turned completely around, the people's prospects are better—even hopeful. The Persians have allowed and even encouraged the exiles of Judah to return to their homeland in the Levant. They authorized the Torah as the imperial law for the people living in the Persian province of Yehud. What is most important of all, they encouraged and supported the construction of a new temple for YHWH in Jerusalem. With the temple rebuilt, the service of YHWH has been resumed under the direction of the priests and Levites. Chronicles tells the story of the Kingdom of Judah with a strong emphasis on the temple and the worship of YHWH that takes place there. Chronicles offers no hint about any future for the national state with its native dynasty (the Davidides), but it connects the story of the Kingdom not only with the ancestors of the Israelite tribes but with the very beginning of the human family. That perspective offers a sense of stability and permanence to the story of Judah and its people. Here, then, is the principal difference between the story told in Samuel and Kings and the story told in Chronicles. Samuel/Kings leads to the question, "Have you rejected us?" Chronicles calls its readers/hearers to begin their adventure with their God again.

Epilogue

The story of the people of ancient Israel in the land promised to their ancestors is told in the Books of Joshua, Judges, Samuel, and Kings. The theological perspective through which this story is told comes from the Book of Deuteronomy, which warns Israel about the consequences of infidelity and idolatry:

> When you have had children and children's children, and become complacent in the land, if you act corruptly by making an idol in the form of anything, thus doing what is evil in the sight of the LORD your God, and provoking him to anger, I call heaven and earth to witness against you today that you will soon utterly perish from the land that you are crossing the Jordan to occupy; you will not live long on it, but will be utterly destroyed. The LORD will scatter you among the peoples; only a few of you will be left among the nations where the LORD will lead you. (Deut 4:25–27)

The story of the rise and fall of the Israelite kingdoms as told in Samuel and Kings recounts the failure of kings and people to heed this warning. The story ends with the people of Judah in exile far from their homeland, leading the reader/hearer to wonder about the prospects for the future of the Jewish people. When arriving at the conclusion of the story of Israel in its land, the first to hear and read this story no doubt asked, "Have you forgotten us completely?" (Lam 5:22).

The exile ended following the fall of Babylon to Cyrus, king of Persia. Cyrus encouraged the Jewish exiles to return to Jerusalem and rebuild the temple to YHWH. The temple was rebuilt and the worship of YHWH was resumed there. The restoration of worship in the Jerusalem temple led circles responsible for leading the temple rituals to suggest that there was another way to tell the story of the rise and fall of the Israelite kingdoms. These circles produced the Books of Chronicles, which offer an alternative narrative to the one found in Samuel and Kings. Chronicles does make use of material from Kings in offering its account of the rise and fall of the Israelite kingdoms. In doing so, however, Chronicles reshapes this material according to its belief that repentance leads to restoration and that authentic worship of YHWH is the key to Jewish identity. Chronicles does not ignore the infidelity of kings and people but rests on the conviction that there is a future for Israel as a worshiping community.

How did that future pan out? The temple and its rituals did become the center of Jewish life in the centuries following the appearance of Chronicles. This work places before the reader/hearer Israel's "golden age," the time of David and Solomon. As Chronicles presents it, these two kings committed themselves totally to the worship of YHWH in the temple. David prepared for the construction of the temple; Solomon executed the plans for the temple laid out by David. What Chronicles suggests to its readers/hearers is that their worship of YHWH stands in continuity with that of Solomon's temple. The Second Temple, then, is the new source of Jewish unity and identity. Over time, however, it became clear that the temple, its priests, and its rituals did not provide sufficient nourishment for all the people's life with God—especially when the Hasmonean kings began expanding their control over larger portions of the territories of the former Israelite kingdoms. Some Jews found themselves too far from the temple to participate in its services except on rare occasions. To nourish their religious life, Jews began assembling in their villages and towns for prayer and the reading of the Scriptures. The "synagogue" grew in popularity because synagogues were a practical way for Jewish people to nourish their religious life.[1]

The destruction of the Second Temple in 70 CE was a serious blow to Jewish religious life as presented in Chronicles. The temple in Jerusalem, its rituals, and its priesthood were central concerns in Chronicles. In addition, the expulsion of the Jews from

168

Jerusalem after the Second Revolt against Rome (135 CE) compounded the problem. Finally, the growth of the Jewish Diaspora forced a reexamination of the basis of Jewish religious life. For Chronicles, Jewish identity, destiny, and unity were based on the worship of Yhwh in the temple of Jerusalem. But that temple was no more. The synagogue was in a position to become the principal institution to maintain Jewish identity, unity, and religious life.

These circumstances led Jews to take a closer look at the narratives in Joshua–2 Kings and the Deuteronomic perspectives that provided the theological underpinnings for telling the story of Israel in its land. There were two key theological assumptions of the story of Israel in its land. First, there was the notion that Israel was responsible for choosing its future:

> See, I have set before you today life and prosperity, death and adversity. If you obey the commandments of Yhwh your God that I am commanding you today, by loving Yhwh your God, walking in his ways, and observing his commandments, decrees, and ordinances, then you shall live and become numerous, and Yhwh your God will bless you in the land that you are entering to possess. But if your heart turns away and you do not hear, but are led astray to bow down to other gods and serve them, I declare to you today that you shall perish; you shall not live long in the land that you are crossing the Jordan to enter and possess. (Deut 30:15–18)

The story of the rise and fall of the Israelite kingdoms in Samuel and Kings provides an explanation of the failure of Israel to remain in the promised land. That failure was the consequence of Israel's infidelity to Yhwh, their ancestral Deity.

The second key element in the story of the Israelite kingdoms is the centrality of "the book of the Torah." The written, authoritative law provided the Jewish people of Israel with guidance for their life in the promised land. Indeed, the story of Israel in its land begins with this exhortation: "This book of the law shall not depart out of your mouth; you shall meditate on it day and night, so that you may be careful to act in accordance with all that is written in it. For then you shall make your way prosperous, and then you shall be successful" (Josh 1:8). The rest of the story illustrates the failure of Israel's people and kings to remain loyal and committed to YHWH. Still, judgment was not God's final word. Israel had a new opportunity to live in commitment and fidelity to YHWH.

The destruction of the Second Temple, however, brought about a new crisis. The response to that crisis required a recentering of the religion of ancient Israel from its foundation in the service of YHWH in the temple and its sacrificial worship. A focus on the study and observance of the written authoritative book of the law emerged in response to this new crisis. The synagogue, with its reading of the Torah in the context of worship, became the new center of Jewish life. Those responsible for nourishing the religious life of the Jewish people were not priests and Levites who served in the temple but scribes and rabbis, who were the teachers of the Torah. Chronicles links the identity and future of the people of Yehud with the authentic worship of YHWH in the Jerusalem temple. To accomplish this, Chronicles offers an idealized portrait of David and Solomon and their reigns, suggesting that the people of Yehud be as totally committed to the service of YHWH as were David and Solomon. Samuel and Kings presents a more critical and realistic account of these two kings. Readers/hearers were able to identify with David the repentant sinner as depicted in 2 Samuel 12. Also, the book of the law was "portable." It could accompany Jews wherever they may find themselves. Finally, the synagogue was not tied down to a specific place. The assembly of Jews for the reading of the Torah and prayer constituted a synagogue no matter where Jews may find themselves.

Both accounts of the rise and fall of the Israelite kingdoms serve as warnings of the consequences of Israel's divided loyalty and lack of commitment to their ancestral Deity. Chronicles identifies the future of the Jewish people with the maintenance of authentic worship in the temple of Jerusalem. With its insistence on living in accord with the prescriptions of the "book of the law" as the key to the future, Deuteronomy and Joshua–2 Kings helps prepare Jews for living in a world without a temple. That will be their new world, to be sure, but the Torah provides instruction of how to live in that world with fidelity and commitment to the God of Israel.

Appendix:
Table of Israelite Kings

EARLY ISRAELITE MONARCHY				
Name	Manner of accession	Length of reign	Manner of death	Evaluation of reign: Samuel/Kings Chronicles
Saul	prophetic designation and popular acclamation	20 years*	suicide	negative none
David	prophetic designation and popular acclamation	40 years	natural death	mixed positive
Solomon (Jedidiah)	dynastic succession	40 years	natural death	mixed positive

*Neither 2 Samuel nor 1 Chronicles notes the length of Saul's reign. Twenty years is a scholarly estimate.

THE KINGDOM OF JUDAH				
Name	Manner of accession	Length of reign	Manner of death	Evaluation of reign: Kings Chronicles
Rehoboam	dynastic succession*	17 years	natural death	negative negative

The Rise and Fall of the Israelite Kingdoms

KINGDOM OF JUDAH *continued*

Name	Manner of accession	Length of reign	Manner of death	Evaluation of reign: Kings Chronicles
Abijam (Kings) Abijah (Chronicles)	dynastic succession	3 years	natural death	negative positive
Asa	dynastic succession	41 years	infection of the feet	mixed mixed
Jehoshaphat	dynastic succession	25 years	natural death	mixed mixed
Jehoram (Joram)	dynastic succession	8 years	Kings: natural death Chronicles: bowel disease	negative negative
Ahaziah (Jehoahaz)	Kings: dynastic succession Chronicles: popular acclamation	1 year	assassination during Jehu's rebellion	negative negative
Athaliah	palace coup	7 years	assassination	negative negative
Jehoash (Joash)	popular revolution	37 years	assassination	negative mixed
Amaziah	dynastic succession	29 years	assassination	negative mixed
Azariah (Uzziah)	Kings: dynastic succession Chronicles: popular acclamation	52 years	leprosy	mixed mixed
Jotham	dynastic succession	16 years	natural death	mixed positive
Ahaz	dynastic succession	16 years	natural death	negative negative
Hezekiah	dynastic succession	29 years	natural death	positive positive
Manasseh	dynastic succession	55 years	natural death	positive mixed

Name	Manner of accession	Length of reign	Manner of death	Evaluation of reign: Kings Chronicles
Amon	dynastic succession	2 years	assassination	negative negative
Josiah	dynastic succession	31 years	died in battle	positive mixed
Jehoahaz	dynastic succession	3 months	deposed by Egypt and died in exile	negative none
Jehoiakim (Eliakim)	enthroned by Egypt	11 years	natural death	negative negative
Jehoiachin (Jeconiah)	dynastic succession	3 month	deposed by Babylon and died in exile	negative negative
Zedekiah (Mattaniah)	enthroned by Babylon	11 years	deposed by Babylon; died in exile (presumably)	negative negative

*All monarchs of the Kingdom of Judah belonged to the Davidic dynasty except for Athaliah.

THE KINGDOM OF ISRAEL				
Name	Manner of accession	Length of reign	Manner of death	Evaluation of reign*
Jeroboam I	prophetic designation and popular acclamation	not specified; probably 21 years	natural death	
Nadab	dynastic succession	2 years	assassinated	
Baasha	coup d'état	24 years	natural death	
Elah	dynastic succession	2 years	assassinated	
Zimri	military coup	7 days	suicide	
Omri	military coup	12 years	natural death	
Ahab	dynastic succession	22 years	died in battle	

KINGDOM OF ISRAEL *continued*

Name	Manner of accession	Length of reign	Manner of death	Evaluation of reign*
Ahaziah	dynastic succession	2 years	died of injuries from a fall	
Jehoram (Joram)	dynastic succession	12 years	assassination	
Jehu	military coup	not specified; probably 28 years	natural death	
Jehoahaz	dynastic succession	17 years	natural death	
Jehoash (Joash)	dynastic succession	16 years	natural death	
Jeroboam II	dynastic succession	41 years	natural death	
Zechariah	dynastic succession	6 months	assassination	
Shallum	coup d'état	1 month	assassination	
Menahem	coup d'état	10 years	natural death	
Pekahiah	dynastic succession	2 years	assassination	
Pekah	military coup	not specified; probably less than 1 year	assassination	
Hoshea	coup d'état	9 years	deposed and exiled by Assyria; presumably died in exile	

*The Books of Kings offer a negative assessment of all the kings of the Kingdom of Israel because Kings considered the worship at the royal sanctuaries of Dan and Bethel to be idolatrous. The Books of Chronicles do not even mention most of the kings who ruled in the north. Of those that Chronicles does mention, all receive a negative evaluation.

Notes

INTRODUCTION

1. Deuteronomy uses this word eighteen times. The NRSV renders the Hebrew as "your Israelite kin" for the sake of inclusivity.

2. Martin Noth, *The Deuteronomistic History*, JSOTSup 15 (Sheffield, UK: JSOT Press, 1981). This is a translation of the first part of Noth's *Überliferungsgeschichtliche Studien* (Tübingen: M. Niemeyer, 1957). Some scholars have raised objections to Noth's hypothesis. See Gary N. Knoppers, "Is There a Future for the Deuteronomistic History?" in *The Future of the Deuteronomistic History*, ed. Thomas Römer (Leuven: Peeters, 2000), 120.

3. Frank Moore Cross, "The Structure of Deuteronomic History," *Perspectives in Jewish Learning*, Annual of the College of Jewish Studies (Chicago: College of Jewish Studies, 1968), 9–24. Reprinted as "The Themes of the Book of Kings and the Structure of the Deuteronomistic History" in his *Canaanite Myth and Hebrew Epic: Essays in the History of the Religion of Israel* (Cambridge, MA: Harvard University Press, 1973), 274–89.

4. For a concise description of the various approaches to the redactions of the Deuteronomistic History, see Mark A. O'Brien, *The Deuteronomistic History Hypothesis: A Reassessment*, Orbis Biblicus et Orientalis 92 (Freiburg, Switzerland: Universitätsverlag, 1989), 3–21.

5. Steven L. McKenzie, *The Chronicler's Use of the Deuteronomistic History*, HSM 22 (Atlanta: Scholars Press, 1985).

6. Gary N. Knoppers, "Rethinking the Relationship between Deuteronomy and the Deuteronomistic History," CBQ 63, no. 3

(July 2001): 398. The term *Deuteronomic* generally refers to the traditions and perspectives of the Book of Deuteronomy, though some scholars also use this word to speak of the traditions in Joshua–Kings. This book will use the term to refer to traditions and perspectives that Joshua–Kings shares with Deuteronomy.

7. Louis Jonker, "Who Constitutes Society? Yehud's Self-Understanding in the Late Persian Era as Reflected in the Books of Chronicles," *JBL* 127, no. 4 (2008): 724.

8. Chronicles twice mentions Manasseh's prayer of repentance but does not provide a text. The Septuagint, however, contains a prayer ascribed to Manasseh. The Codex Alexandrinus appends it to the Book of Psalms, and Jerome placed it in an appendix to the Vulgate.

9. The Babylonian Chronicles provide a date for the breaching of the walls of Jerusalem as the equivalent of March 16, 597. See Ernst Kutsch, "Das Jahr der Katastrophe: 587 v. Chr. Kritische Erwägungen zu neueren chronologischen Versuchen," *Bib* 55, no. 4 (1974): 520–45.

10. See Svend Holm-Nielsen, "Did Joab Climb 'Warren's Shaft'?," in *History and Traditions of Early Israel: Studies Presented to Eduard Nielsen, May 8, 1993*, ed. André Lemaire and Benedikt Otzen, VTSup 53 (Leiden: Brill, 1993), 38–49.

11. The latter is the position of the so-called minimalists. This hypothesis has developed in Thomas L. Thompson, *The Bible in History: How Writers Create a Past* (London: Pimlico, 1999).

12. Several recently published full-scale commentaries have helped stimulate interest in Chronicles, e.g., Sara Japhet, *I & II Chronicles*, OTL (Louisville, KY: Westminster John Knox Press, 1993); Ralph Klein, *1 Chronicles*, Hermeneia (Minneapolis: Fortress, 2006); Klein, *2 Chronicles*, Hermeneia (Minneapolis: Fortress, 2012); Gary N. Knoppers, *1 Chronicles 1—9: A New Translation with an Introduction and Commentary*, AB 12 (New York: Doubleday, 2003). For a current annotated bibliography on Chronicles, see Steven Shawn Tuell, "1 and 2 Chronicles," in *Oxford Bibliographies*, https://www.oxfordbibliographies.com/view/document/obo-9780195393361/obo-9780195393361-0021.xml?rskey=tLnYu5&result=29.

13. All citations of the biblical text are taken from the 4th edition of the New Revised Standard Version, unless otherwise indicated.

14. The word *Evil* here is not a moral judgment on the king but it is a transliteration of the way the Babylonian king's Akkadian name was rendered in Hebrew.

15. The parallel text in Jeremiah 52:31–34 explicitly mentions Jehoiachin's death.

16. Some commentators see the notice of Jehoiachin's parole as "a glimpse of hope," e.g., T. Raymond Hobbs, *2 Kings*, WBC 13 (Dallas: Word Books, 1985), 368. For a list of those who see Jehoiachin's parole as providing hope for the restoration of the Davidic dynasty, see Donald F. Murray, "Of All the Years the Hopes—or Fears? Jehoiachin in Babylon (2 Kings 25:27–30)," *JBL* 120, no. 2 (April 2001): 246n5. This article also contains a fine summary of scholarship on the ending of 2 Kings 25. Mordechai Cogan and Hayim Tadmor suggest that while the ending of Kings may not offer hope for the restoration of the Davidic dynasty, it suggests an improvement of the prospects for the Judean exiles. See their *II Kings: A New Translation with Introduction and Commentary*, AB 11 (Garden City: Doubleday, 1988), 330. But the text itself does not imply this at all.

17. Murray, "Of All the Years," 245–65, as well as Jon D. Levenson, "The Last Four Verses in Kings," *JBL* 103 (September 1984): 353–54.

18. Noth, *Deuteronomistic History*, 74, 79.

19. Gerhard von Rad, *Studies in Deuteronomy*, trans. David Stalker, SBT 9 (London: SCM Press, 1953), 90–91; trans. of *Deuteronomium-Studien*, FRLANT 58 (Göttingen: Vandenhoeck & Ruprecht, 1947).

20. Christopher Begg, "The Significance of Jehoiachin's Release: A New Proposal," *JSOT* 36 (1986): 54.

21. Irving Finkel, *The Cyrus Cylinder: The Great Persian Edict from Babylon* (London: Bloomsbury Publishing, 2013).

22. The temple was completed in the sixth year of Darius's reign, i.e., 516. See Ezra 6:15.

23. Isaac Kalimi describes Chronicles as an example of "sacred didactic historical writing" that is shaped by the specific time, place, and sociopolitical circumstances of the time during

which it was composed. See his "Placing the Chronicler in His Own Historical Context: A Closer Examination," *Journal of Near Eastern Studies* 68, no. 3 (July 2009): 192.

24. John Van Seters, "The Chronicler's Account of Solomon's Temple-Building: A Continuity Theme," in *The Chronicler as an Historian*, ed. M. Patrick Graham, Kenneth G. Hoglund, and Steven L. McKenzie (Sheffield, UK: Sheffield Academic Press, 1997), 300.

25. Mika S. Pajunen, "The Saga of Judah's Kings Continues: The Reception of Chronicles in the Late Second Temple Period," *JBL* 136, no. 3 (July 2017): 568–69.

CHAPTER ONE: THE PRELUDES

1. The Israelite kingdom never controlled this vast territory in its entirety. They shared this region with the Phoenicians in the northwest and Philistines in the southwest, the Arameans in the northeast, and the Ammonites, Moabites, and Edomites in the east.

2. The cities of Jericho and Ai were virtually unoccupied at the time the Israelite tribes emerged in the Central Highlands. See Kathleen Kenyon, "Jericho: Tell es-Sultan," in *NEAEHL* 2:674–81; Joseph A. Callaway, "Ai," *NEAEHL* 1:39–45. The text of Joshua does not mention Shechem explicitly, but it describes a covenant renewal ceremony on Mts. Ebal and Gerizim (Josh 8:30–35). Shechem is located in the valley between these two mountains.

3. Shiloh became an important Yahwistic shrine in the premonarchic period. It was located in the territory of Ephraim, eighteen and a half miles north of Jerusalem. The shrine at Shiloh was the objective of an annual pilgrimage (Judg 21:19). Shiloh was destroyed by the Philistines following the Israelites' defeat at Aphek (Jer 7:12–14; Ps 78:60). In 1834, Edward Robinson identified the site with the village of Sailun. For results of excavations of the site, see Israel Finkelstein, "Shiloh," *NEAEHL* 4:1364–70.

4. Shechem is located in the tribal territory of Ephraim, in the central highlands forty miles north of Jerusalem. The Bronze and Iron Age site is identified with Tell Balâta. See Edward E.

Campbell, "Shechem," *NEAEHL* 4:1345. It was an important cultic, economic, and political center in the valley between Mt. Gerizim and Mt. Ebal.

5. The NABRE translates the Hebrew phrase *mal'ak yhwh* as "the messenger of the LORD," while the NRSV renders the phrase as "the angel of the LORD." There is nothing in the text that suggests that the person giving the message to Israel is a spiritual being, though the phrase could be taken as a euphemism to speak about an appearance of God. It also could simply be speaking of a human messenger. The phrase is ambiguous.

6. See Spencer L. Allen, *The Splintered Divine: A Study of Ištar, Baal, and Yahweh Divine Names and Divine Multiplicity in the Ancient Near East*, Studies in Ancient Near Eastern Records 5 (Berlin: De Gruyter, 2015).

7. Phyllis Trible, *Texts of Terror: Literary-Feminist Readings of Biblical Narratives*, Overtures to Biblical Theology 13 (Philadelphia: Fortress, 1984).

8. Dafna Langgut, Israel Finkelstein, and Thomas Litt, "Climate and the Late Bronze Collapse: New Evidence from the Southern Levant," *TA* 40 (2013): 149–75.

9. The origin of the Philistines is a matter of some debate among scholars. Recent analysis of DNA from Iron I burials at Ashkelon, one of the Philistine city-states, showed a genetic mixture of the Canaanite population with new elements originating in southern Europe. Cf. Michal Feldman et al., "Ancient DNA Sheds Light on the Genetic Origins of Early Iron Age Philistines," *Science Advances* 5, no. 7 (July 2019): eaax0061. Among the possible candidates responsible for the DNA mixture are refugees who fled from Mycenae when that kingdom fell in the 13th c. BCE. After being repulsed by the Egyptians, they settled along Canaan's southern Mediterranean coast and organized themselves in a loose confederation of five city-states. Their expansion to the north and east threated the Israelite tribes. Assaf Yasur-Landau, *The Philistines and Aegean Migration at the End of the Late Bronze Age* (New York: Cambridge University Press, 2010).

10. In the Second Temple Period, the promise of an eternal dynasty was rehabilitated and made part of Jewish and later Christian eschatology as messianism. See James H. Charlesworth, ed.,

The Messiah: Developments in Earliest Judaism and Christianity (Minneapolis: Fortress, 1992).

11. Ashdod was one of the five Philistine city-states. It was in the tribal territory of Judah but remained in Philistine hands. It was extensively excavated by Moshe Dothan. See his "Ashdod," *NEAEHL* 1:93–102.

12. Leonhard Rost, *The Succession to the Throne of David*, trans. Michael D. Rutter and David M. Gunn (Sheffield, UK: Almond Press, 1982), 9; trans. of *Die Überlieferung von der Thronnachfolge Davids*, BWANT 42 (Stuttgart: Kohlhammer, 1926), 119–253. For a summary of recent scholarship on the Ark Narrative, see Keith Bodner, "Ark-Eology: Shifting Emphases in 'Ark Narrative' Scholarship," *Currents in Biblical Research* 4, no. 2 (2006): 169–96.

13. Karel van der Toorn and Cornelis Houtman, "David and the Ark," *JBL* 113, no. 2 (April 1994): 209–231; Klaas Smelik, "The Ark Narrative Reconsidered," in *New Avenues in the Study of the Old Testament*, ed. A. S. van der Woude (Leiden: Brill, 1989), 128–44.

14. Several towns bear this name in the Bible. The one that is the setting for 1 Samuel 7 is Mizpah of Benjamin (Tell en-Naşbeh), which is located eight miles northwest of Jerusalem. In the monarchic period, it was the northernmost fortress of the Kingdom of Judah. See Jeffrey R. Zorn, "Naşbeh, Tell en-," *NEAEHL* 3:1098-1102.

15. E.g., Gary N. Knoppers, *1 Chronicles 1—9: A New Translation with Commentary*, AB 12 (New York: Doubleday, 2003), 261–63; James T. Sparks, *The Chronicler's Genealogies: Towards an Understanding of 1 Chronicles 1—9* (Atlanta: SBL, 2008), 29; Simon J. De Vries, *1 and 2 Chronicles* (Grand Rapids: Eerdmans, 1989), 22; Yitazk Berger, "Chiasm and Meaning in 1 Chronicles," *The Journal of Hebrew Scriptures* 14 (2014): DOI:1-.5508jhs.2014. v14.a1. Still, chiasms, like beauty, are in the eye of the beholder. If one is looking for a chiastic structure in a text, one will usually find it.

16. 1 Chronicles 5:1 explains Reuben's "demotion" as the consequence of his incestuous relationship with Bilhah, one of Jacob's secondary wives (Gen 35:22; 49:4).

17. Sara Japhet, "Exile and Restoration in the Book of Chronicles," in her *From the Rivers of Babylon to the Highlands of Judah:*

Collected Studies on the Restoration Period (Winona Lake, IN: Eisenbrauns, 2006), 331.

CHAPTER TWO: THE EARLY ISRAELITE MONARCHY

1. David's marriages had political implications, serving to provide support for his position as king. See Jon D. Levenson and Baruch Halpern, "The Political Import of David's Marriages," *JBL* 99, no. 4 (December 1980): 507–18.

2. The historical value of stories about Jerusalem of the tenth–ninth centuries BCE is a matter of debate between those who claim that the biblical narratives are historically reliable and those who assert that these stories are a figment of the biblical writer's imagination. For a brief discussion of these positions, see Joe Uziel and Itzhaq Shai, "Iron Age Jerusalem: Temple-Palace, Capital City," *Journal of the American Oriental Society* 127, no. 2 (2007): 161–62. This issue, though important, is not immediately relevant to this study, which focuses on the theological dimensions of biblical text in its final form.

3. Yigal Shiloh, "The Rediscovery of the Ancient Water System Known as 'Warren's Shaft,'" in *Ancient Jerusalem Revealed*, ed. Geva Hillel (Jerusalem: Israel Exploration Society, 1994), 46–54. See also Ronny Reich and Eli Shukron, "The System of Rock-Cut Tunnels near Gihon in Jerusalem Reconsidered," *RB* 107, no. 1 (January 2000): 5–17.

4. Nadav Na'aman, "The Interchange between the Bible and Archaeology: The Case of David's Palace and the Millo," *BAR* 40, no. 1 (January–February 2014): 57–69.

5. Leonhard Rost, *The Succession to the Throne of David*, trans. Michael D. Rutter and David M. Gunn (Sheffield, UK: Almond Press, 1982).

6. Cf. Karel van der Toorn and Cornelis Houtman, "David and the Ark," *JBL* 113, no. 2 (April 1994): 209–231; Klaas Smelik, "The Ark Narrative Reconsidered," in *New Avenues in the Study of the Old Testament*, ed. A. S. van der Woude (Leiden: Brill, 1989), 128–44.

7. Dennis J. McCarthy, "II Samuel 7 and the Structure of the Deuteronomistic History," *JBL* 84, no. 2 (June 1965): 137.

8. Wolfgang Roth, "Deuteronomic Rest-Theology: A Redaction-Critical Study," *Biblical Research* 21 (1976): 5–14.

9. Pancratius C. Beentjes, "Transformation of Space and Time: Nathan's Oracle and David's Prayer in 1 Chronicles 17," in *Sanctity of Time and Space in Tradition and Modernity*, ed. Alberdina Houtman et al. (Leiden: Brill, 1998), 27–44.

10. Michael Avioz, *Nathan's Oracle (2 Samuel 7) and Its Interpreters*, The Bible in History 5 (Bern: Peter Lang, 2005).

11. For an assessment of more recent approaches on the Succession Narrative, see Serge Frolov, "The Succession Narrative: A 'Document' or a 'Phantom?,'" *JBL* 121, no. 1 (February 2002): 81–104.

12. This Aramean kingdom was located in the southern part of the region now known as the Golan Heights. Excavation of et-Tell (Bethsaida) suggests that it may have been the capital of the kingdom of Geshur. Cf. Nadav Na'aman, "The Kingdom of Geshur in History and Memory," *Scandinavian Journal of the Old Testament* 26, no. 1 (2012): 88–101.

13. George G. Nicol, "The Wisdom of Joab and the Wise Woman of Tekoa," *Studia Theologica* 36, no. 1 (1982): 97–104.

14. Rost, *Succession*, 252.

15. E.g., Graeme A. Auld, "David's Census: Some Textual and Literary Links," in *Textual Criticism and Dead Sea Scrolls Studies in Honour of Julio Trebolle Barrera*, ed. Andrés Piquer Otero and Pablo A. Torijano Morales (Leiden: Brill, 2012), 19–34; Nicolas Wyatt, "David's Census and the Tripartite Theory," *VT* 40, no. 3 (1990): 352–60.

16. Gary N. Knoppers, "Images of David in Early Judaism: David as a Repentant Sinner in Chronicles," *Bib* 76, no. 4 (December 1995): 469.

17. For a detailed discussion of the portrait of Solomon in Kings, see Gary Knoppers, "The Deuteronomists and the Deuteronomic Law of the King: A Reexamination of a Relationship," *ZAW* 108, no. 5 (1996): 332–34.

CHAPTER THREE: THE TWO ISRAELITE KINGDOMS

1. The "house of Joseph" refers to the tribes of Ephraim and Manasseh, named after Joseph's sons. These two tribes were the most populous and dominant of the northern tribes.

2. Shechem is located in the central highlands forty-one miles north of Jerusalem in an area home to the tribe of Ephraim. It has an impressive Israelite pedigree, having connections with Abraham (Gen 12:6–8), Jacob (Gen 33:18–19), and Joseph (Josh 24:32). The Book of Joshua locates the assembly of the tribes there at the end of the settlement period (Josh 24:1). G. Ernest Wright and Bernard W. Anderson directed the excavation of Shechem (Tell Balâtah) from 1956 to 1968. They concluded that in the early monarchic period, Shechem was a "modest, unwalled town." Cf. Edward F. Campbell, "Shechem," *NEAEHL* 4:1352. Though Wright and Anderson did not complete a final report on the excavations at Shechem, the project was well known as a training ground for a generation of American field archaeologists.

3. Shoshenq I, known in the Bible as Shishak, ruled Egypt from 945 to 924 BCE. Shishak led a raid into the territory of the two Israelite kingdoms. This raid began with attacks on fortifications in the Negev and ranged as far north as Megiddo. See Andrew D. H. Mayes, "Pharaoh Shishak's Invasion of Palestine and the Exodus from Egypt," in *Between Evidence and Ideology*, ed. Bob Becking and Lester L. Grabbe (Leiden: Brill, 2011), 129–44. Shishak commemorated this raid with an inscription in the Karnak temple in Luxor.

4. Penuel is located in the Transjordan on the Jabbok River. It was the site of a shrine associated with the story of Jacob's encounter with God. There he receives the name "Israel" (Gen 33:22–32). Whether Jeroboam resided in Penuel or simply fortified the city is not clear from the text.

5. Judges 18 presents the cult at Dan as idolatrous from its inception. This is characteristic of literature that reflects the preference for Jerusalem as the divinely chosen setting for the worship of YHWH.

6. Kings uses this expression thirteen times as it tells the story of the Kingdom of Israel and its kings who maintained the shrines at Dan and Bethel. The maintenance of these shrines is the preeminent sin of the kings of Israel. This phrase does not appear in Chronicles because Chronicles all but ignores the Northern Kingdom and its kings.

7. Bethel was located at the southern extremity of the Kingdom of Israel, just twelve miles north of Jerusalem. Only Jerusalem is mentioned more often in the Old Testament.

8. Josiah came to the throne two hundred years later and does profane the altar of Bethel (2 Kgs 23:15–19). Kings places great store on prophecy and fulfillment. This is, however, an example of *vaticinium ex eventu* (prophecy after the fact). The same is true regarding the mention of Samaria in v. 32.

9. Tirzah was another of Jeroboam's residences. It has been identified with Tell el-Far'ah, which is seven miles northeast of Shechem. See Alain Chambois, "Far'ah, Tell el- (North)," *NEAEHL* 2:433, 439–40.

10. Since Chronicles and Kings use different forms of the name, when treating the portrayal of the king in each of the two versions, the present discussion uses the name proper to that version.

11. Gerhard von Rad, *Old Testament Theology*, trans. D. M. G. Stalker, 2 vols. (New York: Harper and Row, 1962), 1:353; Rudolf Mosis, *Untersuchungen zur Theologie des chronistischen Geschichtswerkes*, Freiburger theologische Studien 92 (Freiburg: Herder, 1973), 173.

12. Gary Knoppers, "'Battling against Yahweh': Israel's War against Judah in 2 Chr 13:2–20," *RB* 100, no. 4 (1993): 522. Knoppers characterizes the conflict between Judah and Israel as a "sacral war," avoiding the more commonly used term *holy war*. It should be noted that neither expression appears in the Scriptures.

13. Both the NRSV and the NABRE translate this word as "queen mother." This is misleading. For information about the role and status of the *gəbîrâ*, see "Excursus: The *gəbîrâ*," pp. 95–98.

14. Patrick H. Vaughan: *The Meaning of "bāmâ" in the Old Testament: Study of Etymological, Textual and Archaeological Evidence*, Society for Old Testament Study Monograph Series 3 (Cambridge: University Press, 1974).

15. The Hebrew text identifies the leader of the invading force as "Zerah, the Cushite," who is otherwise unknown. The term *Cush* refers to the area directly south of Egypt.

16. Susan Ackerman, "The Queen Mother and the Cult in Ancient Israel," *JBL* 112, no. 3 (1993): 385–401; Niels-Erik A. Andreasen, "The Role of the Queen Mother in Israelite Society," *CBQ* 45, no. 2 (April 1983): 179–94; Zafrira Ben-Barak, "The Status and Right of the *GĔBÎRÂ*," *JBL* 110, no. 1 (1991): 23–34; Nancy R. Bowen, "The Quest for the Historical *Gĕbîrâ, CBQ* 64, no. 4 (October 2001): 597–618; Marcin Sosik, "*GEBIRA* at the Judaean Court," *Scripta Judaica Cracoviensia* 7 (2009): 7–12. For a monograph on this topic, see Ginny Brewer-Boydston, *Good Queen Mothers, Bad Queen Mothers: The Theological Presentation of Queen Mothers in 1 and 2 Kings*, CBQMS 54 (Washington: CBA, 2016).

17. E.g., Gösta W. Ahlström, *Aspects of Syncretism in Israelite Religion* (Lund: Gleerup, 1963), 118. John Gray, *I & II Kings*, OTL (Philadelphia: Westminster, 1963): 265; Andreasen, "Role of the Queen Mother," 188.

18. The Hebrew text is confusing and may be corrupt. The NRSV does not attempt a translation of *gəbîrâ* in this verse. The NABRE renders it as "his own wife."

19. Andreasen, "Role of the Queen Mother," 184–87.

20. Sosik, "*GEBIRA*," 9–11.

21. 1 Kings 10 and 2 Chronicles 9 use this title in the story of the visit of the Queen of Sheba to Solomon. In 1 Kings 11:19, the title is used for the pharaoh's wife. The Book of Esther uses this title for Vashti and Esther. Song of Songs 6:8, 9 uses the plural form to speak of royal women in general. See Athalya Brenner, *The Israelite Woman: Social Role and Literary Type in Biblical Narrative* (Sheffield, UK: JSOT Press, 1985), 17.

22. Ackerman, "Queen Mother," 391, 400.

23. Ackerman, "Queen Mother," 396–97.

24. Klein, *2 Chronicles*, 231. Sosik agrees ("*GEBIRA*," 8). Bowen prefers to leave the word untranslated (*The Quest*, 598).

25. Israel Finkelstein, "Stages in the Territorial Expansion of the Northern Kingdom," *VT* 61, no. 2 (January 2011): 234.

26. The NRSV corrects the Hebrew by identifying Omri as Athaliah's grandfather. The NABRE translates the Hebrew literally by identifying Athaliah as the daughter of Omri.

27. E.g., see Jeffrey K. Kuan, "Was Omri a Phoenician?" in *History and Interpretation: Essays in Honour of John H. Hayes*, ed. M. Patrick Graham, William P. Brown, and Jeffrey K. Kuan, JSOT-Sup 173 (Sheffield, UK: JSOT Press, 1993), 231–44; Patricia Berlyn, "The Rise of the House of Omri," *Jewish Bible Quarterly* 33, no. 4 (2005): 229; Winfried Thiel, "Omri," *ABD* 5:17.

28. 1 Kings 16:24 asserts that the city took its name from Shemer from whom Omri bought the land on which the city was built. More probably the city's name is derived from the Hebrew root *šmr* (to watch). The city's name in Hebrew, *šōmrôn*, probably means "watchtower." Samaria was built on a hill. For an account of excavations, see Nahum Avigad, "Samaria (City)," *NEAEHL* 4:1300–1310.

29. Walter Bayerlin, ed., *Near Eastern Religious Texts Relating to the Old Testament*, OTL (Philadelphia: Westminster, 1978), 238. John S. Emerton examines the hypothesis that the Moabite Stone was a fictious text written after the time of King Mesha of Moab and finds that hypothesis unconvincing. See his "The Value of the Moabite Stone as an Historical Source," *VT* 52, no. 4 (2002): 483–92.

30. Gale A. Yee suggests that the name Jezebel as found in the Masoretic Text is a parody on *zəbûl*, a title of Baal, that was distorted into *zebel*, i.e., dung. See her "Jezebel," *ABD* 3:848.

31. This is a reference to the palace that Ahab built. The walls of the palace were decorated with beautiful ivory carvings. See Avigad, "Samaria (City)," 1305.

32. David Ussishkin, "Jezreel, Samaria and Megiddo: Royal Centers of Omri and Ahab," in *Congress Volume Cambridge 1995*, ed. John A. Emerton (Leiden: Brill, 1997), 351–64.

33. Nadav Na'aman, "Ahab's Chariot Force at the Battle of Qarqar," *TA* 3 (1976): 89–106.

34. A wadi is a riverbed that contains runoff water only in the rainy season. After the rains cease, a wadi will be dry. The vocalization of *h'rbym* in the Masoretic Text leads to the translation "ravens" in 1 Kings 17:4, 6. A slightly different vocalization would translate this word as "Arabs."

35. It is unclear what this phrase designates. Damascus is a city located in a well-watered basin along the Barada River.

36. Ahab is not mentioned by name in ch. 22 until v. 20. This is similar to ch. 20, an account of another war with Aram. In that chapter Ahab is mentioned by name only three times (vv. 2, 13–14). This has led to the suggestion that the conflicts with Aram actually took place at a later time and were retrojected into Kings' story of Ahab. Kings wishes to portray Ahab as an impious and unjust ruler, and so they fit Kings' purpose well.

37. Jehoram and Joram are two variations of the same name. To add to the confusion, a king of Judah named Jehoram ruled about the same time.

38. Not all this material fits together from a historical perspective. Kings, however, is shaped by a theological vision.

39. The mention of the "king of Edom" in this passage is anachronistic since the kingdom of Edom did not exist in Jehoram's time.

40. Second Kings 1:1 states that Moab's rebellion took place in Ahaziah's reign, though it is more likely that it happened in Jehoram's time.

41. The asherahs ("sacred poles") of 2 Chronicles 17:6 probably refer to the cult objects associated with the worship of the Canaanite goddess Asherah, considered the consort of the supreme Canaanite deity El, and the mother of the gods. What the asherah was is not certain. It could have been a wooden pole or even a living tree, symbolizing the goddess. Some members of Judah's royal court promoted the worship of Asherah alongside of Yhwh (1 Kgs 15:13; 2 Kgs 21:7). An inscription from Kuntillet Ajrud refers to "Yhwh and his Asherah," suggesting that the worship of Asherah was also an element of popular religion. See Nadav Na'aman and Nurit Lissovsky, "Kuntillet 'Ajrud, Sacred Trees and the Ashera," *TA* 35, no. 2 (2008): 186–208.

42. This is the only time Chronicles mentions Elijah. According to Kings' story of Elijah, the prophet had been "taken up" *before* the reign of Jehoram of Judah (2 Kgs 2:9–12).

43. The name means "Yhwh has seized." Second Chronicles 21:17 and 27:23 reverse the two elements of this name and call the king Jehoahaz. Second Chronicles 22:6 distorts his name to

read Azariah. It is clear from the parallel texts in Kings that all three forms refer to Ahaziah of Judah.

44. The location of Beth-haggan is unknown, but it was likely to the south of Jezreel.

45. It was not until the Hasmonean period that another woman would rule Judah as queen. Following the death of Alexander Yannai, his wife Salome (Shlomzion) Alexandra claimed the throne. She ruled from 76 to 67 BCE and was the last Jewish monarch to rule a fully independent Judah, which became a Roman dependency in 63 BCE.

46. The story of Joash's repairs on the temple inspired the production of a stele with an inscription that has been determined to be a forgery. Cf. Edward L. Greenstein, "Methodological Principles in Determining that the So-Called Jehoash Inscription Is Inauthentic," in *Puzzling Out the Past: Studies in Northwest Semitic Languages and Literature in Honor of Bruce Zuckerman*, ed. Marilyn J. Lundberg, Steven Fine, and Wayne T. Pitard (Leiden: Brill, 2012), 83–92; Ernst Axel Knauf, "Jehoash's Improbable Inscription," *Biblische Notizen* 117 (2003): 22–26; Israel Eph'al, "The 'Jehoash Inscription': A Forgery," *IEJ* 53, no. 1 (2003): 123–28.

47. Sela has been identified with Umm-el-Bayyârah. This site, which overlooks Petra, is forty-seven miles south of the Dead Sea and east of the Arava Valley. No evidence of Edomite occupation of this site earlier than the seventh century BCE has been found. A site slightly to the north, el-Sela', is a possibility since it does show Edomite occupation from the 9th to the 7th centuries BCE.

48. The difference between the two names in Hebrew is not as great as it is in English translation. The Hebrew consonants of the two names are the same, except for the *resh* (r) in the name as it appears in Kings.

49. Yohanan Aharoni credits Uzziah with building fortresses at Kadesh-barnea and Ramath-gilead. See his *Archaeology of the Land of Israel* (Philadelphia: Westminster, 1982), 251.

50. To say that Uzziah's army numbered 307,500 is obviously an exaggeration. Broshi and Finkelstein estimate that the entire population of the two Israelite kingdoms in the 8th century BCE was 400,000. See Magen Broshi and Israel Finkelstein, "The

Population of Palestine in Iron Age II," *Bulletin of the American Schools of Oriental Research* 287 (August 1992): 47.

51. Tiglath-pileser III of Assyria claims to have defeated Uzziah in 740. Neither Kings nor Chronicles mentions this. The Assyrian incursion into Judah may have been a raid with no lasting consequences for Judah.

CHAPTER FOUR: THE DECLINE AND COLLAPSE OF THE TWO KINGDOMS

1. For a description of the various forms of divination, see Anne Marie Kitz, "Prophecy as Divination," *CBQ* 65, no. 1 (January 2003): 22–42.

2. The popularity of divination continued unabated despite the strictures of Deuteronomy 18. For example, astrology was popular into the Byzantine period among religious Jews, as shown by the use of the zodiac in synagogue decoration. See Rachel Hachlili, "The Zodiac in Ancient Jewish Synagogal Art: A Review," *Jewish Studies Quarterly* 9, no. 3 (2002): 219–58; Jodi Magness, "Heaven on Earth: Helios and the Zodiac Cycle in Ancient Palestinian Synagogues," *Dumbarton Oaks Papers* 59 (2005): 1–32.

3. Of course, there are exceptions, e.g., the lot oracle employing the 'ûrîm and *tummîm* is permitted. Saul uses this lot oracle to determine who was responsible for his army's defeat by the Philistines (1 Sam 14:41–42). The use of lots assumes that God controls how the lots fall. Another example of the use of divination by lots is the story of the restoration of the Twelve in Acts 1:15–26.

4. An apotropaic ritual is some religious activity like a sacrifice, prayer, or wearing of an amulet that is designed to ward off evil. For an excellent study of such rituals in the Bible and the ancient Near East, see Marion A. Broida, *Forestalling Doom: "Apotropaic Intercession" in the Bible and the Ancient Near East*, AOAT 417 (Münster: Ugarit-Verlag, 2014).

5. Wolfgang Roth claims that the miracle stories of Elijah and Elisha in Kings served as the model for Mark's depiction of Jesus's miracles. See his *The Hebrew Gospel: Cracking the Code of Mark* (Oak Park, IL: Meyer-Stone Books, 1988).

6. An example of such a conflict appears in Jeremiah 28. In that story the prophet Hananiah asserts that the exiles from the 597 BCE revolt against Babylon would soon return to Jerusalem along with the treasures taken from the temple. Jeremiah, on the other hand, maintains that the people of Judah must submit to the yoke of the Babylonians for the foreseeable future.

7. Gary Knoppers, "Democratizing Revelation? Prophets, Seers and Visionaries in Chronicles," in *Prophecy and Prophets in Ancient Israel: Proceedings of the Oxford Old Testament Seminar*, ed. John Day (New York: T&T Clark, 2010), 393.

8. Nathan (1 Chr 17:1–5 from 2 Sam 7:–17); Gad (1 Chr 21:9–13 from 2 Sam 24:11–14); Shemaiah (2 Chr 11:2–4 from 2 Kgs 12:22–24); Micaiah ben Imlah (2 Chr 18:5–27 from 1 Kgs 22:6–28); and Huldah (2 Chr 34:23–28 from 2 Kgs 22:15–20).

9. Asaph (2 Chr 29:30); Azariah (2 Chr 15:1–8); Eliezer (2 Chr 20:37); Hanani (2 Chr 16:7–10; 19:2); Heman (1 Chr 25:5); Jahaziel (2 Chr 20:14–17); Jeduthun (1 Chr 25:3; 2 Chr 35:15); Jeremiah (2 Chr 36:12, 21); Obed (2 Chr 28:9); Zechariah (son of Jehoiada) (2 Chr 24:20).

10. The absence of Jeremiah from Kings is surprising given the literary relationship between the Book of Jeremiah and Kings. For example, Jeremiah 52 is a virtual duplicate of 2 Kings 24:18—25:30. Also, it appears that the final form of the Book of Jeremiah underwent editing by the same circles that produced Joshua–2 Kings.

11. Knoppers, "Democratizing Revelation?," 397.

12. This passage appears to speak of two groups: "messenger" and "prophets." Pancratius C. Beentjes asserts that it is obvious that Chronicles is speaking of two distinct groups, though he does not support this assertion. See his "Constructs of Prophets and Prophecy in the Book of Chronicles," in *Constructs of Prophecy in the Former and Latter Prophets and Other Texts*, ed. Lester L. Grabbe and Martti Nissinen, SBL Ancient Near East Monographs 4 (Atlanta: SBL, 2011), 24. Sara Japhet claims that the two terms stand in parallel and should be considered synonymous. See her *I & II Chronicles*, OTL (Louisville, KY: Westminster John Knox Press, 1993), 1071. Japhet's suggestion is more persuasive.

13. According to 1 Kings 19:16, YHWH ordered Elijah to anoint Jehu. That commission was fulfilled by Elisha.

14. The king referred to in this verse is probably Ahab and the *gĕbîrâ* is Jezebel. This is the only time this title is used of a queen of the Kingdom of Israel. For more information on the *gĕbîrâ*, see "Excursus," 95–98.

15 . These forty-one years (788–747 BCE) likely included a period of coregency with his father Jehoash.

16. Jan Kees de Geus, "Die Gesellschaftskritik der Propheten und die Archäologie," *Zeitschrift des deutschen Palästina-Vereins* 98 (1982): 55.

17. Sargon II may have completed the punitive campaign against Israel initiated by his predecessor Shalmaneser V.

18. Jeremiah 20:2 calls this gate the "Gate of Benjamin." There King Zedekiah sat in judgment to answer the petition of the Ethiopian official in Zedekiah's court to have Jeremiah released from confinement in a cistern. The Gate of Benjamin also is mentioned in Ezekiel 9:2.

19. Kings omits the name of Ahaz's mother in the formula introducing his reign. This is most unusual. The only other occurrence of such an omission is in the formula introducing Joram's reign (2 Kgs 8:17).

20. The prophet Isaiah advised against asking for help from the Assyrians. He was convinced that the coalition would collapse in short order. The prophet challenged Ahaz to trust in God (Isa 7:1–9). When the king demurs, Isaiah utters the well-known "Emmanuel prophecy" (Isa 7:14) that Matthew asserts is fulfilled in Jesus (Matt 1:23).

21. The action of Ahaz immolating his child in fire was likely an apotropaic ritual designed to ward off the threat posed by the Israel-Aram coalition.

22. John P. Meier suggests that Luke's parable of the Good Samaritan was developed from this story. See his *Probing the Authenticity of the Parables*, vol. 5 of *A Marginal Jew: Rethinking the Historical Jesus* (New Haven, CT: Yale University Press, 2016), 207. Like Chronicles, the Gospel of Luke shows a positive attitude toward the people of Samaria.

23. Images of serpents were common enough in the ancient Near East. The presence of a bronze serpent in the temple is legitimated by associating it with the story of Moses, who made such an image during the wandering in the wilderness. Anyone who looked

upon it would be healed of a deadly snake bite (Num 21:4–9). Hezekiah decided to have the bronze serpent removed from the temple because people were worshiping it as a god. The name "Nehushtan" is play on the Hebrew words for "bronze" (*nəḥōšet*) and "serpent" (*nāḥāš*).

24. Nadav Na'aman, "Five Notes on Jerusalem in the First and Second Temple Periods," *TA* 39 (2012): 99.

25. Lachish was the second most important city in Judah. It is thirty-eight miles from Jerusalem and guards the approach to the city from the south. Sennacherib decorated the walls of his palace with reliefs depicting his siege and conquest of Lachish. See David Ussishkin, "The 'Lachish Reliefs' and the City of Lachish," *IEJ* 30 (1980): 174–95.

26. Jeremy Goldberg, "Two Assyrian Campaigns against Hezekiah and Later Eighth Century Biblical Chronology," *Bib* 80, no. 3 (1999): 360–90.

27. There are some who suggest that Manasseh's military activities prepared for a revolt against Assyria, e.g., Roy Gane, "The Role of Assyria in the Ancient Near East during the Reign of Manasseh," *Andrews University Seminary Studies* 35, no. 1 (Spring 1997): 25. It is unlikely that any such activity on Judah's part would not have escaped Assyria's notice.

28. The text says that Manasseh made his son "pass through fire." The NABRE renders this phrase as "he immolated his child by fire," suggesting that Manasseh sacrificed his child. The act of the king's passing his son through fire probably was an apotropaic ritual that sought to avert some catastrophe for Manasseh himself or for his kingdom. Such rituals sometimes followed upon the receipt of an unfavorable omen. Deuteronomy also connects the act of passing a child through fire with the practice of divination (cf. Deut 18:6–14). Kings portrays Manasseh as guilty of the most heinous crimes, including child sacrifice.

29. Asserting that Manasseh was imprisoned in Babylon rather than Nineveh is problematic. Babylon was a center of resistance to Assyrian rule while Nineveh was Assyria's capital city.

30. William M. Schniedewind suggests that there was a tradition about Manasseh's prayer that was the origin of the story of the king's conversion. See his "The Source Citations of Manasseh: King Manasseh in History and Homily," *VT* 41, no. 4 (1991): 451.

Schniedewind does not identify this prayer with the later apocryphal Prayer of Manasseh (p. 460). For the Prayer of Manasseh, see James H. Charlesworth, "The Prayer of Manasseh," in *The Old Testament Pseudepigrapha*, ed. James H. Charlesworth, 2 vols. (Garden City, NY: Doubleday, 1985), 2:625–33. The Prayer of Manasseh is a second–first-century BCE work that is a prayer of repentance. A different and shorter prayer of Manasseh written in Hebrew was found among the Dead Sea Scrolls (4Q381). See Mika S. Pajunen, "The Prayer of Manasseh in 4Q381 and the Account of Manasseh in 2 Chronicles 33," in *The Scrolls and Biblical Tradition*, ed. George J. Brooke (Leiden: Brill, 2012), 143–61.

31. For a thorough treatment of repentance in Chronicles, see Hugh G. M. Williamson, *1 and 2 Chronicles*, New Century Bible Commentary (Grand Rapids: Eerdmans, 1982), 389–93.

32. The biblical text calls this group "the people of the land." Here this designation refers to Judean landowners who enjoyed a prominent place in the kingdom. These people were the elite of Judean rural society. The classical statement of this identification is found in Ernst Würthwein, *Der ʿamm haʾarez im Alten Testament*, BWANT 17 (Stuttgart: Kohlhammer, 1936). The meaning and usage of this phrase, however, developed in the biblical and post-biblical periods. See John Tracy Thames Jr., "A New Discussion of the Meaning of the Phrase *ʿam hāʾāreṣ* in the Hebrew Bible," *JBL* 130, no. 1 (2011): 109–25. The "people of the land" had a major role in maintaining the Davidic dynasty in troubling times. They installed three kings, each one after a king's death: Joash following the assassination of Ahaziah (2 Kgs 11:17–20); Azariah/Uzziah following the assassination of Amaziah (2 Kgs 14:21); and Jehoahaz (2 Kgs 23:30b) following Josiah's death in battle. See Shemaryahu Talmon, "The Judaean 'Am ha'Ares' in Historical Perspective," in Fourth World Congress of Jewish Studies, *Papers* (Jerusalem: World Union of Jewish Studies, 1967), 1:71–76.

33. David A. Glatt-Gilad has developed the idea of "personal" and "public" moments in Josiah's reform. See his "The Role of Huldah's Prophecy in the Chronicler's Portrayal of Josiah's Reform," *Bib* 77, no. 1 (January 1996): 16–31.

34. Wilhelm M. L. de Wette, *Dissertatio critico-exegetica qua Deuteronomium a prioribus Pentateuchi Libris diversum, alius cuiusdam recentioris auctoris opus esse monstratur* (Jena, 1805) (ET:

A critical exegetical discussion that shows that Deuteronomy is a work that differs from the first books of the Pentateuch and is the work of another author). The most convenient access to the work is Wilhelm M. L. de Wette, *Opuscula Theologica* (Berlin: G. Reimerum, 1830), 149–68. De Wette maintained that, since Deuteronomy contained ideas that reflected a later period of Israelite theological reflection, it could have been the lawbook found in the temple in Josiah's time.

35. Roland de Vaux, *Ancient Israel: Its Life and Institutions* (New York: McGraw-Hill, 1961), 338.

36. David Henige offers an excellent survey of contemporary scholarly opinions on the identity of the lawbook as he explores the plausibility of the biblical narrative. See his "Found but Not Lost: A Skeptical Note on the Document Discovered in the Temple under Josiah," *Journal of Hebrew Scriptures* 7 (2007): 1, doi:10.5508/jhs.2007.v7.a1.

37. Henige, "Found but Not Lost."

38. Jonathan Stökl, "Female Prophets in the Ancient Near East," in *Prophecy and Prophets in Ancient Israel: Proceedings of the Oxford Old Testament Seminar*, ed. John Day (New York: T&T Clark, 2010), 47–64.

39. See, e.g., Christopher T. Begg, "The Death of Josiah," *Ephemerides Theologicae Lovanienses* 64 (2005): 157–63; Christine Mitchell, "The Ironic Death of Josiah in 2 Chronicles," *CBQ* 68, no. 3 (2006): 421–35.

40. Jehoahaz is probably a throne name. The king's given name was Shallum (1 Chr 3:15).

41. The tribute Egypt demanded as one talent of gold and one hundred talents of silver (2 Kgs 23:33; 2 Chr 36:30). A talent of these precious metals was an incredibly large sum. In today's money, the cost to the people of Judah would be in excess of $12 billion. The Septuagint reads "a hundred talents of gold" and the Peshitta reads "ten talents of gold" in place of the Hebrew text's one talent of gold. In either case, it would be impossible for Judah to pay such an amount.

42. Determining the specifics regarding Jehoiakim's death is a matter of guesswork. There are conflicting traditions. Second Kings 24:6 implies that Jehoiakim died a peaceful death. Second

Chronicles 36:6 says nothing about his death but implies that he was taken to Babylon as a hostage. Jeremiah predicted that Jehoiakim would die a violent death (perhaps by assassination) and would go unlamented by his people (23:13–19; Jer 36:30).

43. The Talmud remembers Jehoiakim as the prototypical arrogant and evil king (Sanhedrin, 103). Matthew omits Jehoiakim from his genealogy of Jesus and presents Jehoiachin rather than Jehoiakim as the son of Josiah (Matt 1:11).

44. This was probably a throne name. This king's given name was Jeconiah (1 Chr 3:16–17; in Matt 1:11–12 he is Jechoniah). He was also known by a shortened form of his given name: Coniah (Jer 22:24, 28; 37:1).

45. The Babylonian day began and ended at sunset. This makes it impossible to give a precise date for the fall of Jerusalem. The Babylonian date is 7 Adar of the seventh year of Nebuchadnezzar's reign. This overlaps with two days in the modern calendar.

46. According to 2 Chr 26:10, Mattaniah was Jehoiachin's brother. Following the Hebrew of this text, both the NABRE and the NRSV read "brother." The Septuagint of this text has "his father's brother," i.e., his uncle that corresponds with 2 Kgs 24:17.

47. The NRSV gives him the title of "governor," a word that does not appear in the Hebrew text. The NABRE provides a more literal rendering of 2 Kings 25:22. What status Gedaliah actually had is not apparent from the text. A more complete story of events that immediately followed the fall of Jerusalem can be found in Jeremiah 40—43.

48. Tell en-Naṣbeh has been identified as the biblical Mizpah. Remains from the Iron I stratum suggest that it was a border fortress, protecting the western approach to Jerusalem. The Iron II stratum does not show the destruction that befell Jerusalem and the other cities of Judah. In the Babylonian period, it became a provincial capital and the town plan was altered. See Jeffrey R. Zorn, "Naṣbeh, Tell En-," *NEAEHL* 3:1098–1102.

49. Norbert Lohfink, "Die Gattung des 'Historischen Kurzgeschichte' in den letzten Jahren von Juda und in der Zeit des Babylonischen Exils," *ZAW* 90, no. 3 (1978): 323–27.

EPILOGUE

1. Here *synagogue* refers to the religious assembly itself rather than a structure to house such an assembly. The question about the origins of the synagogue as a religious assembly, the elements of synagogue rituals, and the beginning of single-purpose buildings used for such assemblies are still debated issues that are beyond the scope of this study. An excellent discussion of these issues can be found in Lidia D. Matassa, *The Invention of the First-Century Synagogue*, Ancient Near East Monographs 22 (Atlanta: SBL Press, 2018), 1–36.

Bibliography

BOOKS

Aharoni, Yohanan. *Archaeology of the Land of Israel*. Philadelphia: Westminster, 1982.

Ahlström, Gösta W. *Aspects of Syncretism in Israelite Religion*. Lund: Gleerup, 1963.

Allen, Spencer L. *The Splintered Divine: A Study of Ištar, Baal, and Yahweh Divine Names and Divine Multiplicity in the Ancient Near East*. Studies in Ancient Near Eastern Records 5. Berlin: De Gruyter, 2015.

Avioz, Michael. *Nathan's Oracle (2 Samuel 7) and Its Interpreters*. The Bible in History 5. Bern: Peter Lang, 2005.

Bayerlin, Walter, ed. *Near Eastern Religious Texts Relating to the Old Testament*. OTL. Philadelphia: Westminster, 1978.

Brenner, Athalya. *The Israelite Woman: Social Role and Literary Type in Biblical Narrative*. Sheffield, UK: JSOT Press, 1985.

Brewer-Boydston, Ginny. *Good Queen Mothers, Bad Queen Mothers: The Theological Presentation of Queen Mothers in 1 and 2 Kings*. CBQMS 54. Washington, DC: CBA, 2016.

Broida, Marion A. *Forestalling Doom: "Apotropaic Intercession" in the Bible and the Ancient Near East*. AOAT 417. Münster: Germany: Ugarit-Verlag, 2014.

Charlesworth, James H., ed. *The Messiah: Developments in Earliest Judaism and Christianity*. Minneapolis: Fortress, 1992.

———, ed. *The Old Testament Pseudepigrapha*. 2 vols. Garden City, NY: Doubleday, 1985.

Cogan, Modechai, and Hayim Tadmor. *II Kings: A New Translation with Introduction and Commentary*. AB 11. New York: Doubleday, 1988.

Cross, Frank Moore. *Canaanite Myth and Hebrew Epic: Essays in the History of the Religion of Israel*. Cambridge, MA: Harvard University Press, 1973.

de Vaux, Roland. *Ancient Israel: Its Life and Institutions*. New York: McGraw-Hill, 1961.

de Wette, Wilhelm M. L. "Dissertatio critico-exegetica qua Deuteronomium a prioribus Pentateuchi Libris diversum, alius cuiusdam recentioris auctoris opus esse monstratur." In *Opuscula Theologica*, 149–68. Berlin: G. Reimerum, 1830.

Finkel, Irving. *The Cyrus Cylinder: The Great Persian Edict from Babylon*. London: Bloomsbury Publishing, 2013.

Gray, John. *I & II Kings*. OTL. Philadelphia: Westminster, 1963.

Hobbs, T. Raymond. *2 Kings*. WBC 13. Dallas: Word Books, 1985.

Japhet, Sara. *I & II Chronicles*. OTL. Louisville, KY: Westminster John Knox, 1993.

———. *From the Rivers of Babylon to the Highlands of Judah: Collected Studies on the Restoration Period*. Winona Lake, IN: Eisenbrauns, 2006.

Klein, Ralph. *1 Chronicles*. Hermeneia. Minneapolis: Fortress, 2006.

———. *2 Chronicles*. Hermeneia. Minneapolis: Fortress, 2012.

Knoppers, Gary N. *1 Chronicles 1—9: A New Translation with an Introduction and Commentary*. AB 12. New York: Doubleday, 2003.

Matassa, Lidia D. *The Invention of the First-Century Synagogue*. Ancient Near East Monographs 22. Atlanta: SBL Press, 2018.

McKenzie, Steven L. *The Chronicler's Use of the Deuteronomistic History*. HSM 22. Atlanta: Scholars Press, 1985.

Meier, John P. *Probing the Authenticity of the Parables*. Vol. 5 of *A Marginal Jew: Rethinking the Historical Jesus*. New Haven, CT: Yale University Press, 2016.

Mosis, Rudolf. *Untersuchungen zur Theologie des chronistischen Geschichtswerkes*. Freiburger theologische Studien 92. Freiburg: Herder, 1973.

Noth, Martin. *The Deuteronomistic History.* JSOTSup 15. Sheffield, UK: JSOT Press, 1981.

O'Brien, Mark A. *The Deuteronomistic History Hypothesis: A Reassessment.* Orbis Biblicus et Orientalis 92. Freiburg, Switzerland: Universitätsverlag, 1989.

Rost, Leonhard. *The Succession to the Throne of David.* Translated by Michael D. Rutter and David M. Gunn. Sheffield, UK: Almond Press, 1982. Translation of *Die Überlieferung voη der Thronnachfolge Davids.* BWANT 42. Stuttgart: Kohlhammer, 1926.

Roth, Wolfgang. *The Hebrew Gospel: Cracking the Code of Mark.* Oak Park, IL: Meyer-Stone Books, 1988.

Sparks, James T. *The Chronicler's Genealogies: Towards an Understanding of 1 Chronicles 1—9.* Atlanta: SBL, 2008.

Thompson, Thomas L. *The Bible in History: How Writers Create a Past.* London: Pimlico, 1999.

Trible, Phyllis. *Texts of Terror: Literary-Feminist Readings of Biblical Narratives.* Overtures to Biblical Theology 13. Philadelphia: Fortress, 1984.

Vaughan, Patrick H. *The Meaning of "Bāmâ" in the Old Testament: Study of Etymological, Textual and Archaeological Evidence.* Society for Old Testament Study Monograph Series 3. Cambridge: University Press, 1974.

von Rad, Gerhard. *Old Testament Theology.* Translated by D. M. G. Stalker. 2 vols. New York: Harper & Row, 1962.

———. *Studies in Deuteronomy.* Translated by David Stalker. SBT 9. London: SCM Press, 1953. Translation of *Deuteronomium-Studien.* FRLANT 58. Göttingen: Vandenhoeck & Ruprecht, 1947.

Williamson, Hugh G. M. *1 and 2 Chronicles.* New Century Bible Commentary. Grand Rapids: Eerdmans, 1982.

Würthwein, Ernst. *Der ʿamm haʾarez im Alten Testament.* BWANT 17. Stuttgart: Kohlhammer, 1936.

Yasur-Landau, Assaf. *The Philistines and Aegean Migration at the End of the Late Bronze Age.* New York: Cambridge University Press, 2010.

ARTICLES

Ackerman, Susan. "The Queen Mother and the Cult in Ancient Israel." *JBL* 111, no. 3 (1993): 385–401.

Andreasen, Niels Erik A. "The Role of the Queen Mother in Israelite Society." *CBQ* 45, no. 2 (April 1983): 179–94.

Auld, Graeme A. "David's Census: Some Textual and Literary Links." In *Textual Criticism and Dead Sea Scrolls Studies in Honour of Julio Trebolle Barrera*, edited by Andrés Piquer Otero and Pablo A. Torijano Morales, 19–34. Leiden: Brill, 2012.

Avigad, Nahman. "Samaria (City)." *NEAEHL* 4:1300–1310.

Beentjes, Pancratius C. "Constructs of Prophets and Prophecy in the Book of Chronicles." In *Constructs of Prophecy in the Former and Latter Prophets and Other Texts*, edited by Lester L. Grabbe and Martti Nissinen, 21–40. SBL Ancient Near East Monographs 4. Atlanta: SBL, 2011.

————. "Transformation of Space and Time: Nathan's Oracle and David's Prayer in 1 Chronicles 17." In *Sanctity of Time and Space in Tradition and Modernity*, edited by Alberdina Houtman et al., 27–44. Leiden: Brill, 1998.

Begg, Christopher T. "The Death of Josiah." *Ephemerides Theologicae Lovanienses* 64, no. 1 (2005): 157–63.

————. "The Significance of Jehoiachin's Release: A New Proposal." *JSOT* 36 (1986): 49–56.

Ben-Barak, Zafrira. "The Status and Right of the GĔBÎRÂ." *JBL* 110, no. 1 (1991): 23–34.

Berger, Yitzhak. "Chiasm and Meaning in 1 Chronicles." *The Journal of Hebrew Scriptures* 14 (2014). https://doi.org/10.5508/jhs.2014.v14.a1.

Berlyn, Patricia. "The Rise of the House of Omri." *Jewish Bible Quarterly* 33, no. 4 (2005): 223–30.

Bodner, Keith. "Ark-Eology: Shifting Emphases in 'Ark Narrative' Scholarship." *Currents in Biblical Research* 4, no. 2 (2006): 169–96.

Bowen, Nancy R. "The Quest for the Historical Gĕbîrâ." *CBQ* 64, no. 4 (October 2001): 597–618.

Broshi, Magen, and Israel Finkelstein. "The Population of Palestine in Iron Age II." *Bulletin of the American Schools of Oriental Research* 287 (August 1992): 47–60.

Callaway, Joseph A. "Ai." *NEAEHL* 1:39–45.

Campbell, Edward E. "Shechem." *NEAEHL* 4:1345–54.

Chambois, Alain. "Far'ah, Tell el- (North)." *NEAEHL* 2:433–40.

Charlesworth, James H. "The Prayer of Manasseh." In *The Old Testament Pseudepigrapha*, edited by James H. Charlesworth, 2:625–37. Garden City, NY: Doubleday, 1985.

Cross, Frank Moore. "The Structure of Deuteronomic History." In *Perspectives in Jewish Learning*, 9–24. Annual of the College of Jewish Studies 3. Chicago: College of Jewish Studies, 1968.

de Geus, Jan Kees. "Die Gesellschaftskritik der Propheten und die Archäologie." *Zeitschrift des deutschen Palästina-Vereins* 98 (1982): 50–57.

Dothan, Moshe. "Ashdod." *NEAEHL* 1:93–102.

Emerton, John S. "The Value of the Moabite Stone as an Historical Source." *VT* 52, no. 4 (2002): 483–92.

Eph'al, Israel. "The 'Jehoash Inscription': A Forgery." *Israel Exploration Journal* 53, no. 1 (2003): 123–28.

Feldman, Michal, et al. "Ancient DNA Sheds Light on the Genetic Origins of Early Iron Age Philistines." *Science Advances* 5, no. 7 (July 2019): eaax0061.

Finkelstein, Israel. "Shiloh." *NEAEHL* 4:1364–70.

———. "Stages in the Territorial Expansion of the Northern Kingdom." *VT* 61, no. 2 (January 2011): 227–42.

Frolov, Serge. "The Succession Narrative: A 'Document' or a 'Phantom?'" *JBL* 121, no. 1 (February 2002): 81–104.

Gane, Roy. "The Role of Assyria in the Ancient Near East during the Reign of Manasseh." *Andrews University Seminary Studies* 35, no. 1 (Spring 1997): 21–32.

Glatt-Gilad, David A. "The Role of Huldah's Prophecy in the Chronicler's Portrayal of Josiah's Reform." *Bib* 77, no. 1 (January 1996): 16–31.

Goldberg, Jeremy. "Two Assyrian Campaigns against Hezekiah and Later Eighth Century Biblical Chronology." *Bib* 80, no. 3 (1999): 360–90.

Greenstein, Edward L. "Methodological Principles in Determining that the So-Called Jehoash Inscription Is Inauthentic." In

Puzzling Out the Past: Studies in Northwest Semitic Languages and Literature in Honor of Bruce Zuckerman, edited by Marilyn J. Lundberg, Steven Fine, and Wayne T. Pitard, 83–92. Leiden: Brill, 2012.

Hachlili, Rachel. "The Zodiac in Ancient Jewish Synagogal Art: A Review." *Jewish Studies Quarterly* 9, no. 3 (2002): 219–58.

Henige, David. "Found but Not Lost: A Skeptical Note on the Document Discovered in the Temple under Josiah." *Journal of Hebrew Scriptures* 7 (2007): 1. http://doi.org/10.5508/jhs.2007.v7.a1.

Holm-Nielsen, Sven. "Did Joab Climb 'Warren's Shaft'?" In *History and Traditions of Early Israel: Studies Presented to Eduard Nielsen, May 8, 1993*, edited by André Lemaire and Benedikt Otzen, 38–49. VTSup 53. Leiden: Brill, 1993.

Jonker, Louis. "Who Constitutes Society? Yehud's Self-Understanding in the Late Persian Era as Reflected in the Books of Chronicles." *JBL* 127, no. 4 (December 2008): 703–24.

Kalimi, Isaac. "Placing the Chronicler in His Own Historical Context: A Closer Examination." *Journal of Near Eastern Studies* 68, no. 3 (July 2009): 179–92.

Kenyon, Kathleen. "Jericho: Tell es-Sultan." *NEAEHL* 2:674–81.

Kitz, Ann Marie. "Prophecy as Divination." *CBQ* 65, no.1 (January 2003): 22–42.

Knauf, Ernst Axel. "Jehoash's Improbable Inscription." *Biblische Notizen* 117 (2003): 22–26.

Knoppers, Gary N. "'Battling against Yahweh': Israel's War against Judah in 2 Chr 13:2–20." *RB* 100, no. 4 (1993): 511–32.

———. "Democratizing Revelation? Prophets, Seers and Visionaries in Chronicles." In *Prophecy and Prophets in Ancient Israel: Proceedings of the Oxford Old Testament Seminar*, edited by John Day, 391–409. New York: T&T Clark, 2010.

———. "The Deuteronomists and the Deuteronomic Law of the King: A Reexamination of a Relationship." *ZAW* 108, no. 5 (1996): 329–46.

———. "Images of David in Early Judaism: David as a Repentant Sinner in Chronicles." *Bib* 76, no. 4 (December 1995): 449–79.

———. "Is There a Future for the Deuteronomistic History?" In *The Future of the Deuteronomistic History*, edited by Thomas Römer, 119–34. Leuven: Peeters, 2000.

————. "Rethinking the Relationship between Deuteronomy and the Deuteronomistic History." *CBQ* 63, no. 3 (July 2001): 393–415.

Kuan, Jeffrey K. "Was Omri a Phoenician?" In *History and Interpretation: Essays in Honour of John H. Hayes*, edited by M. Patrick Graham, William P. Brown, and Jeffrey K. Kuan, 231–44. JSOTSup 173. Sheffield: JSOT Press, 1993.

Kutsch, Ernst. "Das Jahr der Katastrophe: 587 v. Chr. Kritische Erwägungen zu neueren chronologischen Versuchen." *Bib* 55 no. 4 (1974): 520–45.

Langgut, Dafna, Israel Finkelstein, and Thomas Litt. "Climate and the Late Bronze Collapse: New Evidence from the Southern Levant." *TA* 40 (2013): 149–75.

Levenson, Jon D. "The Last Four Verses in Kings." *JBL* 103 (September 1984): 353–61.

Levenson, Jon D., and Baruch Halpern. "The Political Import of David's Marriages." *JBL* 99, no. 4 (December 1980): 507–18.

Lohfink, Norbert. "Die Gattung des 'Historischen Kurzgeschichte' in den letzten Jahren von Juda und in der Zeit des Babylonischen Exils." *ZAW* 90, no. 3 (1978): 323–27.

Magness, Jodi. "Heaven on Earth: Helios and the Zodiac Cycle in Ancient Palestinian Synagogues." *Dumbarton Oaks Papers* 59 (2005): 1–32.

Mayes, Andrew D. H. "Pharaoh Shishak's Invasion of Palestine and the Exodus from Egypt." In *Between Evidence and Ideology*, edited by Bob Becking and Lester L. Grabbe, 129–44. Leiden: Brill, 2011.

McCarthy, Dennis. "II Samuel 7 and the Structure of the Deuteronomistic History." *JBL* 84, no. 2 (June 1965): 131–38.

Mitchell, Christine. "The Ironic Death of Josiah in 2 Chronicles." *CBQ* 68, no. 3 (July 2006): 421–35.

Murray, Donald F. "Of All the Years the Hopes—or Fears? Jehoiachin in Babylon (2 Kings 25:27–30)." *JBL* 120, no. 2 (April 2001): 245–65.

Na'aman, Nadav. "Ahab's Chariot Force at the Battle of Qarqar." *TA* 3 (1976): 89–106.

————. "Five Notes on Jerusalem in the First and Second Temple Periods." *TA* 39 (2012): 93–103.

————. "The Interchange between the Bible and Archaeology: The Case of David's Palace and the Millo." *BAR* 40, no. 1 (January/February 2014): 57–69.

————. "The Kingdom of Geshur in History and Memory." *Scandinavian Journal of the Old Testament* 26, no. 1 (2012): 88–101.

Na'aman, Nadav, and Nurit Lissovsky. "Kuntillet 'Ajrud, Sacred Trees and the Ashera." *TA* 35, no. 2 (2008): 186–208.

Nicol, George G. "The Wisdom of Joab and the Wise Woman of Tekoa." *Studia Theologica* 36, no. 1 (1982): 97–104.

Pajunen, Mika S. "The Prayer of Manasseh in 4Q381 and the Account of Manasseh in 2 Chronicles 33." In *The Scrolls and Biblical Tradition*, edited by George J. Brooke, 143–61. Leiden: Brill, 2012.

————. "The Saga of Judah's Kings Continues: The Reception of Chronicles in the Late Second Temple Period." *JBL* 136, no, 3 (July 2017): 565–84.

Reich, Ronny, and Eli Shukron. "The System of Rock-Cut Tunnels near Gihon in Jerusalem Reconsidered." *RB* 107, no. 1 (2000): 5–17.

Roth, Wolfgang. "Deuteronomic Rest-Theology: A Redaction-Critical Study." *Biblical Research* 21 (1976): 5–14.

Schniedewind, William M. "The Source Citations of Manasseh: King Manasseh in History and Homily." *VT* 41, no. 4 (1991): 450–61.

Shiloh, Yigal. "The Rediscovery of the Ancient Water System Known as 'Warren's Shaft.'" In *Ancient Jerusalem Revealed*, edited by Geva Hillel, 46–54. Jerusalem: Israel Exploration Society, 1994.

Smelik, Klaas. "The Ark Narrative Reconsidered." In *New Avenues in the Study of the Old Testament*, edited by A. S. van der Woude, 128–44. Leiden: Brill, 1989.

Sosik, Marcin. "GEBIRA at the Judaean Court." *Scripta Judaica Cracoviensia* 7 (2009): 7–12.

Stökl, Jonathan. "Female Prophets in the Ancient Near East." In *Prophecy and Prophets in Ancient Israel: Proceedings of the Oxford Old Testament Seminar*, edited by John Day, 47–64. New York: T&T Clark, 2010.

Talmon, Shemaryahu. "The Judaean 'Am ha'Ares' in Historical Perspective." In Fourth World Congress of Jewish Studies, *Papers*, 1:71–76. World Union of Jewish Studies: Jerusalem, 1967.

Thames, John Tracy, Jr. "A New Discussion of the Meaning of the Phrase *'am hā'āreṣ* in the Hebrew Bible." *JBL* 130, no. 1 (2011): 109–25.

Thiel, Winfried. "Omri." *ABD* 5:17.

Tuell, Steven Shawn. "1 and 2 Chronicles." In *Oxford Bibliographies*. https://www.oxfordbibliographies.com/view/document/obo -9780195393361/obo-9780195393361-0021.xml?rskey= tLnYu5&result=29.

Ussishkin, David. "Jezreel, Samaria and Megiddo: Royal Centers of Omri and Ahab." In *Congress Volume Cambridge 1995*, edited by John A. Emerton, 351–64. Leiden: Brill, 1997.

———. "The 'Lachish Reliefs' and the City of Lachish." *IEJ* 30 (1980): 174–95.

Uziel, Joe, and Itzhaq Shai. "Iron Age Jerusalem: Temple-Palace, Capital City." *Journal of the American Oriental Society* 127, no. 2 (2007): 161–70.

van der Toorn, Karel, and Cornelis Houtman. "David and the Ark." *JBL* 113, no. 2 (April 1994): 209–31.

Van Seters, John. "The Chronicler's Account of Solomon's Temple-Building: A Continuity Theme." In *The Chronicler as an Historian*, edited by M. Patrick Graham, Kenneth G. Hoglund, and Steven L. McKenzie, 283–300. Sheffield, UK: Sheffield Academic Press, 1997.

Wyatt, Nicolas. "David's Census and the Tripartite Theory." *VT* 40, no. 3 (1990): 352–60.

Yee, Gale A. "Jezebel." *ABD* 3:848.

Zorn, Jeffery R. "Naṣbeh, Tell En-." *NEAEHL* 3:1098–1102.

Praise for *The Rise and Fall of the Israelite Kingdoms*

"In this book, Leslie Hoppe draws on the knowledge he
has accumulated from decades studying and teaching
the Historical Books of the Old Testament in order to
present a critical overview of the Deuteronomistic history
and Chronicles in comparison to one another. Hoppe
emphasizes the different settings and theological interests
of the biblical writers to account for their differences in
interpreting the history of Israel and Judah. What emerges
is a theology of the Deuteronomistic history and Chronicles
that will complement any careful study of their contents."

—Steve McKenzie, prof. of Hebrew Bible/Old Testament, Spence
L. Wilson Senior Research Fellow, Rhodes College, Memphis, TN

"Leslie Hoppe's book is a masterful synthesis of the Old
Testament's Historical Books. By examining the Books of
Samuel and Kings together with the often-overlooked Book
of Chronicles, Hoppe shows the different ways that biblical
writers tried to make sense of their own history in the wake
of the destruction of Jerusalem and the Babylonian Exile.
Hoppe's reading of Israel and Judah's history offers lessons
to any community that seeks to understand its past and is
determined to rebuild itself for the future."

—Andrew R. Davis, assoc. prof. of Old Testament,
Boston College School of Theology and Ministry, Brighton, MA

Praise for *The Rise and Fall of the Israelite Kingdoms*

"With seasoned scholarship and prosaic clarity, Leslie Hoppe, OFM, sets forth the distinctive character of the rise and fall of the Israelite kingdoms as narrated in the Deuteronomistic history and in the Chronicler's account. As Hoppe observes, the story in Samuel/Kings ends by leaving Judah's king and many of its inhabitants in exile due to idolatry and infidelity. It also leaves readers wondering about the identity and future of the Jewish people. By contrast, the Chronicler's account retells the same story in the Persian era, one-hundred fifty years later, when the exiles had returned and faithful worship in Jerusalem had been reestablished. Reshaping the Deuteronomistic account, the Chronicler ties the identity and future of the Jewish people to authentic worship of Yahweh. In the process, Hoppe not only skillfully illuminates the distinct theological horizons crafting each of these two historical narratives; he also reveals how different historical contexts have a determining impact upon how the story of a people's past is told. Such disclosures grant reading this work an excess of rewards for both students and scholars alike."

—Gina Hens-Piazza, Joseph S. Alemany Prof. of Biblical Studies, Jesuit School of Theology, Santa Clara Univ., Berkeley, CA

Praise for *The Rise and Fall of the Israelite Kingdoms*

"In this volume one can follow the process of growth, development, decline, and dissolution of the Israelite kingdoms of Israel and Judah. This has often been done by historians, but they usually present the story described either in Samuel/Kings or in Chronicles, with occasional cross-references to the other document. Hoppe's presentation interweaves significant movements and details as the 'story' he is telling develops, but he also extends the history in time by characterizing the events and theology that extend long past the events being narrated. We could say that Hoppe rehabilitates the story and religious instincts of Chronicles, especially by comparing it with the content and theological underpinning of Samuel/Kings; in doing this he turns 'Israel's past into a sermon,' a guide for hearers/readers for their future. Frequently Hoppe anchors his positions in very concise reviews of the history of scholarship on this literature; as well he deftly incorporates recent archaeological results that shift our angle of vision. He accomplishes all this in a prose style that often seems to draw readers on the path of an investigation. You can count on this volume to amplify issues for readers either of Chronicles or Samuel/Kings—or better, both at the same time. It is indispensable for study of these two kingdoms, of Israel and of Judah."

—John Endres, SJ, emer. prof. of Sacred Scripture and Old Testament, Jesuit School of Theology, Santa Clara Univ., Berkeley, CA